MONEY CREATORS

Who Creates Money?
Who Should Create It?

by

GERTRUDE M. COOGAN

OMNI PUBLICATIONS

Hawthorne, California 90250

Library of Congress Catalog Card Number 67-28926

First Printing February 1935
Second Printing April 1935
Third Printing June 1937
Fourth Printing April 1938
Fifth Printing November 1938
Sixth Printing January 1939
Seventh Printing November 1939
Eighth Printing November 1943
Ninth Printing October 1963
Tenth Printing November 1967
Eleventh Printing - February 1971
Twelfth Printing Nov. 1974
Printing 1982

Printed in U. S. A.

PREFACE

How long shall we allow our leaders, spiritual and political, to pretend that they see nothing, hear nothing, and know nothing? How long shall we tolerate organs of education and information, public and private, commercial and religious, which are drugged? How much longer shall we silently consent to have the strong kept in a trap, the wise surrounded by fog, and the sincere millions caused to suffer needlessly?

There can be no Liberty without Economic Freedom — America can have no Economic Freedom without an honest money system — one removed from the controls of the socially irresponsible private Money Creators.

The problem facing us today is not the formation of a new political party. It is to inform the constituents of every Congressional District so that they may put such pressure upon our Congressmen and Senators as to leave them no alternative but to do the will of the people. The people must *demand* of them an honest money system. The illicit political machines and numerous rackets will pass into oblivion when an honest money system is set in operation. The controllers of our money system are the controllers of our illicit political machines.

VICTIMS!

Do you want money made honest *for you* by the National Government; or kept "sound" for the Money Creators by mis-government?

Do you want U. S. dollars in sufficient number to keep the "wolves of depression" from your door; or do you want dollars in such overwhelming numbers as to deprive them of all value, as the Money Creators have done in other countries?

The reader will ask: "Why have not business leaders known that our money system is dishonest? They are intelligent, aggressive people who seem equal to anything." The answer is found in the fact that with few exceptions business men are honest, and, as honest men, believe that few men are dishonest.

The situation resulting from this concept has set the stage for any confidence game, large or small. The Money Creators have truly operated a confidence game.

Our home town and city bankers are, with few exceptions, honest men. Through intrigue and manipulations of gold and government debts they have become mere pawns in the world monetary confidence game.

They and their predecessors inherited a system which, because it *is*, they believe always *was*. If they would look into the origin of the system, and examine its nature, originated sub-rosa and only through centuries of legislative trickery congealed into Law, they would demand that the system be demystified, made non-collapsible, and honest in essence; for they would see that the near-by destiny of the system is ruin for them as well as for others.

January 29, 1935

FOREWORD

TO THE AMERICAN PEOPLE:

It gives me special pleasure to have the opportunity to explain the principles and purposes of this book, written by Miss Gertrude M. Coogan of Chicago.

The facts that Miss Coogan was awarded a Master's Degree in Economics and Finance by Northwestern University; was for eight years a Security Analyst for The Northern Trust Company of Chicago; that from the beginning she had a deep desire to understand the fancied enigma of money, have given her a great insight into monetary science.

The basic principles of monetary science are simple. It is a sound axiom of monetary science that the value of money depends upon the available supply of money in relation to the goods to be exchanged with it. Knowledge of the science has been made difficult by those who have converted these simple principles into an enigma. They have done so with ponderous volumes written on prices and on the processes of production, transportation, distribution and allied topics; weaving into the subject matter deceptive terms so that the public has been grossly misled by the use of words which contain accepted false premises.

The intentional use of deceptive terms has made monetary science obscure. For example; the so-called monetary experts and financial writers use the word Inflation to stigmatize justified expansion in the volume of money, when Inflation actually means *unjustified* expansion. They use Deflation, which means justified contraction of a previous unjust expansion; that is, contraction of previous inflation, as synonymous with *unjustified* contraction, in order to commend that unjust contraction.

They use the word Money as meaning gold and currency alone, when the word Money really means, as Webster's dictionary truly says: "anything having a conventional use as a medium of exchange and a measurement of value." That is, Money means bank checks and bank demand deposits principally. It is through this deceptive use of the word Money that they say there is no relation between the volume of money and our domestic price levels. It is with this false use of the word Money that they deny the quantitative facts of money.

They use the term Gold Standard deceptively because the weight of the gold exchangeable for a currency dollar has no standard measure of value, and cannot have. The value of a fixed number of grains of gold exchangeable for a dollar, fluctuates directly with the expansion or contraction of bank credit money. It was easy to fix the currency price of gold, but the creators and controllers of bank credit money fixed the *goods* price of gold.

The number of grains of gold exchangeable for a currency dollar is of very minor importance from a domestic standpoint. It is only in the purchase of foreign exchange, the currencies of other countries, that the number of grains of gold exchangeable for a dollar is of vital importance. When other countries change the grains of gold exchangeable for their currency units, it is necessary that the United States do likewise, if we wish to enter export markets.

In a really scientific money system, gold should not have a fixed price. The number of grains of gold exchangeable for a unit of currency, in reality, should fluctuate as the purchasing power of the dollars themselves change. Fixing the weight of gold exchangeable for a unit of currency has been the means by which the price levels of each country have been altered at the pleasure of foreign Bankers.

My own interest in this matter arose when I was a boy

of 17 in the Panic of 1873. Then, the value of my father's property was completely destroyed and my mother, from a life of abundance, was suddenly compelled to earn her living by teaching music.

I determined to solve that question and have continued to give it consideration throughout my whole life.

Opportunity favored me. In 1877, I was graduated in six languages; was awarded the Degree of Master of Arts; was Valedictorian of my class; received the Debater's Medal; and later had conferred upon me the Degree of LL.D. and was elected to Phi Beta Kappa. During my entire life I have been a serious student.

In 1890, I had the opportunity of establishing the first national bank chartered in Oklahoma; was its President ten years, and have been elected a Director for 45 successive years. I knew the causes of the Panic of 1893 and conducted that bank through that panic.

I was a delegate to the National Democratic Convention in 1896 and made a resolute fight to commit the Democratic Party in its platform to a pledge to protect the people of the United States against panics and depressions. An attempt was made to remonetize silver. Hon. William Jennings Bryan himself strenuously demanded the establishment of an honest money system—money whose purchasing power should remain the same. Bryan was defeated solely by a studied and expressive campaign of deception and ridicule, the threat of panic and the use of money.

In 1898 I went to Europe and studied the methods by which Europe stabilized credit and the value of money. After having studied at first hand the Bank of England through its Governors; the Bank of France through its Governor and expert advisers, and the Reichsbank through its Directors, I wrote many articles describing how the purchasing power of money could be stabilized in America.

Many articles were written by me at that time to show what principles could be applied to an American system.

In 1900 I devised a plan to protect this country against the evils of monetary panics by providing for the issuance of United States legal tender money when national production necessitated an increase in the supply of money.

In December 1907, I entered the United States Senate and served there for 18 years. Within ninety days after I entered the Senate, on the 25th day of February 1908, I analyzed completely the Panic of 1907; showed its causes, how it could be cured, and how depressions could be prevented in the future. My text was *stability* in the value of money.

I was made Chairman of the Committee on Banking and Currency of the United States Senate on March 5, 1913, and immediately drafted a Bill called the Federal Reserve Bill. In drafting this Bill I was greatly assisted by the results of four years work done by the National Monetary Commission. That Commission's report consisted of 32 volumes, and an auxiliary library of 2500 volumes. It had been established on my request from the floor of the United States Senate.

In July 1913, Hon. Carter Glass joined me in presenting to the Senate and to the House the so-called Federal Reserve Bill which had been prepared by me the previous March, but which had been expanded, and contained provisions with which I was not entirely content. My Committee was immediately called together to take testimony on this Senate Bill, and after 3,000 pages of printed testimony had been taken, my colleagues in the Senate authorized me to write another Bill. I thereopon had the Senate strike out the Bill that had been prepared in the House and substitute the Bill which I had originally prepared. The Senate adopted the Bill written by me without a change of word. In the Bill introduced in July, in which the Hon. Carter Glass joined me, I had inserted a provision *requiring* that the powers of the Reserve System be employed in the service of commerce and to promote a *stable* price level. The meaning of this, of course, was to establish and maintain the stable value of money under mandate. This *mandatory* provision was stricken out in the House under the leadership of Hon. Carter Glass. I was unable to keep this mandatory provision in the Bill because of the secret hostilities developed against it, the origin of which at that time I did not fully understand.

Under the administrations of Wilson, Harding, Coolidge and Hoover, this Act was diverted from its proper purpose on the advice of some who controlled the policies of a number of the largest banks.

In the campaign of 1920, under the pretext of lowering the cost of living, those in charge of some of the largest banks demanded the contraction of credit and currency. This was done in spite of nine protests I had made on the floor of the Senate between January and June of 1920. Policies pursued by those in charge of the Central Federal Reserve Banks resulted in raising the value of money 80%, from an index of 60 in May 1920 to an index of 107 in June 1921.

Again, under President Hoover, the contraction of credit took place on such a colossal scale as to force the dollar index (purchasing power) to 166. The consequence was universal bankruptcy, every bank in the United States being forced to suspend operations at the close of Hoover's services.

The purpose of this book is to bring before the American people the knowledge that they must have regarding the nature and manipulations of their money system. In my opinion, America faces a crisis which may result in the loss of our Representative Constitutional Government unless every man and woman, rich or poor, young or old; doctor, lawyer, merchant, laborer, educator, clergyman, social worker, society leader; will bestir himself or herself toward the problem of bringing the fundamental truths of monetary science to every fireside.

It is time for intelligent Americans to examine their money system and learn how to make simple but fundamental changes. Those who own insurance policies and savings accounts must bestir themselves to protect those accumulations. It is an obvious fact that the value of savings accounts and insurance policies will be destroyed unless correct measures are taken to restore property values, employment, and equitable raw material price levels. Instead of allowing our entire social order to be changed, we should examine the fundamental cause of our economic chaos. Making a few intelligent and scientific changes in the operation of our money system will eliminate the dangers of our being afflicted by false principles.

It is hopeless to think that a few public-spirited citizens in some of the key cities of the United States can accomplish this enormous benefit. They cannot; their handicaps are many. The truths themselves are very simple, but many of the newspapers and publishing companies allow themselves to be used to carry misinformation to the American public, while neglecting to print the truths. Honest money principles are understandable to every one when the money subject is presented in its true light. America will remain in a deplorable condition only so long as the "Let George do it" attitude continues. Americans must bestir themselves to eliminate the causes of this business depression and social disorder, and restore prosperity and opportunities to the American people. Loyal Americans realize that the possession of knowledge carries with it the responsibility of dissemination.

It required the assistance of every loyal American to help win the World War. In my opinion, the American people have more at stake today than they had at the time of the World War, not that I at all deprecate the glorious services rendered by men in uniform. But I believe the future of our nation and the principles for which it has stood, were less in jeopardy then than they are today. It is not necessary that you make the sacrifices you made at the time of the World War, but the cooperation of every one in this important educational program is absolutely necessary.

The solution of the problem to protect our homes does not rest with a few leaders in a distant city. It is necessary that every man and woman appoint himself and herself a leader. Honest Money Groups must be formed in every block, in every precinct throughout the United States, and in every rural community. The rural community centers and schoolhouses can be most profitably employed this winter in showing the American farmers how simply they can solve all of their own problems. Their grave troubles have been caused not by overproduction, but by money manipulations frequently executed upon foreign advice and to harmonize with foreign "policies." The result has been the extraction of dollars of a distorted purchasing power from the American farmer. Collecting dollars of such unfair purchasing power has deprived many American farmers of their homes, and all farmers of their share in the industrial products which this nation is so well equipped to manufacture and distribute.

The principal reason for endorsing this book is that I feel it is an intelligent vehicle for the dissemination of the truths which must be understood in every home and crystallized into legislation as quickly as possible.

While I was considering practical plans to reach the American people, Miss Coogan brought the manuscript to me. It was read to me and its purpose and intent explained. I found that this young American woman had a masterful knowledge of the so-called money enigma. She asked me to recite my means of knowledge and experience in connection with the subject matter, and to write a word of explanation.

I am glad to commend it; to give the book my blessings in its principles and purposes to restore and maintain honest money through the powers of the Congress of the United States. This book is worthy of careful study by American citizens who wish to understand the principles that govern the value and the volume of money in the United States and in other countries. It contains scientific truths—not quackery.

This book can be used as a text book to enlighten the American people as to the simple principles of monetary science which have been befogged by the learned economists. The learned economists, in my opinion, fulfill a description I once heard of a gentleman who "was an encyclopedia of undigested misinformation."

This writer is informed. The information is sound. It has been digested. It is written in an attractive way with an engaging style, and it conveys to the American people truths of the very first magnitude.

When these truths are known, and the American people demand their constitutional right of an honest money system, this country will enter upon an era of material and physical prosperity; of opportunity, and spiritual and cultural advancement that will not only charm and delight its own people but will become a model for the rest of the human race.

ROBERT L. OWEN,
New York City,
October 29, 1934.

CONTENTS

CONTENTS

To the American People, from Whom the Truth Has Been Too Long Withheld.

In honor of Alice Coogan
In memory of Michael Coogan
1858-1916

Why This Book Was Written

"With adequate knowledge of the physical realities that dominate the economic affairs of peoples, the road is clear for unlimited progress and the attainment of universal peace and prosperity. The evils that in the past have paralyzed the very heart of nations lie patent and beyond concealment. So they pass beyond the power of further harm. Only that rarest kind of courage—intellectual fearlessness and honesty to face things as they are and not as they appear—is required to abolish poverty and economic degradation from our midst..."

—*Wealth, Virtual Wealth and Debt,* by Frederick Soddy.

"A great industrial nation is controlled by its system of credit. Our system of credit is concentrated. The growth of the nation, therefore, and all our activities are in the hands of a few men . . . We have come to be one of the worst ruled, one of the most completely controlled and dominated Governments in the civilized world — no longer a Government by free opinion, no longer a Government by conviction and the vote of the majority, but a Government by the opinion and duress of small groups of dominant men."

—Woodrow Wilson, 1916.

Democrats were ousted; Republicans came and went. Democrats are back—what has been done to destroy this illicit power so clearly defined by a President who was later forced to follow its dictates?

"What is it we want of our currency? . . . We want a dollar that will, in the language of the President, 'not change its purchasing and debt paying power during the succeeding generation' . . .

"What are the points to be taken into consideration? First and foremost, that Congress should assume the responsibility laid on it by the Constitution of regulating the value of money. We now know that a given weight of gold is not an unchanging standard of value. That fact is dawning slowly on the most conservative and obstinate minds."

—Frank A. Vanderlip, 1935.
Former Pres. National City Bank,
of New York.

CHAPTER I

WHY?

When Lincoln wanted to issue constitutional money, he was violently opposed by the "Bullion Brokers," as the international bankers were called in those days. Lincoln was, perhaps, the greatest exponent of honesty and of the Constitution that this country has had since Washington. He persisted in demanding honest money, until he was silenced.

Abraham Lincoln, by the following quotation, proved that he understood the private control of money:

"As a result of the war, corporations have been enthroned and an era of corruption in high places will follow, and the money power of the country will endeavor to prolong its reign by working upon the prejudices of the people until wealth is aggregated in the hands of a few and the Republic is destroyed. I feel at this moment more anxiety for the safety of my country than ever before, even in the midst of the war."

President Garfield publicly stated that the hand that controls the money supply, rules the nation. What hand sent Guiteau?

An honest, constitutional money system is the *one* thing that international money magicians will *not* stand for. Woe to the scientific man who attempts to teach the people common sense in money systems, as envisioned by the founders of the Nation.

Benjamin Franklin, in his autobiography, stated that the refusal of George III to allow the colonies to continue to operate an honest colonial money system, which permitted freedom of the ordinary man from the clutches of manipulators, was probably the prime cause of the American Revolution. Franklin was perhaps the wisest man this continent has ever produced; he was a great thinker and statesman.

You are invited to consider what we have in America. Have you consented to be "tricked" out of your heritage, your children's and your grandchildren's? You are asked to decide whether both you and your descendants wish to live in peace and prosperity, secure under the kind of money system visualized by the Founders of this Nation, and their faithful disciple, Abraham Lincoln; or in slavery, starvation and chaos.

We now witness:

America in a financial cramp — and no relief in sight!

What a spectacle!

The world's greatest nation (richest in raw materials) laid low and writhing in an agony of monetary starvation. Factories idle, while abundant raw materials are at hand but unused, and workmen starving while they linger about the gates hoping for them to be thrown open; farmers hard at work growing their crops in sufficient abundance, but unable to find buyers at decent "prices" — that mysterious index of prosperity.

Business men able and willing to put their brains and factories to work on what is needed by the people at large, yet restrained from so doing because there is a lack of purchasing power upon which all commercial activity depends.

Clouds of "mystery" everywhere, and on every mountain top a prophet of gloom and doom in cap and gown.

We now hear:

Tirades against the Constitution and assertions

that it is an antiquated failure by those who have never tried to give even a hint of how matters can really be improved within the framework of that document which is effectually fitted to human nature.

"Humanists," "Liberals," "Socialists," "Internationalists" and "Communists" (but not Bolshevists strangely enough) crying for Economic Justice for the oppressed, the weak, the able and disabled, the widows and orphans, and meaning every word of their Jeremiads.

Speakers crying out against Capitalism, without a thought as to what happens to Christian people and institutions under Bolshevism — the *secret* inevitable of the "reforms" these same speakers are demanding at the expense of the God-given right of every rational human being to own property and enjoy the fruits of his own labors.

We never hear the following truths:

Capitalism is that system of political economy which recognizes the right of individuals to own, use and control private property. The right to own private property conforms to the basic laws of human nature—the reward to the individual for effort and attainment. Equality of opportunity is part of our fundamental code. However, individuals differ; some desire and will assume responsibilities, others decline them. Since natural endowments differ, and individuals differ in their desire to work, the rights of individuals to obtain possessions and distinctions are God-given and inherent in human nature.

Capitalism includes the right of a working man to own his cottage; his right to his instruments of production; his automobile, etc., as well as the employer to own the factory which employs him in turning out products which civilization needs. This is the point which the internationalists are not making clear.

Capitalism is not a means of exploiting the masses for the benefit of the few. In America, as in other countries, in recent years, particularly since the World War, the masses have been thoroughly exploited, and that exploitation was made possible and executed only because class legislation and dishonest and maliciously controlled private money creation and cancellation powers—fraudulently granted—became the weapons through which the few, most of whom were internationalists, accomplished the exploiting.

NOW!

That that exploitation has been accomplished — great wealth and power having become concentrated in the hands of a very few—discussions and cartoons are being widely circulated attempting to teach that Capitalism itself is a system of government which keeps a few *very rich* and all the rest *very poor.* This is being done to make the people of the United States believe that Capitalism should be abandoned.

It is a very sinister element that is trying to tell us that Capitalism is wrong. The bolder are stating that we have outgrown Capitalism; the more dishonest are claiming that science and invention have necessitated discarding Capitalism and adopting a Socialistic form of government. Those who are responsible for such misstatements would have the United States abandon Capitalism in order to further entrench the wealth and power of these internationalists.

We hear Capitalism has failed! No, the right and pride of ownership of private property has *not failed* and will *never cease* while man is man.

The error lies not in Capitalism but in our having permitted it to be abused, and allowing a small minority, through malicious operation of the monetary system, to destroy the economic security and peace of all others.

Capitalism has now, because of the suffering of the masses, become a target at which the demagogues are aiming the very arrows fashioned by their own masters—those masters are the internationalists, the manipulators of unconstitutional and dishonest money powers. The masters of the demagogues are the real enemies of patriotic Americans.

Under three unjust super-commandments the World is ruled by the International Money Masters:

"*Thou shalt not make honest the money system.*"

"*Thou shalt not follow the money mandates of the Constitution of the United States.*"

"*Thou shalt not examine the money subject except under our direction.*"

And even the prominent spiritual leaders obey their dictates!

And patriotic organizations formed ostensibly to "defend and uphold" the Constitution are strangely, but it seems intentionally, *silent* on the most flagrant violation of the Constitution—the delegation to private individuals of the most important national prerogative — "the power to coin money and regulate the value thereof."

That violation is the principal cause of our overwhelming depression and Socialistic onrush. Without *Economic* Liberty there can be no lasting political liberty, or religious liberty. All forms of liberty depend upon Economic Liberty.

But are the International Money Creators the Bolshevists' supporters and sympathizers?

Are the international money masters and their

domestic pawns the holders of money-creating privileges, contrary to the plain words of the Constitution? Are they the real generators, financiers, controllers, and profiteers of Communism, Socialism, Bolshevism and social disorder of all kinds?

Let the reader decide from the evidence, to which the keys are given herein, and confirmed by many other American volumes.

Let the reader also decide as to the remedy.

Thinking in terms of "*how?*" and "*why?*" on the part of every American, and the exercise of the political sense demonstrated by his predecessors (the founders and builders of this Nation) are the only means of salvation for America, as well as for the rest of the World.

It makes no difference to which Political Party your Congressman belongs. He is *your* servant. He must do what his constituents demand. Our enemies operate only while we American people remain uninformed. *Inform yourself and your fellowmen.*

"Truth is Simple"; "Knowledge is Power." The question is: Is our knowledge of truth or of falsehood? If the former, it imposes the duty of dissemination; if the latter, that of exposure and rectification. The possession of a modicum of knowledge also imposes another obligation, viz.: that of aggregation; and still another: to properly use the power thus acquired; for, while knowledge is power it is a power for evil as for good, according to the use made of it by its possessor.

John Adams wrote to Thomas Jefferson in 1787:

"All the perplexities, confusion and distress in America arise, not from defects in their Constitution or Confederation, not from want of honor or virtue, so much as from downright ignorance of the nature of coin, credit and circulation."

Our Constitution, repeatedly analyzed by eminent students of political science, has been pronounced the key to the science of government. Shall we destroy a government of laws based upon reason and supinely accept the only alternative—a government based upon force, violence, intimidation, and the negation of man's right to use his God-given reason? Our Constitution, as written, recognized the basic fundamentals of human nature.

"Human law is law only in virtue of its accordance with right reason; and thus it is manifest that it flows from the eternal law. And in so far as it deviates from right reason it is called unjust law: in such case it is not law at all, but rather a species of violence."—St. Thomas of Aquinas, Summa Theologiae, Qxciii, Art. iii.

Our economic and social chaos will be increased as we depart further from the rule of reason upon which this country's laws were based. Our economic and social chaos can be eliminated only by restoring an honest money system and, through that step, open the way for a return to the scientific principles of government upon which human progress must be based.

Shall we be driven back to the primitive life of barter for exchange of goods and services, or shall we push aside the human obstacles and set up an honest, simple money system adequate for making all of our exchanges of goods and services readily, and with universal convenience and permanent prosperity?

CHAPTER II

THE SETTING FOR THE "MYSTERY"

THE CONGRESS SHALL HAVE POWER: TO COIN MONEY, REGULATE THE VALUE THEREOF AND OF FOREIGN COIN.

(*Article I, Section 8, Part 5—Constitution of the United States*)

HOW LONG SHALL WE CONTINUE TO ALLOW OUR PRESENT UNCONSTITUTIONAL MONEY SYSTEM TO KEEP OUR NATION ARTIFICIALLY POOR?

"Congress shall have power to coin money, and regulate the value thereof." This well-defined authority contains the hope of preserving from destruction our entire civilization. Fortunately, for Americans and for the entire world, the founders of this country, the authors of the Constitution of the United States, knew well the supreme importance of a scientific and honest money system. Farsighted and intelligent, they took the enormous precaution of placing the power to coin money and regulate its value, with Congress alone. That power is the greatest power inherent in any people who constitute a civilized nation, because with money we make our exchanges of goods and services.

The founders of this nation, being learned men, knew well the effects of allowing money creation to be made a privilege and function of private individuals. The phrase "to regulate the value thereof" gives power to control the purchasing power of all money in the nation. Wide and sudden gyrations in the purchasing power of money have been the direct cause of more human misfortune and suffering than any other single force in the experience of civilized peoples. To entrust that power to private individuals gives them controls which can actually jeopardize the welfare of every individual in a nation.

The subject of money has been presented in all countries as a mystery beyond the wit of all save a few "supermen" to understand. "High finance" has been considered magic, controlled by forces unintelligible to the real producers of wealth — those who plan and labor to produce the things which people and nations need to sustain life.

Industrialists and agriculturists have been duped and the working classes have been made slaves, not because they are incapable of producing all things necessary for every family to live well; that is, to have houses, food, clothing and opportunities for culture and recreation, but simply because they did not understand the nature and operation of the money system of the United States. Had it been honestly explained, they would never have allowed its practices to continue. A money system, if based upon correct and honest principles, is very simple. Those who succeeded in inducing Congress to grant unconstitutional money powers have spent many millions in political racketeering and subsidizing the teaching of false economic and monetary principles. The possessors of these unconstitutional privileges, in reality, govern the United States. This was well demonstrated in President Hoover's administration. He privately admitted that he knew the monetary policies in force should be changed. When asked why, as President of the United States, he did nothing to effect this change, he answered that those in charge of the Federal Reserve policies would not allow him to act, or even make his knowledge known to the public.

Truth is Simple

Only falsehoods and false principles need be discussed in mysterious terms. Any citizen of ordinary mentality can readily understand the money system of this country. In studying it he will observe that there are two important phases: (1) he will see how it works in the distribution of goods, domestically produced and consumed; (2) he will see how our money system connects with the money systems of other countries. Because the United States is a 95% self-contained country, the all important object should be to operate the system to provide domestic purchasing power. Since 1920, that object has been disastrously sacrificed.

A correct understanding of the nature and operation of our money system will bring a concerted demand from all real patriots for correction of the present unconstitutional, unscientific and dishonest money-creating privilege serving a few private individuals. Some individuals have used those unconstitutional powers to destroy the economic and social fabric of our could-be great America for their own selfish advantages.

Not content with possessing these vast, dishonestly acquired privileges, which have concentrated the nation's wealth in their hands, they have proceeded to use the power of this wealth to rob loyal Americans also of their personal liberties, and reduce them to slaves in the category of mere animals. Socialism and Communism, as preached and practiced in the world today, and *recognized by most Americans as false doctrines,* have already to a considerable degree been saddled and bridled upon this people. Originated and fostered by foreign beneficiaries of our institutions, these false doctrines have been used to betray America, and, under the guise of "reform" and high-sounding humanitarian appeals to laborers of all classes, are now being used to weld the chains of tyranny and oppression around the limbs, and place shackles on the brains of all save the Elect few;—in fact, to induce Americans to assist in forging their own fetters.

For the past twenty years a handful of selfish vested international interests have controlled our money system, and with it the power to manipulate our entire economic life. If that control is not taken away from them, there is only one answer — the United States Government will be destroyed, millions of lives will be lost, years of starvation, chaos and sorrow will follow—the French and Russian Revolutions will be duplicated in America. Those international interests who seek complete world control will have their own possessions in real property and in gold. When other people's properties pass into the hands of the internationally-controlled Government, under the guise of Socialism and Communism, they will, in reality, pass into their hands; because the Government will be in their hands, as in Russia.

A revolution for America is in the World Plan of the Internationalists. It can be averted only if every loyal American will rise to the occasion and help, by such means as he is blessed with, be it knowledge, wise counsel, information, and personal services or money for spreading facts, warnings and encouragement,—and, I repeat, help those individuals who now endeavor to preserve, not only America, but all nations from a return of the Dark Ages, which followed the fall of the Roman Republic;—and will surely follow the fall of our own. The same financiers who brought terror, starvation and murder to Russia are at work in America.

In order to destroy intangible claims on wealth,

such as insurance policies and bonds of all kinds, they can execute a complete destruction of currency through a vicious inflation. A vicious inflation results from printing and putting into circulation unlimited amounts of currency, and continuing that process until the currency is outstanding in such enormous volume that it actually has no value. In the early stages of a vicious currency inflation, only the extremely shrewd can detect the process. Excess money dilutes the purchasing power of all the money in circulation. As soon as vicious currency inflation is recognized by the masses, they hasten to turn all money into actual physical property. When that stage is reached the entire money structure of the nation is quickly destroyed. It was done after the issue of assignats during the French Revolution; it was repeated after the Russian Revolution. To brave and informed people "Only that is inevitable which has already happened."

CHAPTER III

THE ORIGIN OF THE PRACTICES

The Origin of the Practices of our Mysterious and Unconstitutional System of Money

Fundamentally, only the Government of a nation should create money. It should be created by the imprint of a National Government, and paid into circulation in the first instance as government expenditures. As people's ability to produce the necessities and luxuries of life increases, in other words, as the people learn how to use tools and machinery instead of hand labor, they are capable of producing more crops, minerals, houses, clothing, etc., etc. As more of these things are being produced, more money is necessary in order that distribution can take place among the people constituting a nation. Were the money system of a nation in the hands of conscientious men, they would carefully observe the growth of actual production, and as it increases, they would enlarge the supply of money, and put it into circulation in payment for some governmental operation. When issued to pay for necessary government buildings or to pay the legitimate and reasonable costs of carrying out the government's real purpose—to protect the person and property of private individuals—all governmental costs do not have to be met by taxation. But additional money can only be issued as physical production increases. Otherwise, the purchasing power of all money outstanding would be diluted.

If money were placed in circulation out of proportion to the physical goods actually produced, it would cause prices to rise, that is, the purchasing power of money would be less. The object of an honestly operated money system is not to do that. The object is to keep a flow of money adequate to permit distribution to take place among all producers of the nation. That kind of money system is both scientific and honest.

Before the advent of private money-creating power, if any private individual created money and caused the imprint of a government to be put upon it, he was guilty of counterfeiting. What he was doing was really stealing from all of the other people in the nation, because as he counterfeited money and put it into circulation, he was not only obtaining purchasing power for himself, but he was diluting the purchasing power of all holders of money in the nation. In other words, he was increasing the flow of money without any regard to the actual physical goods existing within a nation. His increasing the volume of money raised prices for all other people in the nation which, of course, meant that the money belonging to all other people would have less purchasing power. When caught, he was punished very severely by the National Government, for counterfeiting is a very serious offense. It is theft from every person having any purchasing power (money).

Any increase or decrease in the flow of money should be the function of the people acting through their duly elected representatives, Congress, and it should affect all producers of wealth in exactly the same manner.

A Beginning in Monetary Chicanery

In earlier periods of human existence, trade was conducted with various media of exchange; cows (*pecca,* hence the word pecuniary), sheep, gems, salt (mined in Italy and carried over the via salaria, the salt road; hence the word salary), skins, shells, and the wampum or beaded shells of the American Indian, as well as gold and silver.

Eventually, as population grew and trade increased, money became scarce. Then a group of money lenders conceived the idea of using gold and silver as a basis for the issue of paper money; whereupon they proceeded to obtain legal monopolies of issue in the various countries, which carried with it the power of manipulation and economic control.

Of course, well informed people know that money itself is not wealth. Money is simply a medium used as a reckoner or counter of wealth. Wealth classifies into two distinct types and functions: (1) Consumer goods, or perishable goods which are consumed or destroyed in actually motivating life; e.g., food, clothing, etc.; (2) Capital goods, or producer goods, which do not motivate life itself, but are instruments used in the production of consumer goods; e.g., a factory, a freight car, a machine, etc. These deteriorate and grow obsolete, but are not consumed by living beings directly.

Those who conceived the idea of using gold and silver as bases for money issue were able to "sell" that idea to their fellow citizens. There was really nothing the matter with using gold and silver tokens for money, so long as the nation using them was capable of obtaining enough of these metals to increase the flow of money whenever it became necessary due to the people's increasing ability to produce physical goods.

When people accepted the idea of using gold and silver tokens as the counters used in reckoning the actual physical wealth exchanged, they sought to have those precious metals kept in safe places. A farseeing individual among them realized that if he would build a strong room, people would hire him to store their precious metals. He thereupon went into business and was paid a fee for storing precious metals until the owners needed them to make whatever purchases they desired. Those who turned over precious metals to the owner of the strong room obtained receipts for their deposits.

The people soon found that it was inconvenient to go to the strong room keeper when they wanted precious metals and, since everybody was assured that precious metal was safe in the strong room, it soon became a common practice to simply turn over the receipts for the precious metals in exchange for goods. It was more convenient to pass a piece of paper which gave evidence that the precious metal existed, than it was to go and get the heavy metal to make the exchange. The new owner of the receipt did not take it to the strong room keeper because he felt that when he wanted to pass it on he could simply turn over the piece of paper. These pieces of paper were, in reality, the strong room keeper's promises-to-pay precious metals upon demand.

This was the original public error. The public error lay not in trusting the private banker with their real money, but in carelessly allowing the private banker to issue *his slips* of paper in *substitution* and later in multiplicate for *real money*. This placed his private seal on a parity with the seal of the Government on its lawful money. This was the step by which eventually the money seal of the private banker actually took precedence over the money seal of the Government itself.

The strong room keeper was in touch with others in the same business throughout his nation. We may be sure that no measures were overlooked by which the laws of nations would be made to legalize practices which were rooted in secretly established precedents rather than on honest and sound principles.

Whenever any modern Government has attempted to establish a common sense, honest, simple money system, such attempts have always been defeated by law makers who inserted trick clauses in the legislation.

It was a fatal mistake to turn over the money metal to private custodians in return for private receipts, and allow them to secretly issue multiplicate receipts, which then became money—the medium of exchange.

That was only one-half of the mistake; the other part lay in the stupidity of the nation in legalizing this fraudulent practice, as has our Congress.

The Strong Room Keeper Sees Opportunities

The keeper of the strong room was a clever and observant man. He soon noticed that the people were exchanging his promises-to-pay the precious metals with one another. He learned this upon noticing that some of those who brought these receipts to his strong room were not the ones to whom he had originally issued them, but he was perfectly willing, if people desired, that business be done in that way.

The second observation he made had very far-reaching effects. He noticed that only a small percentage of the people presented receipts for their precious metals on any given day. In other words, he noticed that about 90% of his total stock of gold remained in his vaults entirely undisturbed, and that only about 10% of the stored metal was necessary to take care of disbursements and receipts in the course of business.

A temptation entered his mind! Since approximately only 10% of the owners of metal ever wanted it at once, why not issue more receipts than metal actually existed in the vaults? He knew the principle was dishonest, but the temptation was great.

After thinking the matter over carefully, and finally succumbing to the temptation, he decided to begin in a small way issuing receipts for more metal than he held in the vaults. In other words, he would increase his promises-to-pay metal beyond the amount of metal that actually existed, and collect interest on this fictitious money. This was the original fraud, which exists even today, and is the root of all our economic ills. Let the bankers defend the practice as they will, *the fact* remains that when they loan their "credit" at interest they are simply creating private money, which they can recall and destroy at will to the distress and impoverishment of the borrower, who periodically finds himself forced through artificial scarcity of "credit" money to pay back real property for the "credit" dollars borrowed.

He quietly looked around for some business man who might need more money to conduct his business. The business man he sought was a good hard-working honest man. When approached with the idea that the keeper of the strong room would lend him money at interest, he thought that the promise-to-pay which the strong room keeper was offering to lend him, was a receipt for precious metal which actually belonged to the strong room keeper himself. He had no thought that it was simply a fictitious claim created by the stroke of the pen of the strong room keeper and that the gold to which it was a claim did not exist.

When the strong room keeper issued these promises-to-pay metal which did not exist, he secured from each borrower a mortgage—on his home or business—as security for the return of an equivalent amount of metal receipts. This of course, was dishonest because he was demanding real security for his promises-to-pay fictitious gold; more than existed in his vaults. He simply had created that promise by a stroke of the pen. Furthermore, he gave no security to the actual owners of the metal in his vaults when he began to issue more promises-to-pay than metal existed.

After a while the strong room keeper grew still bolder and less principled. The business man to whom he loaned a receipt for fictitious precious metal agreed to pay interest for the use of that money and agreed to return a receipt for metal on a given date. The strong room keeper then found that his income was increasing. He was not only getting a fee for safe-guarding metal but he was getting interest on receipts for metal which did not exist. However, the business man was totally unaware that he was a party to a dishonest practice.

Business went along well and the strong room keeper sought other business men to whom he agreed to lend receipts for precious metal. With the increasing of these receipts for precious metal, loaned at interest, prices began to rise and people began to notice an acceleration in the rate of business, due to the increasing supply of money which allowed more men to work and produce by supplying the medium for making their exchanges. Business men found their profits increasing and sought to expand their businesses. Other men hearing of the loans which the strong room keeper had made, applied for loans themselves, because they saw in a rising price structure, a chance to earn more profits.

The strong room keeper was actually causing inflation (bankers' money inflation), that is, he was increasing the amount of money in circulation at a faster rate than physical goods were being increased. This was *inflation,* of which the people of the community were entirely unaware.

The Strong Room Keeper Reaches His Limit

While the strong room keeper was increasing his promises-to-pay at a rate faster than the community was able to produce goods, prices were rising sharply. Rising prices are always caused by increasing the money flow faster than the actual physical volume of goods is increased. If the two are increased in the same proportion, production and distribution of increasing amounts of goods can take place without sharp price rises. While this sharp price rise was taking place, business activity was at high levels. There not only was no unemployment in the community, there was an actual shortage of labor. The community was happy. The members of every family who wanted to work were employed and had the purchasing power to buy the shoes, clothes, food, furniture, houses, etc., which were being produced.

The teachers in all of the schools had noted that the children were doing very good work. They came to school well fed and clothed and they radiated the happiness that prevailed in their homes. The charitable organizations in the community found their services unnecessary. Crime almost disappeared. The people wanted to work; there existed the raw materials and machinery with which to work, and there was a sufficient supply of money which made it possible for them to exchange their products for those of other workers.

There was not too much money in the community, but it had been issued too quickly and had caused sharp price rises. Had it been increased only as production was increased, those unhealthy price rises could not have taken place, but there was *not* too much money.

There was, however, one very *dangerous* aspect

in the situation. *Ninety percent* of the *money* which was in circulation had been created dishonestly by the strong room keeper. It consisted of his promises-to-pay precious metal which he did not have. He had issued them as loans and *he alone had complete control* over them.

The people did not realize that he had issued receipts for non-existent precious metal, and they were unaware that the strong room keeper had power to take away their opportunity to earn a livelihood and, hence, their happiness. We observed before that the strong room keeper in issuing these promises-to-pay, had taken mortgages on homes, farms and factories. He now held mortgages on a substantial part of the people's physical properties.

The strong room keeper realized that he must not expand beyond ten times the amount of metal he had in his vaults, for his experience had taught him that even in a rising price structure, it would be very dangerous to issue promises-to-pay in a greater ratio than ten to one.

He needed real money (precious metal) equivalent to about 10% of his promises-to-pay in order to keep up his deception, for about 10% of the transactions over his counter were in real money! Today the practice is accepted as "sound" because it is ancient and has been unwittingly legalized; it is so accepted only because of plausible arguments propagated by those who profit thereby.

Once those promises-to-pay fictitious metal had been spent by clients who borrowed from him, the new holders had exactly the same claim on the gold in his vaults as did those first individuals who had actually brought gold to his vaults. If something should happen to disturb the "confidence" of the people (every one knows "confidence" is the essence of this kind of banking, even today), he might be confronted very quickly with demands for more gold than he had in his vaults.

As soon as the strong room keeper stopped lending additional promises-to-pay, he noticed that prices ceased to rise. He began to wonder if some of the later borrowers might not have difficulty in selling their products, due to the fact that the volume of money was now stationary. He decided to curtail somewhat. He also saw an opportunity to take an *undue* advantage of all the people in the community.

Remember, he held mortgages on a number of their businesses and homes. His borrowers had given him these mortgages in good faith, believing that he had loaned them receipts for actual precious metal; never understanding that he was building up a collapsible money structure. They had no idea that they had borrowed and were paying interest on receipts for fictitious metal, and that the strong room keeper by merely calling in these receipts for non-existent metal could cause a serious collapse in prices and values.

The strong room keeper decided to act. He thereupon summoned the owner of one of the local factories before his loan period expired. He called him to his office and after a few very courteous inquiries, he told him that he felt the "business situation" warranted that some of his loans should be recalled. He very carefully explained to the factory owner that he, as the strong room keeper, was really the guardian of all business in the community and that he was bound to see that the business men keep their operations within reasonable limits.

The factory owner was very much surprised. He knew that he had given ample security for the loan, for he had given a mortgage on his factory, worth many times the amount of the loan. He also knew that his business was in good condition for he was showing very satisfactory profits, and he had no accumulation of inventories. He began to tell this to the strong room keeper. The strong room keeper grew very serious. After all, he told the factory owner, the strong room keeper's first obligation was to the entire community. He could observe what was going on in all businesses much better than any individual business man; that, after all, business men were human beings and were readily carried away by enthusiasm, ambition, and even greed. Therefore, the responsibility fell naturally and directly upon his shoulders to keep the business men in line. He further told the factory owner that the most essential thing in any business is to keep one's standing with the strong room owner and that in the name of "sound" lending, it would be necessary for him to curtail at this time.

Of course, he felt very sorry, but he just had to guard the "best interests" of the community. After all, he must be guided by the "laws of economics" alone. He could not be carried away by his desire to see full employment maintained for all of the people, or the community's desire to produce and distribute enough food, clothing and shelter for every family to have a reasonable share, as was possible because of the availability of raw materials and their ability and desire to work.

A Business Depression

The factory owner had no alternative. He left the strong room keeper's office glum and discouraged. Why was it necessary to call his loan; to cancel out what he was using for money? He knew that there were no inventories piling up in any of the businesses in the community. He knew that labor was giving an honest day's work for an honest day's pay. He could not understand why the harbinger of disaster had to descend upon his business. He felt resentful that the strong room keeper had said business men were greedy. He had worked very hard to build up his business and was not in any manner dissatisfied with any of the people who were working for him. If he were forced to realize cash to pay that loan, he would have to curtail his operations. That meant he would have to offer some of his goods for sale at much lower prices, and that he would have to discharge some of his employees. The thought of having to tell them saddened him. Why, when the community was getting along so well, did it have to be disturbed by a "business depression"? The community had demonstrated its ability to produce food, clothing and shelter for all of the people—why did the money man now have to start disturbing that situation?

He thought the matter over very carefully that night but could see no way out, excepting to cancel his orders for more raw material, and sell some of his goods at lower prices for quick raising of cash. The next day he notified his customers that they would have to pay him immediately. Each of them, of course, had to face the same situation that the factory owner faced. Each one in turn had to write to his customers and request the payment of accounts. Once set in motion the force was cumulative. Due to the sudden forced offering of goods, prices began to drop severely in all businesses. Alas! Soon working men began to get slips in their Saturday night envelopes telling them that work had to stop.

Meanwhile, prices continued to drop. The strong room keeper called in other borrowers. Some he ruthlessly told to pay their loans. Others he told he would have to raise the interest rates on their loans. Money was now "scarce" and in order to continue accommodating them, it would be necessary to increase the rate from 4% to 8%. They saw that prices had already fallen and knew they would have to sacrifice their inventories in order to obtain cash, so they agreed to pay the 8%. Collecting 8% meant that the strong room keeper could still, after squeezing his loans by 50%, enjoy the same income he was receiving when all of his promises-to-pay were outstanding.

He kept up the process of calling loans, forcing business men to sell their inventories and discharge their employees, until prices had dropped to the point where some of the business men were not able to sell their inventories and realize sufficient money to meet their loans. These business men he called in and in a very sympathetic tone of voice explained to them that they were simply victims of "economic laws" and that "economic laws" could not be violated. The strong room keeper had "to safeguard the money of the community." Though he disliked to act, it would be necessary for him to foreclose. He thereupon took over their businesses. Of course, he shed a few tears and told the business men he really felt very sorry that such a situation arose, but that his first duty was to safeguard the money of the community and that the "laws" of economics simply could not be violated by mankind.

This meant foreclosures. The business men had borrowed the banker's loans of imaginary or "confidence" money, secretly manufactured, actually sheer counterfeit; and now because the volume had been contracted must repay the "loans" with real wealth.

The business men thus had to turn over to the strong room keeper the results of many years of hard work. They had built their factories and stores over a period of years; they now had to turn them over to the keeper of the strong room and begin all over again, or try to find employment working for some one else. This process went on until the strong room owner had called in one-half of his promises-to-pay, and cancelled one-half of the money in the community. By simply "destroying" one-half of the fictitious money he had created he enriched himself by foreclosing on *real* wealth pledged against the loan of his fictitious money. Business men had pledged their real wealth (factories and properties) to obtain a loan of money which had nothing behind it except the money man's purely imaginary "credit"—on which they had paid interest.

The Community Calls an Economic Conference

The community had changed from a happy prosperous one to a scene of discouragement, disillusionment and poverty. Many working men had been discharged; many business men had lost their businesses and their homes; many farmers had lost their farms. The school children were no longer well fed and clothed. The demands for charity were overwhelming. Dissatisfaction and crime in the community became a serious problem.

The principal Christian clergyman in the town was a kindly, sympathetic gentleman. He wisely suggested that a committee be appointed to discuss the plight of their community, and see if there was not some solution to the serious mysterious trouble.

That suggestion was an excellent one. Therefore, two clergymen, two business men, the Mayor and one of the aldermen were asked to meet with the strong room keeper to discuss the town's problems. The business men were open, frank individuals and when asked for their opinions they said they believed the problem was a monetary one; that there simply was not as much money in the community as there had been before the trouble started. They pointed out that the same farms, factories, men and women were there and that, as they saw it, the one thing lacking was a sufficient amount of money in circulation to carry on production and distribution to effect the exchange of goods between various classes of producers and workers in the community. One of the clergymen spoke and said that he did not claim to understand the intricate "laws of economics," but that he was inclined to believe that the business men were right in their opinions.

However, the Mayor spoke. He said he knew "the people themselves were to blame" for the condition they were in. After all, they had been getting along very well and some of them had grown careless. "Why, some of the working men were even buying new furniture for their homes, and some working men's families had gone so far as to have their children taking music lessons." Of course, he realized that the town had made a great mistake when it had exceeded the bounds of good judgment by building a recreation park for the children. He admitted that the city officials themselves had been carried away, and that they regretted ever having proposed building a recreation park, for now they realized that the people were unable to pay for it because of the business depression. His thought was that it was too bad that the "laws of economics" were so rigid, but that human beings would simply have to obey them, and obeying them meant drastic economy on the part of everybody—and starvation for some of the less fortunate people—in the community.

The strong room keeper smiled at the Mayor and approved of his statements. Here was *one* man who understood "economic laws." Of course, this Mayor did not understand how the strong room had been operated.

The strong room keeper, having heard from the other gentlemen, it was now his turn to speak. He cleared his throat and in a very sad voice told the committee that he "regretted more than any one in the community" that the "laws of economics" were so rigid and did place such burdens on mankind, particularly upon the weaker members of the community. It made him very sad to see undernourished and poorly clad children, and old and emaciated people without the wherewithal to live in peace, but man did not make the "laws of economics" and he, as a guardian of the community's money could do no other than recognize those bitter laws. There was simply no solution to the problem except economy. He pointed out that he knew there was an "over supply" of food, clothing, houses, etc., and at the same time many people in the community were in destitution and want, from living in enforced and illogical idleness. But the community would have to face its problem courageously and they would simply have to economize more until all the debts foolishly contracted had been wiped out; that is, until the people either paid what they owed, or surrendered their property. That was the only "sound" solution. He knew that the people wanted a "sound solution." They certainly had no desire to violate the "laws of economics."

He blamed the business men for contracting debts "foolishly," but carefully glossed over his own origination of the loans, his own earlier approach to those same business men with offers of his "surplus" funds for their business purposes.

The business men were disgusted but they saw it would be folly to incur the wrath of the strong room keeper for, after all, if they did, and things ever did change, they personally would be unable to borrow from the strong room keeper and, hence, would be unable to partake of any future business opportunities. They simply had to accept what common sense told them were false conclusions regarding the "laws of economics."

The strong room keeper suggested that a resolution be drawn up stating that the consensus of opinion was that the community had been extravagant; business men had grown greedy (that is, all but the smug lender of counterfeit money); working men had become careless and shiftless, and that now they were only paying the price of their folly. There was no solution to the problem except "rigid economy." They admitted there was a vast store of unsalable clothes, food and houses in the community and regretted the unfortunate plight of the hungry and destitute, but the community would have to be led by courageous men, and *courageous* men could only recommend economy. Economy meant that they would all have to "tighten their belts" and buy less and, of course, all would have to hold the unfortunate members of the community in "sympathy"; they would have to arrange some method of gathering up a pittance from the more fortunate people in order to prevent actual starvation.

One of the clergymen suggested that every one in the community give a certain percentage of his income into a fund to take care of the destitute. That suggestion did not meet with the approval of the Mayor or the strong room keeper. "It would be unwise to make any mandatory points in the resolution." It should simply be suggested that everybody do what he could and leave it to his own generosity to contribute. That suggestion was especially in concurrence with the strong room keeper's ideas.

CHAPTER IV

A FOREIGN SNARE

The Strong Room Keeper Is Invited to Confer With the Large City Strong Room Keeper

While the depression was in its blackest phases —property was being foreclosed and more people were daily suffering increasingly from want — the strong room keeper received a very carefully written letter from a distant large city. It stated that the strong room keeper in that city had something of great importance to discuss with him. It was in connection with the "welfare" of his community. The large city strong room keeper had noted that a serious business depression prevailed in that section of the country. His own section had also suffered from a depression but it had not been so servere as the one in the community discussed. The strong room keeper was, of course, interested in anything that was for the "welfare" of his own community, because he was vitally interested in "service." He accepted the invitation.

When he reached the large city office on the appointed day, he there met the strong room keepers of several other communities. This must be an important meeting, he thought to himself, and felt flattered that he had been included in the invitation. The large city strong room keeper invited them all to a very sumptuous luncheon. After they had enjoyed plenty of good food and had lighted cigars, he arose to address the group. In a very grave voice he told these men from the smaller communities that he had observed that some of them had quite serious depressions in their districts, but that he supposed each of them knew how to guard himself, and that personally they were now in a better condition than ever before. They probably now owned a great deal of property which had been foreclosed, and that as soon as conditions began to right themselves they all would be in a position to sell those properties they had taken over and thus reap a big profit.

He congratulated them all for their business judgment and acumen and stated that he had a suggestion to make which he felt would be profitable to all present. The strong room keeper felt flattered, in the course of the speech, for he noticed that the large city strong room keeper began to address them as "Bankers." After all, he was a banker, and he was operating in his community on exactly the same principles as was the largest bank in the biggest city.

The large city banker told them he had recently been visited by a banker from London. The London banker had pointed out to him great advantages which would accrue to all bankers in this country, both large city and community, if all would "cooperate." Since all community bankers placed the "welfare" of their communities foremost in their consideration, he felt in conscience bound to call them for a discussion of the proposals of the London bankers. Of course, London typified all that was "learned and dignified" in money matters. The fact that the country in which these community bankers did business was practically self-contained was not to be considered. After all, mankind's highest interest could be furthered only by recognition of that type of "brotherhood" so admirably espoused in internationalism.

The large city banker mentioned his great admiration for the financial acumen of the London banker and felt constrained to accept the plan proposed as infallible for the promotion of world "prosperity" and "good will." Since it was difficult to improve upon the London banker's use of technical terms, the plan could best be presented if the letter prepared by the London banker were read:

"The Community Bankers of America,

"Honorable Gentlemen:

"Realizing the grave responsibilities you carry as the guardians of all industry, and knowing your supreme aim to increase the security of all industry, I feel constrained to recommend most urgently for your wise consideration, a plan for genuine world cooperation.

"I have noted that you have recently had a down swing in the business cycle and I perceive this would be a very propitious time to weld together ties for our mutual benefit. I have suggested to an honorable fellow banker in your leading city that he become the agent for the Bank of England. He is agreeable to the plan and awaits only the concurrence of your infallible decision.

"I have noted that the people in your local communities have, through wisely handled publicity, become convinced that your country is producing too much wheat and other agricultural products. I also note you have demanded payment of about one-half of your promises-to-pay and made very heavy foreclosures. I judge you are about ready to make your plans to begin another upward swing of the trade cycle (credit cycle).

"You must now be in a position where you can soon begin to reissue your promises-to-pay. As this is done, of course, with the rise in raw material prices and real estate values, you and your intimate friends will be able to reap handsome profits through the sale of some of the properties you now hold. I am sure your banks (strong rooms) are in good order and business men will be anxious to cooperate and work doubly hard to rebuild their businesses.

"They have shown that they love work, and you have demonstrated a praiseworthy willingness to allow them to indulge themselves in their peculiar fondness for productive activity—for a consideration to you. Only your willingness to lend your credit has made it possible for your people to make their exchanges. Their confidence in you (your 'credit') has actually been their money! To their interest payments they really should add grateful blessings to you for the vital 'service' rendered by their confidence in you.

"I further note that your country could well undertake some capital expansion. More railroads and steel plants could be built, more farm machinery factories should be added; in the merchandising field I believe you are ready for some mail order houses.

"I have therefore suggested to your worthy leader that some highly regarded British bankers place some of their promises-to-pay (loans) on a long term basis for your country. A New York banker will act as our agent.

"You realize that if large amounts of long term promises-to-pay are placed for your country, it will be necessary to send both interest and principal payments to London in the form of raw materials, particularly wheat, cotton and pork products. An opportunity to export some of your 'surplus' food supplies will most assuredly be a 'blessing' to your good people at this time.

"In order to insure smooth working plans and full cooperation for mutual benefit, it will be necessary that you place a part of your promises-to-pay on the books of your worthy large city banker. These promises-to-pay must constitute a reasonable part of your entire loans and it will be necessary that you follow very carefully all the suggestions made from time to time. You understand that world trade requires constant 'cooperation.'

"We will, in addition to placing large long term promises-to-pay for your country for its development, also assist your country by placing some short term credits with your reliable and worthy leading bankers.

"We will be very happy to have your country ship us quantities of wheat, cotton and pork products. Your country will then have the inestimable benefits of the great Liverpool and Manchester markets. It will be much better for America to have its agricultural price levels for both domestic consumption and export determined entirely in England. England is so experienced and astute. Her markets are so much more reliable than your own ever could be. The great commodity markets in England have been very wisely built, and men throughout the world look with awe at their movements.

"The commodity exchanges in your own country will act as mirrors for the great English markets. They will be efficient branches.

"If, from time to time, we find it necessary to withdraw substantial amounts of our short term promises-to-pay from New York, it will, of course, be essential that you cooperate to the extent of calling in your promises-to-pay simultaneously. If we are to carry the responsibility of determining world markets in all raw materials, we will have to have complete cooperation in all of the great countries. When the 'requirements of business' necessitate our withdrawing large amounts of short term promises-to-pay, it will also be necessary for you to take drastic steps to curtail your loans whenever notified by our agent in your great New York City.

"I shall await your judicious decision. May I wish your great country progress under its worthy Bankers.

Cordially yours,

LORD RIDING."

ONE COMMUNITY BANKER WAS TOO SHREWD—HE SPOKE ALMOST TOO PLAINLY IN THIS INTIMATE GROUP

The community bankers stared at each other. The large city banker saw that the letter had not impressed as he desired. He thereupon hastened to amplify by pointing out that cooperation with the London bankers would give each community banker a much greater diversification on his promises-to-pay. Instead of all of the promises-to-pay being outstanding in the local community, the small banker would be able to place some of his promises-to-pay in New York. In fact, it would even be possible for him to send promises-to-pay to New York simultaneously with his withdrawing them in his local community. In other words, he could create more local business depressions, thereby getting title to more properties, and while they were in progress not be without earning income on as many promises-to-pay as he dared issue.

Then, too, it would be better not to have all of the promises-to-pay in the local community, for there would be much less danger of some local situation disturbing the "confidence" of the people. Even one local situation might cause many people to demand more metal for their promises-to-pay than he actually held, and thus expose his fundamental self-created insolvency. If a substantial part of his promises-to-pay were not in the local community, that danger would be diminished.

After he had gone on with the discussion, a banker from one of the local communities decided to ask some questions. Why wouldn't he, as a small community banker, be jeopardizing himself when he allowed the large city banker, and in turn the London banker, to decide when he had to curtail the volume of his promises-to-pay? He said that he had found his own judgment as to when to curtail very good, and he believed he would be better satisfied to continue operating his strong room in a manner agreeable to himself. He had found that there was no actual overproduction of anything in his community, for when his promises-to-pay were at the maximum levels commensurate with "reasonable safety," the people were able to purchase and consume everything they produced.

He also boldly reminded the group that this country is 95% self-contained. To sacrifice agricultural prices to London control could, if London saw fit to do so, destroy the purchasing power of a large part of the population. If control of the situation were taken out of his hands and placed in the hands of the banker at New York, it might create some very difficult situations. Then, too, he said, if we allow the price levels of all of the raw materials which we produce to be determined in London, London might not adjust those prices high enough to cover the cost of production of most of our farmers. He pointed out that not all farmers had equal costs, and in order for the majority to cover cost of production and have a reasonable profit, it would be necessary to take into serious consideration the varying costs in different parts of the country. He knew what the costs were in his own district and he knew when the price levels were adequate to cover the cost of production and leave a profit. He knew of other districts where actual costs were less than in his own district. He wisely distrusted "average" figures. He, therefore, hesitated very much to place the power to control the price levels of raw materials in London, because London might set a price on basic raw materials which would be high enough for some districts of the United States, but not high enough for most of them.

He pointed out that if the promises-to-pay were adequately expanded in all districts and kept that way, excepting when "depressions" were judicious, there would be no surplus problem. Even under a curtailed volume of promises-to-pay (the result of having intentionally called in loans), he felt that not more than 25% of the wheat could be exported under such conditions. Why should he allow London, which might possibly take 25% of the wheat, to determine the price levels for the 75% which would always be consumed in his own country? He therefore felt that, in his case, it would be much wiser to keep his operations confined to his own district. After all, he might issue some long term promises-to-pay and build some steel plants. He knew of no raw materials which could not be bought in his own country. Of course, it might take longer to develop his district, but if it were done in that way, the country would be under the control of its own bankers.

The large city banker hastened to put him right: "You understand that agriculture is a 'mode of living' only. It is really not a business, and when we are looking at the long term 'welfare' of the country, we should not take into consideration too seriously whether the farmers in any particular districts are able to sell their products at prices adequate to cover their costs and leave a reasonable profit. Raw material prices must always be sacrificed to the promotion of great industry." With a laugh he continued:

"After all, farmers are an illiterate class, and if they are given reasonable profits over too long a period, they might grow shiftless. It's better to keep them in their place and we can do that by controlling their price levels. You understand if price levels of raw materials are kept down, we can then also keep down wages for city laborers. Wages constitute an important cost of production of all manufactured goods and if they are kept low, much better profits will be available to us—the eventual owners of businesses. Laborers also have a tendency to grow lazy and shiftless if they are allowed too much freedom. We can very readily control wage levels, in fact, they can be controlled in all of the industrial countries of the world, by our cooperation with London bankers. You see, London bankers will be placing loans in many other countries.

"As soon as prices of labor begin to rise, due to the fact that a particular country has enjoyed an upward swing in the cycle, it will be very simple for London bankers to keep labor also in its place by suddenly curtailing long term loans in that country. As the operations of that country are curtailed through the withdrawal of long term promises-to-pay, long term promises-to-pay can be placed in other countries which have had less of an upward swing in the business cycle. This constant recurrence of cycles in all of the countries, under the control of London, will tend to make laborers see that it is hopeless for them to expect to enjoy constant purchasing power and they will be satisfied to accept their inevitable periods of unemployment and 'leisure' whenever we find it necessary to curtail and bring about the downward phase of the business cycle."

But another question arose in the community banker's mind. He courageously asked: "If our price levels are determined at London, and we curtail our promises-to-pay whenever ordered to do so by the New York bankers, I presume the London bankers will simultaneously withdraw gold from New York and return it to London. Am I right in that conclusion?"

The city banker responded: "Yes, you are right in that conclusion. It will be necessary for you to curtail and as you curtail we will have to allow London bankers, if they so desire, to withdraw metal from this country. You understand that London is the great gold market of the world. London sets the price of gold and, of course, the currency of our country will be transferred into the currencies of London on a certain gold ratio. For instance, it is proposed that an ounce of gold in New York 0.9 fine will be worth $20.67. When wheat or other raw materials are sold in Liverpool, it will be an easy matter to convert the proceeds in terms of gold into United States dollars. To make transfers of gold from London to New York unnecessary, London bankers will take ample precaution to place sufficient long term promises-to-pay for America in London to force sufficiently large interest payments to offset the value of the raw materials exported to London. If London is to control, gold must always move to London, for gold is the alleged basis of the promises-to-pay. Gold moving out of London would force a collapse of the London money structure."

Still another question arose and the community banker spoke: "Suppose that London should at some time decide to change the number of units of currency for which an ounce of gold could be exchanged. If an ounce of gold could be exchanged for 20.67 dollars in New York, but London increased the number of shillings for which an ounce of gold could be exchanged, a serious disadvantage would arise for the American exporter. With an ounce of gold exchangeable for 20.67 dollars, or approximately 85 shillings in terms of London units of currency, what could prevent London from raising the number of shillings exchangeable for an ounce of gold to 100 or 125, or even 150? The number of shillings exchangeable for an ounce of gold is an arbitrary figure which London gold brokers could alter at their pleasure.

"Or what if London bankers decide to change the number of units of currency exchangeable for an ounce of gold in all of the colonial possessions of Great Britain? In that case, if the American farmer ships raw materials to Great Britain, in transferring his London credits into dollars, he will get fewer units of his own currency than the exporters of other countries will receive units of their currencies. Hence, wouldn't the American farmer be actually getting less units of currency with which he could pay his interest, taxes and overhead, and have fewer dollars left to buy industrial products?"

The community banker realized that the great Liverpool market was the center for the agricultural exports from all of the colonies, and it would be possible for the London bankers to change the currency price of gold in the colonies and, hence, give an unfair advantage to the agricultural products from the colonies.

The large city banker smiled at this apparent lack of faith in the integrity of the London bankers. At the same time, he was disturbed that any of the community bankers could reason out the proposition so clearly. Many of the community bankers were shaking their heads in apparent confusion as to just what was the point of the question raised by the apprehensive community banker.

The large city banker, with a magnanimous gesture, stated that after all, community bankers should realize that London was the "center of integrity" and that they should be honored to be invited to cooperate in the great world plan; that when such an occasion as the community banker was attempting to discuss arose, it would be time enough to worry over that problem. After all, "integrity" was the essence of banking operations and he felt that a simple community banker had no right to question the integrity of the London bankers.

The community banker saw that it was hopeless. He realized that he would not be able to stand out alone. He saw very clearly that the proposition was acceptable to most of the community bankers, mystified though they were. He therefore knew that if he refused to cooperate, he would soon become an outcast and take the chance of having the New York City banker establish some one else in his community who would, over a reasonable time, be able to take his business away from him.

He therefore wisely decided to abide by what he realized would be the vote of the majority, and although he knew the proposition was contrary to his better judgment and would be a serious disadvantage to his community and his country, he was politic enough to realize that it was time to keep those conclusions to himself.

He thereupon rose to tell the great city banker that he agreed and that, after all, London was the center of "integrity" and that his country could well adopt the plans proposed. He felt that world cooperation would be a means of controlling farmers and laborers, which would be an advantage.

CHAPTER V

THE "FEDERAL RESERVE" SNARE

ANOTHER SNARE IS CREATED, THIS TIME FOR THE SUCCESSOR TO THE COMMUNITY BANKER

Many years passed. The successor to the community banker many times regretted that his predecessor had agreed to allow himself to be controlled by London bankers but, now that his nation was dependent upon the Liverpool wheat and Manchester cotton markets and London bankers had placed large volumes of their promises-to-pay for United States in London there was nothing he could do personally but cooperate. Many times he felt that the London bankers were ruthless in curtailing the promises-to-pay at times when it jeopardized most seriously the businesses of farmers and industrialists in his country. However, if he raised his voice, he would simply find himself declared a public enemy by the many newspapers which the London and New York bankers now seemed able to control.

The sub-rosa, dishonest principles originated by the strong room keeper are related to call to the attention of the reader, the actual origin of our unsound and crooked private money creation practices. In the United States we did not actually have the stage of the strong room keeper in our banking system.

The Constitution of the United States was ratified long after the development of private money creation had gone beyond the rudimentary stage of the strong room keeper. The Constitution of the United States was intentionally written to prevent the strong room keeper's thievery becoming the essence of the money system of the United States.

In 1791, after the death of Benjamin Franklin, Alexander Hamilton through connivery, succeeded in getting banking laws passed which were in violation of the Constitution of the United States. These laws re-introduced the private money creation system in this country. They re-inaugurated in toto the dishonest practices instituted by the strong room keeper. The story of how Alexander Hamilton accomplished this dishonest legislation, and the facts regarding his own viewpoint, are told in a later chapter of this book.

The great panics of 1873, 1884, 1893, 1903 and 1907 had been serious handicaps in the development of America, but each time the great industry and thrift of the American people inspired them again to go ahead even though manipulators had repeatedly caused them to lose their properties through intentional well timed curtailment of the supply of money, the supply of their private promises-to-pay.

In 1913 the American Community banker was summoned to a very important meeting in New York. Community bankers from all over the United States were there. Each man was pledged to secrecy, for the discussions at this meeting were of a highly confidential nature and "intelligible only to bankers." The Chairman of the meeting arose in a very affable manner to address the group:

"Gentlemen: I have the great honor of presenting to you today facts and details regarding the accomplishment of one of the greatest blessings ever bestowed upon 'our' country. You realize that 'we' have never had a completely unified banking system. There have been units which have attained great strength and as they grew stronger rendered increasing 'service' to our country. But there have been other lesser units which have remained really local in nature. They have gone along and taken care of the needs of their own communities or districts, but they have never been a vital part of a real international system of banking.

"We all know that real progress is based upon 'international cooperation.' England has done us the great honor of assisting in the development of our country and she now asks us to establish a banking system which will more closely parallel her own system, also the system dominated in France by the privately owned Bank of France, and in Germany by the privately owned Reichsbank. These great banking systems fit with the majestic privately owned banking system of England. America must pattern hers after the learned banking accomplishments of Europe.

"Our great country also should have a system which will make our currency very 'elastic.' It is proposed that 'we' establish twelve great Central Banks in twelve important districts of the United States. Each of these twelve banks will, of course, be 'independent,' but the lesser eleven will be expected to cooperate with the great Central Bank at New York City.

"Our country has reached the stage where, in order to move forward, we must equip 'ourselves' to finance foreign trade. 'We' look with envy upon England who sends her goods over the seven seas. 'We Americans,' if we are to gain world dignity, must prepare to imitate England in our humble way. Under 'our' present banking arrangements, it is very difficult to finance foreign loans and trade. Some large banks have done financing of that kind, but they wish to offer similar opportunities to the banks in all parts of the country.

"Supposing one of our great South American neighbors desired to purchase some steel rails. Their railroads are backward and they must be developed. She could not place orders for steel in the United States unless our banking structure was equipped to handle the financing. If South America is to buy steel rails or any machinery in 'our' country, we must be equipped to finance long term loans (promises-to-pay) to South American countries. Of course, you understand South America would not order steel rails in our country if the prices here were higher than they were in England, but with a banking system such as we propose, we can take good care to keep our costs of manufacturing steel rails or other machinery in line with those of England.

"We all understand that if export trade is to be carried on, domestic purchasing power must always be curtailed because if domestic purchasing power is adequate to absorb the products of manufacture, the public can really see no need in seeking export markets. Some of our shrewd business men will say: 'Why should we seek foreign markets? Our own country is practically self-contained; is able to absorb the output of our factories, so why should we not be wise enough to allow our own people to buy, use and enjoy our own products? Why should we be interested in sending our products to foreign countries and receiving from them merely promises-to-pay us at some future date? Wouldn't it be much better if we would lend our own promises-to-pay to people in our own country, that our products be used in our own country?'

"But, ah, gentlemen, if we are shrewd, we can prevent our business men from seeing those points. If, when we are anxious to make international loans, we take good care to call in enough of our domestic promises-to-pay to collapse domestic purchasing power, our manufacturers will be only too glad to seek foreign markets, for they will believe that there is no chance to sell their entire volume of output in this country. When they are faced with an output capacity which is greater than the domestic purchasing power will absorb, they will readily fall into the scheme we plan. They will be very anxious to seek foreign markets.

"You understand, though, that in order for them to be able to obtain foreign markets, our wage levels have to be adjusted to the price levels of every other industrial country; that means that our domestic purchasing power has to be stifled, otherwise, our wage levels will be higher than those of other industrial countries which have a scarcity of natural resources and less modern machinery.

"We all realize that America is endowed with magnificent natural resources, also that our problem, if we bankers are to control the situation and make business men desirous of seeking foreign markets, is to control wage scales and keep them low enough so that domestic purchasing power will never be adequate to absorb the output of our factories. We can control domestic purchasing power simply by contracting and expanding the domestic monetary structure (loans) at our discretion. That exportable surplus which will determine the domestic price levels as long as Liverpool controls the world's markets will give us complete control over the domestic price and wage levels, and will make all business men subject entirely to our views.

"This proposed banking system will be known as the 'Federal Reserve System.' It will make it possible for us to create much wider gyrations in the price structure. Hence, we will be able to have bigger and better business cycles. The minimum 'reserves' required will be much smaller than under our present banking laws and you will, therefore, be able to issue a great many more promises-to-pay. When it is time to call in these promises-to-pay and curtail the purchasing power of the people, you will be able to reap a rich harvest in real wealth by means of foreclosures. Then too, it will be much easier to charge higher rates of interest on your promises-to-pay because we can raise rates throughout the whole country simultaneously. That will prevent business men from raising protests against high rates, because they will have noted that the bankers in other districts have raised their rates similarly. Uniformity of rates, when they are high, is really very essential to harmony.

"Of course, this system will be 'Federal' in name only. The private bankers will own it. Originally we will promise to share with the government the heavy profits on our monetary franchise which the government will thus place in our hands; but later on, when profits are ready for distribution, doubtless ways can be found to avoid too generous a sharing of the proceeds derived from our management.

"Under the proposed system you community bankers in the smaller cities will be required to keep only 13% 'reserve' against your demand deposits (promises-to-pay) and 3% against your time deposits. You see, this will give you greater leeway. In reality, for every dollar of real money deposited as a demand deposit, you can expand 7 plus times, and for every dollar deposited as a time deposit, you can expand 33 times. This will provide immense possibilities for the creation of broad business cycles.

"You will keep your reserves in the Central Bank of your district. The Central Bank of your district will be required to keep a 35% gold reserve against your deposits ('reserves'). This will mean that since only 35% gold reserve against deposits (your reserves at Central Bank) is necessary, $1.00 of gold in the vaults of the Central Federal Reserve Bank will support a maximum of $30.00 in your private promises-to-pay, which the people have been taught to regard as money."

The large-city banker demonstrated further how a community bank could multiply its loans (promises-to-pay), and illustrated, arithmetically, figures presented in the preceding paragraph.

$100,000	Demand Deposits
.13	Required Reserve
$13,000	Reserve Required
$50,000	Time Deposits
.03	Required Reserve
$1,500	Reserve Required
$13,000	plus $1,500 equals $14,500.

"The Community bank must have on the books of one of the twelve Central Banks a deposit of $14,500. Against this deposit (reserve) the Central Bank must have a 35% gold reserve; 35% of $14,500 equals $5,075. Therefore, $5,075 in gold will support $150,000 deposits (loans) in the community bank. In other words, $1.00 in gold will support $30.00 in promises-to-pay of the community bank, for $150,000 is approximately 30 times $5,075.

"This Federal Reserve System will enable us to use Government bonds (tax payers' promises-to-pay given to private bankers in exchange for private bankers' unsecured promises-to-pay) as a part of our reserves in a much more efficient way than we have ever done before. We will be able to carry on what are known as 'open market operations.' That simply means expanding or contracting the volume of the community bank reserves on the books of the Central

Bank, by taking Government bonds in or out of community banks.

"For instance, if a community bank desired to increase its own promises-to-pay it could, by simply selling one of its Government bonds to the Central Bank, increase its reserves on the books of the Central Bank. A $1,000 bond sold by the community bank to the Central Bank will create a deposit of $1,000 on the books of the Central Bank. That deposit of $1,000 on the books of the Central Bank will be sufficient reserve to support $7,000 in demand deposits, or $33,000 in time deposits. It will be a very simple thing to expand and contract the volume of promises-to-pay by the Central Bank purchasing Government bonds from the community banks, or selling Government bonds to the community banks. Visualize your earnings under this great European system!!

"Another great weapon will be the rediscount rate. You understand that if one of you community bankers wishes to sell to the Central Bank one of your promises-to-pay, which is secured by the obligation of one of your local business men, you may do so. The Central Bank will, in reality, simply take that piece of paper (a business man's promise-to-pay which has previously been given by him in exchange for the banker's promise-to-pay) and advance you the proceeds on it, the 'cash' of course being deposited to your reserve account on the books of the Central Bank. What the Central Bank will really do is credit to you the amount that the piece of paper calls for, less the unearned interest. The rate charged for that unexpired time is what will be known as the *rediscount* rate. That rediscount rate will have a tremendous influence because it will, in reality, determine the going rate of interest on all commercial and Government loans.

"By raising it very quickly, say from 3% to 6%, or even to 8% or 9% if we wish to create a real crisis, we can bring about sudden changes in the volume of reserves. For example: if the Government bonds in your portfolio are carrying a 3% coupon rate and we raise the rediscount rate to 8%, then it would no longer be possible for the Government to finance at less than 6%. If the new Government bonds carry a rate of 6%, no one would be willing to buy the 3% bonds excepting at a discount. Therefore, the 3% bonds would automatically drop in price. For example: a bond due in ten years, at the rate of 3%, while the new bonds due in ten years were 6%, the 3% bonds would drop in price to approximately 80. If the bonds in the portfolio of the community bank dropped to 80 its 'reserves' would be impaired and it would have to sell some of the bonds or call some of the loans of the business men, in order to increase its reserves at the Central Bank. You can readily see that the rediscount rate is a powerful weapon. Business men will never have the wit to understand that by arbitrarily raising the rediscount rate, we will be able to control the value of Government bonds. The value of Government bonds will, in turn, control the size of the bank reserves and these, in turn, will control the volume of promises-to-pay (privately issued money) which all community banks will be able to have outstanding.

"The volume of bankers' promises-to-pay outstanding, of course, plus the actual currency, constitutes the volume of actual purchasing power (money) of the nation. Rapidly curtailing it causes collapses in the price structure. This forces business men into tight places. It forces them, in order to raise cash, to sell their inventories at a loss; carried far enough, it forces them to sacrifice their assets in foreclosure.

"You see, the Federal Reserve System will really give us a great weapon to force business crises, and enable us to scoop up businesses and farms whenever we so desire. In that way, we can eventually control practically all of the wealth of the country and business men can be kept in their places just as are farmers and laborers. Of course, the public will be told that the object of the new system is to act as a '*stabilizer,*'" laughed the internationalist.

One community banker gathered sufficient courage to ask a few questions: "Will it not be dangerous to place in the hands of a small group of men such absolute power over the lives of every one in the United States? Might they not be tempted to use it to their selfish advantage? We individual community bankers, of which there are thousands, are known by our customers intimately, and I do not believe we would have the courage or ruthlessness to go as far in collapsing our own communities as would the great Central Bankers. After all, the Central Bankers never have to face the customers, and they are not in direct touch with the suffering incurred by collapsing the money structure. They sit off in a distant city and are entirely unreachable by the local business men. Even though I realize that primarily we would make a great deal less money by not having a great Central Banking System, I would be better satisfied to go along controlling the affairs within my own community."

The banker, trained in European ways, presiding at the meeting smiled benignly at the community banker and politely told him that: "After all, you must realize that these great Central Bankers would always keep the welfare of the country foremost in their minds. Money is no object to them, and they will only be interested in controlling price structures to the extent of controlling greedy business men. You know, business men are a greedy lot and unless they are controlled by altruistic bankers, they will always let their ambition and their desire to get on in the world overcome their better judgment. The Central Bankers will be the handmaids of industry.

"Business men dream and plan of great institutions and go so far, at times, as to want their employees to partake in a substantial way in their accomplishments. When they are going along, they grow generous and raise the wages of their employees. Some of them even give part ownership of their plants to employees. Of course, such practices will never do if we are to have great international cooperation, because high wages and employee-plant ownership always create high domestic purchasing power and we cannot have high domestic purchasing power and real cooperation for humanity's best interests.

"Then too, well-paid and well-fed employees can never be whipped into accepting even altruistic bankers' domination. American bankers cannot afford to have laboring men more independent and free than the laboring men of England, France or Germany where for generations we have taught them their places. If this were allowed to go on, America would soon tend to lead all countries. That would not do, for England is the natural leader of mankind. Our country would soon have a great immigrant problem because men and women who saw how their efforts would be rewarded in America, would seek to come to America to establish their homes.

"Gentlemen! I must not talk further. I have already told you of the great benefits you, as individuals, and our country as a whole, will derive from our mutual cooperation under the Federal Reserve System. I am sure that all of you will return to your homes and begin telling your customers of the wonderful system we are about to install in America. Tell them that it is modeled after the Bank of England, the Bank of France and the Reichsbank, and that with it, they will be able to enjoy great foreign markets, and that the length and intensity of business depressions can be better controlled.

"Be sure to see that your newspapers carry very favorable stories regarding the proposed Federal Reserve System, and as soon as practicable, see that the text books used in your communities extol the glories of the Federal Reserve System. Young America must be taught 'modern' banking."

CHAPTER VI

THE MONEY CREATORS' HARVEST

The Great War

The Federal Reserve Act was passed December 23, 1913. Some parts of that Act seem to have been altered at the instigation of those who apparently knew that a great war was being planned. Financing a war would require a great central bank, which would manufacture billions of new "credit money" to finance the huge production for destruction.

The World War had not progressed very far when, lo and behold, great England began to borrow in America. The American national debt to foreign nations, which Americans had been so carefully taught was a "blessing" to our nation, and which had existed for many decades through the operations of the London bankers who needed to keep our money system closely geared to the British System in order to bring about depressions at their pleasure, had been wiped out by our shipping goods to Europe. America was no longer in debt to the foreign bankers. America was soon to become their *creditor*. It was a *great moment* in history which has never been even mentioned in our schools of Business Administration.

All of the community bankers issued as many promises-to-pay as possible, and these promises-to-pay went to ammunition manufacturers, and various producers of food and clothing. As soon as the community bankers had reached their limit of safety, the great Federal Reserve System was brought in to help with its super "credit money" expansion franchise. Some of the private bankers in the largest city had already made advances to England. One of the private bankers, it is reliably reported, had advanced credits beyond the bonds that had been sold to Americans, to the extent of four hundred million dollars.

If the war were to go on, it was necessary for the American tax payer to begin paying the piper. Therefore, America had its first "Liberty" Loan Drive. The process through which this financing was done was really very simple, due to the fact that we had this great Central Banking System. The community banks advanced 5% of the amount of the proposed loan to the Central Reserve Bank. The Government printed the bonds and sent them out to the community banks. Upon the receipt of bonds, the community banks credited to the deposit account of the United States Government the total amount of the bonds. It was simply a legalized method, whereby the community banks created by making bookkeeping entries 95% of the funds advanced to the United States Government. The United States Government, of course, was magnanimous and was willing to pay interest to these community banks in return for their great privilege of creating money to lend to the United States Government. After all, it is a magnanimous government that allows a few private individuals to create its money for it, and then allows the dear hard-working private citizens to buy those creations, and pay tribute ever after in interest.

As soon as the Government began to spend these enormous amounts of money for ammunition, food, clothing, etc., prices began to rise very rapidly. As prices began to rise, business men began to expand their facilities. The community bankers, upon pressure from the Central Banks, expanded their promises-to-pay and advanced to business men the loans with which to expand their plants and inventories. A really worth-while credit cycle was created. As business profits increased enormously, due to the rising price structure, and as wages also began to rise, peoples' incomes began to be sufficient to permit them to absorb some of the Government bonds. The banks thereupon sold these Government bonds to the American public. In many cases the banks loaned the entire amount of the purchase price of Government bonds to individuals.

The bonds carried a 4¼% coupon and the banks charged an individual 6% or 7% on the unpaid balance of the purchase price of the bonds. Of course, it was patriotic, and an American patriot didn't mind paying 2 or 3% extra into the huge coffers of the unpatriotic banks. After all, the bands played every day, and occasionally some bank contributed toward the Red Cross fund. It was only being a good citizen to help the banks make the profits from which to supply an occasional check to the Red Cross.

The war went on and on. Government obligations piled higher and higher. Millions of the world's young soldiers were losing their lives. The war was really a huge success.

The "Federal" Reserve "credit" money not only "paid" for Europe's war supplies, but America's as well. All together the American Government had borrowed "Federal" Reserve Credit and had given its interest-bearing bonds to create a debt of billions for goods sent to the Allies and other billions for our own share of the war destruction.

During the course of the War, it never occurred to the great bankers of the United States that, after all, our participation in the World War was a community affair and the only just way to have financed it would have been to print good constitutional government currency bearing the imprint of the United States, and have the United States issue it in exchange for war supplies and to defray war costs. That, of course, would have been an honest way, because it would have spread the burden of payment equally by diluting the purchasing power of every one's dollar equally and would not have created a gigantic *collapsible* structure absolutely controlled by international bankers, plus an unbearable burden of debts, the proceeds of which were used to buy consumer goods destroyed in conducting the War.

(The writer wishes to emphasize parenthetically the grave necessity of the United States maintaining at all times a great army, navy and air force for self protection and defense, at least until the money power, which also is the war power, is destroyed. Those with sinister purposes are preaching "Pacifism" in America for one reason only—to have us entirely unprotected while Russia and the European nations are fully armed and ready to destroy us if we refuse to submit to the rule of the international money exploiters.)

CHAPTER VII

"COOPERATION"

London "Cooperation" Became Exploitation

The War was over.

America had made "the world safe for democracy." Agricultural prices were high, as were also costs of production. In the World War America had been called upon to supply raw materials. Farmers had been told that the success of the war depended upon them, for a soldier had to have a full stomach.

The "Peace" Treaty of Versailles had been signed, Germany would "never again" threaten the world with autocracy and militarism. She had been drawn and quartered; her gold taken to Paris and London (that was all-important to the manipulators), her Saar iron and coal region was gone; her colonies lost, her sources of raw materials placed under the control of others.

But England's position as the world's financier had been destroyed forever *unless* the great America would again "cooperate."

Why? Because England was no longer the world's creditor. America was now the world's creditor to the amount of about fifteen billions in private credits and loans, and twelve billion dollars in war debts; a gigantic lever, greater than England ever possessed. With this lever, if honestly used, America could enforce world peace for a Century.

We had been cooperating many years, in fact, we had been "cooperating" ever since we started to allow our agricultural price levels to be determined in Liverpool, London and Manchester; ever since we had been foolish enough to believe back in the 1860's and

1870's that we had to borrow and pay interest on England's promises-to-pay in order to buy *our own* raw materials and hire *our own* workmen to build *our own* railroads and factories. Our "cooperation" with England had really been most magnanimous.

During the 50 years which climaxed with the beginning of the World War, England had controlled not only her colonies but the United States, through her control of the London gold market and through placing international loans in various countries. Her international loans made it possible for her to play one country against another, for the collapsible banking structures in all of her colonies and the United States made it possible for her bankers, the Rothschilds and other internationalists, to create or lift business depressions at will.

So before the close of the World War the United States was in a position for the first time since Civil War days, to have bid good-by to London control and operate her money system for the benefit *of the American people*. This important fact was never emphasized in our university schools of business or in the press. Unfortunately, America was betrayed by those who were vested with power to determine and carry out the policies of the privately owned Federal Reserve System; that gigantic accordion-like banking structure which can create or destroy prosperity at will.

During the course of the World War, America had not only paid her debt to England—but had become a huge creditor to England and all of the Allies. The international bankers had now perpetrated the trick of having the Allies borrow our private bankers' promises-to-pay.

Some of the British colonies were also practically

out of debt to London. This was due to the fact that London had been calling upon them to supply vast amounts of raw materials, and there was less finished goods going back to the colonies.

Our Central Bankers' Part in the "Cooperation" With London

A secret bankers' meeting was held on May 18, 1920, in Washington, D. C. In the name and style of The Orderly Deflation Committee of the American Bankers Association, a secret resolution was passed declaring for the contraction of money and credits. The published proceedings of this secret bank meeting show that it was held in the name and style of the Federal Reserve Board, the Federal Advisory Council and the Class "A" Directors of the Federal Reserve Banks. The action prescribed was taken on a resolution assuming to be presented by the American Bankers Association.

The names of all men present at that meeting, and the statements made by them, can be obtained by any one who will take the trouble to write to the Superintendent of Documents, Washington, D. C., and request Document No. 310 of the 67th Congress, 4th Session. Those who attended were warned to hold the proceedings in sacred secrecy.

Those who have the Congressional Record are referred to Page 4858, Proceedings of February 28, 1923. An account of the secret meeting will be found in Volume 64, Part 5 of the 67th Congress, Fourth Session. Hon. Finly H. Gray described the meeting:

"The manipulating financiers and bankers, the master minds of frenzied finance, engineering this gigantic secret movement, were not there, present and in person, but were pulling the wires, directing and prompting their tools, puppets and catspaws from afar.

Maybe these catspaws were not fully aware of the destruction they were bringing down upon their unsuspecting fellow men. The Chairman of the meeting said:

" 'We all know that if the bankers in any community, large or small, were to clasp the screws on tight, they could bring disaster upon the community which might spread to other communities.'

"A Mr. Smith was there and said, 'Of course, contraction of money and credits would result in low prices and an easing up of business.' These bankers knew the effect of the contraction of money and credit upon farm values and price levels. Another Mr. Smith was there, claiming to have secured the farmers' consent to reduce farm values and the price level, and, assuming to speak from personal conversation directly with farmers said: 'The farmers with whom I have talked are in thorough accord with it.'

"Now this Mr. Smith had probably met these farmers standing around on the streets of New York, wearing overalls and cowhide boots, carrying their forks and scoop shovels, and there he secured their consent to reduce farm values and the price level.

"Mr. John Skelton Williams, Comptroller of the Currency, when this contraction of money was proposed, explained his efforts to stop the resolution being drawn. In relating his efforts to the late John A. Simpson, he said: 'I told the other members of the board, Do you know that this will break lots of little country banks? They cold bloodedly answered me, They ought to break—there are too many of them. I then told them, Don't you know it's going to ruin lots of farmers, and they cold bloodedly replied to me, They ought to be ruined—they are getting so prosperous they will not work.' " Congressional Record, May 2, 1933.

I wonder if these members of the Federal Reserve Board had in mind the farmers' "failure to work" to produce the food supplies necessary in carrying on the War by which the world money creators were enriched?

Thus, the Federal Reserve Banks, under *orders* of the Federal Reserve Board, pursuant to the secret resolution of May 18, 1920, without notice or warning, began to raise the rediscount rates from 2% to 5%, to 7%, to 8%, to 9% and until, for some farm banks, the rates were much higher.

Simultaneously with this drastic increase in the rates, the Central Reserve Banks began selling Government bonds. This selling continued until the price of "Liberty" bonds dropped to 80. The people who remember their own efforts to get anything like the price they paid for Liberty Bonds, which they had to sell to live, will recall the type of purchasers who opened over-the-counter places in which these bonds were bought at bargain levels. Had these bond buyers been particularly noted for their patriotism during the War?

Falling bond prices decreased the "reserves" of the community banks. Decreasing reserves made it imperative that the community banks call in their local loans and force all borrowers to pay. This brought a terrific liquidation of all agricultural products. Almost in the twinkling of an eye, agricultural prices tumbled to ruinously low levels.

Within seven months farm prices dropped to ruinous levels. In May 1920, the United States Bureau of Labor Statistics showed farm products at 244 contrasted with 100, the average price in 1913. From 244 the farm products index dropped to 136 by January 1, 1921. In eight months wheat fell from $3.00 to $1.60 per bushel. Corn fell from $1.50 to 35c.

At the same time, the finished goods which the farmer had to buy, and his interest and taxes, did not drop accordingly. By May, 1921, the index of farm products stood at 117. In other words, the farmer was getting only 17% more for his products than he was receiving in 1913 before the War. But the indices of clothing were 181; fuel and lighting 194; lumber and building material 202, and house furnishings 262. Thus, the farmer was robbed of his purchasing power. This was premeditated: the farmer had to be ruined and kept ruined if Americans were to be financially subjected and eventually bolshevized.

Rural banks could accept farmers' deposits, but could not loan farmers' money to farmers; such loans were "unsound" by decree of the Federal Reserve dictators. Thus the sluices were prepared for draining the rural money to industrial centers, and thus via speculation into the hands of the internationalists.

On this sudden fall of the price levels, the confiding and unsuspecting farmers and other citizens of the agricultural districts, saw their property, crops and produce sinking in a vortex of falling values, forcing down and destroying their buying power, their tax-paying power, their interest, debt and mortgage paying power. These things were done for two reasons: (1) to "cooperate" with London because London wanted low agricultural prices, and (2) to undermine the entire economic fabric of the United States; but with the knights of finance still in the saddle.

The United States is a 95% self-contained country. Thirty-five million people are directly dependent upon agriculture for purchasing power, and twenty million additional citizens of small communities are indirectly dependent upon the prices of agricultural products for purchasing power. Destroying raw material prices, and forcing them down below the cost of production drained all purchasing power of the agricultural sections, and made it impossible for those people to meet their obligations and be customers of the industrial world. This destructive policy was pursued intentionally. It was not an experiment. Hon. Finly Gray said that they knew exactly what the result would be.

It was done to further cooperate with England—not the real English people, for honest English statesmen were very much opposed to England's deflating the Empire sufficiently to allow the pound sterling to be brought back to its former gold parity. They knew that the best interests of humanity should be paramount, but others sacrificed humanity in order to bring the price of an ounce of gold back to its former arbitrary price. This was done to deflate all raw material producing countries and enable the internationalists to foreclose on real property.

It is interesting to note that at the time of the agricultural collapse in the United States, some in charge of the destructive policies sent their paid agents out into the agricultural states to misinform and mislead farmers. The purpose was to promote dissension and radicalism. Those who instigated these movements were the paid agents of the very ones who were responsible for placing the terrible economic pressure on farmers. Their object was to make the American farmer lose faith in his own institutions and innocently become a party to the destruction of his own country.

If the Federal Reserve policies had been honest, we would never have cooperated with England in such a deflationary movement. If England's policy had been right, England would have left the raw material prices high, because the debt structure piled up on all of the Allies made a high raw material price level imperative *unless* the whole economic and social fabric of the countries were to be undermined.

A number of Britons were strongly opposed. They knew that England should have repriced the ounce of gold at that time and gone forward with the relatively high price levels throughout the world. In that case deflation would have been unnecessary. Viscount Rothemere, British publisher, on September 27, 1931, said: "We were fools to force the pound up to its old gold level of six years ago. It benefited only the bankers by restoring prestige to our currency and all the international money lending and the money dealings that go with it."

By mid-year 1921, all of the agricultural sections had been paralyzed. Their undermining had been started and has been continued right down to the present time (1935).

In July 1921 the Central Reserve Banks reversed their process. They began to buy Government bonds in the open market and they lowered the rediscount rates. This process increased the reserves of the city banks. However, agricultural banks were not benefited, due to the fact that our price levels for agricultural products were, as of old, being determined in Liverpool and Manchester, and were kept low by the manipulations previously described and by the banks being prevented from extending local loans. England saw to it that the banking structures of all of the colonies were kept in a weakened condition.

When the bank reserves in the cities of the United States had been increased, it was possible for the city banks to again begin creating additional promises-to-pay, in other words, to start another upward phase of the "business cycle."

In 1923 the United States began some of the most disastrous financing that could have been conceived in human minds, no matter what degree of trickery one could imagine. The promises-to-pay in the United States were used to buy bonds of foreign countries. We began to play a game for the benefit of the money lender in London. We were keeping our agricultural prices low, which was undermining all of our agricultural sections, and we were making foreign loans in order to create foreign exchange for the benefit of England. We made loans to many countries of Europe and South America. Many of these loans were for fantastic purposes and the borrowers had no intention of ever paying them. To begin with, this country had no business making foreign loans, because we did not desire to control the people of any other country, and honestly operated governments never need foreign money to pay for domestic purchases.

Again, Europe already owed us many billions and was "welching." What could we possibly gain by increasing the already uncollectibles?

The only logical reason England ever had for making foreign loans was to control the price levels and, hence, the people in all of her colonies. She had made loans to us for that reason alone. What stupidity, therefore, or rather, what dishonesty, was manifested in the "cooperation" which we have given England from 1920 down to date!

The internationalists had failed in their efforts to conquer the world through militarism. Now they would conquer it by destroying the financial and social fabric of every country. They deliberately set out to do that, and are continuing the process right down to the present moment.

America's Further "Cooperation"

In August of 1927 America presented a queer

spectacle. Her agricultural sections were continuing to deteriorate because her agricultural price levels were artificially and constantly kept below the cost of production.

Industrial sections of the United States were in a vicious phase of an upward swing in a business cycle. It was vicious because the prosperity created was reaching only a small section of society and the "credit" money structure was being forced toward a very dangerous pinnacle.

The strength of the stock market drew money here from all over the world. This caused a flow of gold from Europe to the United States greater than had existed before. England had returned to the old gold value of the pound sterling (driven by the Rothschild controlled Bank of England and in face of the opposition of patriotic British statesmen who knew what the result would be). So the Governor of the Bank of England, Montagu Norman (Norman Montagu) came to New York and persuaded the Federal Reserve Board to agree to reduce the rediscount rate. This reduction of the rediscount rate—when every honest banker knew that it was in direct opposition to what should have been done, as had been promised when the Federal Reserve Act was passed in 1913, was literally forced down the throats of the eleven Reserve Banks outside of New York City. It constituted a public scandal at the time, well remembered by every banker and many others who watch events and marvel at the audacity of the hidden few.

In August of 1927, despite opposition from eleven of the twelve Federal Reserve Banks, who saw the danger, the Central Federal Reserve Banks were ordered to lower their rediscount rates and buy additional Government bonds. In other words, the steps were taken to increase the reserves of the city banks. City banks responded by increasing their promises-to-pay (loans). These loans went almost entirely to finance stock purchases. Loans were made on any and every kind of collateral. It became a very common practice for corporations to issue rights to buy additional stocks, and for individuals exercising those rights to borrow the entire amount at their banks, using the stock as collateral. In other words, banks were creating promises-to-pay and the funds thus created were flowing into the treasuries of corporations, there either to lie idle as deposit cash or to be used in building plants. Of course, these loans were unsound.

This was the actual method of financing the terrific stock market speculation of 1928-29; it was not "prosperity" as many supposed. The rural sections were being deliberately drained of their money by coercing country bankers into calling their local loans and purchasing very questionable domestic bonds and international loans. These orders came from the bank examiners acting under the authority of the United States Treasury which, of course, was dominated by the Federal Reserve policies. Honest country bankers protested that their communities needed whatever funds existed, but they were told to either comply with the examiners' orders or get out of the banking business.

In response to the stimulation of bank loans (promises-to-pay) flowing into the stock market, the price of securities rose higher and higher. Stocks of corporations which had very little property and whose earnings were small, sold at from 20 to 50 times their earnings. Conditions grew more dangerous and spectacular each day.

Thinking people knew that some day the bankers would begin to curtail their privately created money, loaned at interest—and when they did, the securities markets would suffer a terrific crash. That crash would destroy billions of dollars' worth of then existing purchasing power; would cancel the credit money then in use, and wreck countless individuals and businesses.

The newspapers and well publicized paid "Economists" repeated deliberate falsehoods telling the people that America was in a "new era." We were assured eternally rising prices and all of the old measurements of stock values were out-of-date. The New York Stock Exchange was an Aladdin's lamp. The newspapers did everything possible to fan the flames and 16,000,000 people in the United States were active participants in the purchase and sale of securities.

The Day of Reckoning

Rumblings began to sound in September 1929. The Hatry failure in London in September precipitated heavy selling from "informed" sources abroad. Of course, these could not have been the international bankers who could know the day and hour which would record a terrible collapse. All during September and up until the third week of October, while some securities were making new highs, there was heavy liquidation. European sellers of securities were converting into cash and transferring their balances abroad. Gold began to flow to Europe.

On October 24, 1929, at 11:00 o'clock sharp hundreds of thousands of shares in hundreds of issues were offered for sale "at the market." It was a very strange thing that this could have been a mere accident. It was most unusual that thousands of people decided to sell at the same instant. It was also strange that they all decided to sell "at the market." Inexperienced stock traders do not put in "market" orders. That's a trick known only to the "wise boys"—the internationalists and their cohorts, the type of government adviser speculator who says "a speculator has to be right."

The market continued to crash day after day. The new era was over. The internationalists had squeezed the money accordion. It was they who had pumped the air into it and it was now their privilege to let it out. They had no responsibility whatever to inform Mr. and Mrs. American that they had decided to curtail the credit. After all, it was their privilege to contract the volume of promises-to-pay (loans) outstanding; to pull gold out of the country, and to collapse the whole "price" and money structure.

Was it not they who had expanded it? It was "legally" their instrument; theirs was the exclusive franchise to play it for private pleasure—and personal profit.

You know, business men are a dutiful lot. They take the responsibility of building great factories, of furthering science and invention, making it possible for many less enterprising human beings to have the physical where-with-all to live. Such ideals as those are entirely too civilized, and if business men were not controlled, it would not be long until labor would really be very independent, because laboring men, if constantly employed at high wage levels, can soon accumulate property. It is therefore necessary that hard working, sincere business men have the wind taken out of their sails by the great guardians of the nation, the international bankers.

American business men, farmers and laborers struggled on. Nearly every day some so-called leader proclaimed loudly; "America is fundamentally sound," and that a "Buy Now Campaign" would solve the nation's problems. Be patriotic—buy now. After all, there is nothing the matter!! Confidence alone is lacking. Confidence must be restored. After all, the whole business cycle is based on "confidence," (misplaced confidence, unfortunately). We have business cycles because for some "mysterious" reason people suddenly, in great numbers, lose "confidence."

The only real mystery however, is why the people have never been told the truth, which is that our very money itself (over 95% of it) is a matter of confidence; it is purely psychological. It exists when certain minds so will it; and it similarly disappears.

The adviser to Presidents was summoned. He had already been the "adviser" to Presidents Wilson, Harding, Coolidge and now President Hoover. It's strange, with his "great knowledge of economics and finance" that he did not advise President Wilson to *properly* issue new *honest* constitutional non-interest bearing currency, having thereon the imprint of the United States Government. Had he, in his "great wisdom" done that, America could never have suffered the terrific collapse that was brought about in 1920, and America could never have had the "farm problem" about which he concerns himself so frequently in the "respectable" press.

This adviser relates that he has devoted great mental effort since 1921 to the "solution" of the farm problem: his word must have influenced much of the farm "relief" legislation for his advice was "sought by Presidents." Certainly his friends got the job plums. Are the farmers pleased with *results?* The records also show that since 1920 "the adviser" has exerted considerable influence upon legislation enacted "to regulate" the commodity exchanges which until 1920 had functioned very efficiently for the farmer.

It was also strange that with his great knowledge, he did not advise President Coolidge against allowing the United States to make *unsound* international loans. His great knowledge of international money movements should have enabled him to know that we were simply drawing the resources out of all of the agricultural sections, and that we were playing a magnanimous international game—manufacturing products and financing their sale to foreign countries by taking the actual money to pay for them away from our own people.

He did not appear to advise President Coolidge in August 1927, when the Federal Reserve Board decided to put new steam into the boilers and push a galloping stock market to higher and higher levels. There were many government offices gathering statistics for him, and he certainly must have known that many stocks were already selling far in excess of the value which the earnings of the corporations warranted. Besides the Government's able services, he might also have consulted Dr. Goldenweiser, Director of Research of the Federal Reserve Board. That able doctor could have furnished him with many valuable statistics pointing out the dangerous road ahead.

Of course, at that time, there was a great question as to whether the United States would be able to manufacture stock certificates fast enough to supply the great need. Perhaps he was advising President Coolidge as to just how the paper and engraving companies could turn out these certificates fast enough.

In the "adviser to Presidents' " own writings, the people are told that he got out of the stock market before the crash in October 1929. It is strange that he did not share his feelings of uncertainty with President Hoover. It is strange, if he had the wisdom to sell his own stocks, that he did not inform President Hoover that there was something "fundamentally wrong." If President Hoover had understood, he would never have so frequently repeated "America is fundamentally sound" or "A business recovery is just around the corner."

Upon word from the "adviser," President Hoover would not have made the great error of calling an "Economic Conference" in January of 1930, at which he urged business men to go ahead spending money for plant extensions. A few sincere business men followed the exhortation of the President and paid for their cooperation by losing their businesses.

And yet, this same adviser continues on and on as adviser to Presidents. He is "unofficial President" in this administration, we are told. We change Presidents but never advisers. Americans should question the next presidential candidate and try a change in advisers.

The Moratorium—June 1931

The business depression went on and on. Bankers' promises-to-pay continued to be contracted. Thousands upon thousands of banks failed. Foreclosures and more foreclosures took place; Politics and the Courts grew more weird, but the perpetrators of the Sunshine Campaign lost no heart.

In June of 1931 America was called upon to make another noble sacrifice. The great Bank of England, the great Bank of France (bursting with gold), also the Reichsbank, the Bank of Italy, and others would be unable to make their war loan payments due June 15, 1931.

President Hoover summoned "the adviser" and the members of the Federal Reserve Board. Presto! America would grant a moratorium to the hard pressed bankers of Europe in their great hour of need. We had cooperated to the extent of getting ourselves into a World War; into collapsing our agricultural sections; into building up a stock market condition which meant only disaster to all but the "informed few," and now we were willing to grant a moratorium. But why was the public not told that an official had privately promised such a moratorium months before?

This meant that America would tell the Allies that, after all, we didn't expect them to pay. We were not a crude, selfish, bloodsucking lot. Our taxpayers, consisting in fact of our farmers and laboring people, could sympathize with the plight of the international bankers. They had hoarded their gold in the vaults under the Seine River. To do so, they had collapsed Europe's banking structure, but that made no difference—their gold was safe in a specially constructed vault under the Seine. Then too, the American people really never did expect these international connivers to pay their honest debts. It would be much simpler to have Mr. Hoover and the Ministers of Finance exchange a few high-sounding notes.

Wrote Garet Garrett:

"Only the United States had the resources to save Germany. England alone was helpless to avert the calamity. France was obscure...such were the circumstances under which President Hoover proposed an international debt holiday . . . and besides that effect, international finance at the same time made a direct loan of one hundred million dollars to the German Reichsbank to meet any emergency. The money was provided by the Federal Reserve Bank of New York, the Bank of England and the Bank of France. On this day's work, international finance heaved a great sigh . . . Then European exporters had been in the habit of leaving their profits on deposit in American banks, thinking the money was safer here than in Europe . . . For the same reason private European capitalists had been sending money to New York to be employed in short-term paper which they could sell at a moment's notice and some of Europe's credit balances in this country *were simply the untouched proceeds of recent American loans*; even the ambulance loans we had made in the summer [of 1931] to avert a financial collapse in Europe . . . There lay the great American gold reserve—five billions of it—exposed and unprotected. She [Europe] had keys to it. The keys were those credit balances in New York banks payable in gold on demand. And where these balances represented, as many of them did, the untouched proceeds of recent American loans to Europe, the keys she had to the American gold were keys we had "*unwittingly*" handed away. The American gold reserve was defenseless . . .

"True, we had enormous bank balances in Europe, but these were either frozen . . . or now payable in paper money . . . The curious and final illustration would be this: that a British holder of a pound sterling note could not go to his own Bank of England and get gold for it, but he could send it to New York, sell it in the foreign exchange market, and take the proceeds in gold . . . We had eased Europe of its obligations to us, without limiting in any way our obligations to them — one way grace — thus the abnormity that owing us more than ten billions in the form of public debt, on which we had granted a one year moratorium; in the form of private debt on which we could get nothing in gold even where it was not in default;

in the form of overdue short-term credits in Germany and Austria which we had agreed not to demand payment of; in the form of bank balances all over Europe that were simply frozen — owing us all of this, Europe nevertheless could demand payment forthwith and payment in gold of all her credit balances in New York, amounting, as we have supposed, to a billion dollars more or less . . . How preposterous! Debtors owing us in all manner of ways . . . themselves protected by grace, by moratorium or by insolvency, are yet able to descend upon the American gold reserve and deplete it wholesale.

"During July and August (1931) Europe swallowed up a billion and a half of American gold . . . In September she is making a run on the American bank system for gold, and the American bank system is helpless."

Every dollar of gold which Europe was withdrawing from America had the effect of collapsing up to thirty dollars of the promises-to-pay outstanding and, hence, the *volume of money*. Where was "the adviser" at that time?

Resuming with Mr. Garrett:

"Europe wanted the gold for its own sake, wanted it while she could get it — the gold itself! The power of possessing it! The American gold! . . . England was not getting it . . . France alone took more than one-third — nearly one-half — she did not need it at all, for already she had actually more gold in her possession than any other country, save only the United States, and relatively more than we ourselves possessed."

But, after all, France does have the world's strongest vaults. We are plainly told that those who conspire to control through World Dictatorship will do so *with the power of gold*. Can we not see that they are concentrating that gold in the specially constructed vaults under the Seine River to keep it safe —for whom?

". . . France has built since the war a treasure chamber unique in the world. Every country has massive burglar-proof vaults for its gold reserves, but France decided, after the War, to make one so deep and strong and mysterious that not even a victorious modern army could break into it. You might blow the Bank of France away with bombs and its gold would be all the safer. The chamber is two and one-half acres in extent; it lies two hundred feet deep in the earth. Over it, first, is forty feet of water, which is a lake they made by damming the subterranean river that flows beneath Paris, and then above the water fifty feet of solid rock. The way to it is through six steel towers with revolving doors moved by electric engines, and the passage of descent can be flooded at a moment's notice. At the signal of alarm a detail of defenders would instantly vanish through this passage, pull the water in after them, and be forgotten — safely forgotten for an indefinite time, or for the duration of a war, because everything has been thought of beforehand. They would find in the gold chamber a kitchen, provisions enough for two or three arctic expeditions, dishes, linen, beds, all the facilities for comfortable housekeeping." (Garet Garrett).

America! Will all of your gold reach those vaults under the Seine River? Will it be sent there by those who plan with their international cohorts to enslave loyal Americans? The Gold Bill of 1934 (surreptitiously forced through Congress in January 1934) gives the Secretary of the Treasury power to place America's gold out of this country!!

Continuing the events of the Fall of 1931: . . .

". . . who could have foreseen that parallel to the raid on the American gold reserve there would run in Europe a campaign of rumor, innuendo and propaganda against the value of the American dollars? . . . In France the campaign was subtle and ingenious; in England frank and brutal. As the Bank of France took gold from New York, rumors of an imminent financial collapse in the United States spread from Paris throughout Europe and the French papers kept saying with one voice that the franc was the sound gold money of the world . . . The British campaign was led by the Rothemere newspapers . . . Day after day these papers printed big headlines . . . proclaiming the downfall of American credit, together with the exhortation to sell dollars and [American] securities while yet there was time to convert them into gold. Examples: '*Bring Your Money Back To Britain*'—'Advices from America indicate a serious state of affairs. This, therefore, offers a favorable moment to sell dollar securities and bring back the money to this country.' Again: '*Sell Dollar and Franc Securities*'—'Don't be trapped. When the break on Wall Street comes, the reaction may be far-reaching.' Another day: '*Who Will Go Off the Gold Standard Next.*' 'The American banking position shows no sign of improvement.' And so on, in such taste and meaning, day after day, with the Bank of England and the British Treasury together owing New York 350,000,000 gold dollars."

Americans! This was our reward for the "cooperation" we had given. They (International Bankers) purposely did everything possible to further collapse our banking structure and bring suffering and chaos in the great America — the simple cooperator, whose officials and advisers had repeatedly betrayed her.

"With the Premier of France on the high seas

[coming to America], and the newspapers running big headlines . . . suddenly we were astonished by the news that the Bank of France had served an ultimatum on the American banking system. The ultimatum is this: France cannot afford to leave her credit balances in New York any longer unless the rate of interest is raised. If the rate of interest is not raised she will feel obliged to call the remainder of her credit balances home [in gold]. And the remainder of these credit balances is $600,000,000."

Apparently, those who own and control the private and misnamed Bank of France, the world's newspapers, munition plants, etc., were not satisfied with the progress of destruction in America.

". . . At all events, the effect," Mr. Garrett goes on to say, was, ". . . to lead to large withdrawals here by other important European countries, more particularly Holland, Belgium and Switzerland."

In September 1931 England was no longer able to meet the demands for gold. England thereupon announced suspension of gold payments and proceeded to carry out the repricing of gold. Any one who can look behind the scenes knows that this was a part of the great scheme to destroy the financial and social fabric of all countries. We now readily understand why it was necessary to put England into the condition she was placed in September 1931. England herself has been betrayed by the same forces that are preying upon America.

CHAPTER VIII

EFFECTS OF REVALUATION

Changing the Currency, Paper Money Units, Exchangeable for An Ounce of Gold

In September 1931, due to the fact that internationalists had maliciously exported gold, London was forced to suspend gold payments. Few people realize that the barbaric gold standard cannot function at all when internationalists are allowed to ship huge amounts of liquid capital in the form of gold from one country to another, wherever they see an opportunity to reap the greatest profit thereby. We know there have been several billion dollars worth of liquid capital which has been transferred about from one country to another since the close of the World War. This has been done to shift gold and create trouble. Moving gold into a country permitted that particular country to expand its monetary structure, so that whenever these internationalists got ready to withdraw the gold they could thereby collapse the money structure and it would fall like a house of cards.

The price levels of practically all countries were controlled by the bankers in London for many years. The two levers used in operating those controls were, first: Control of the movements and the price of an ounce of gold, and second: Through those weapons, control of the price of wheat and other raw materials. Liverpool is still the world's wheat pricing center.

Until recent years the cotton market was controlled at Manchester. Today the New York Cotton market is a more important market than the Manchester market for Americans. This is one case where the internationalists over-reached themselves in their efforts to strangle America.

Since the Napoleonic Wars London has controlled the basic sources of gold (mines). Gold was called the "base" of the collapsible money structure in all of the Colonies and the United States. London had made loans (promises-to-pay) to the Colonies and to the United States. Whenever the Internationalists wanted to collapse the money structure of the United States or the Colonies, they needed only to call some loans or sell some securities — to convert part of their promises-to-pay, or securities bought therewith, into cash; turn the cash into gold, and ship the gold out of New York or the principal financial center of any of the Colonies.

As soon as gold began to leave New York, money became "scarce," as $1.00 of gold "supported" a maximum of $30.00 of bank money. When gold began to move out of the country, all of the community bankers were forced to call in their promises-to-pay, and they were under initial agreements to contract not only the demand loans (their promises-to-pay), but also the currency (bill fold money) within the community by retiring Federal Reserve Notes.

We trusting Americans, and especially our "economists," have been taught that gold leaves a country when price levels begin to fall and trouble seems imminent; the exact reverse is the case. It is not a "natural" and "mysterious" force that causes gold to move from one country to another, but the deliberate intention of manipulators to cause price fluctuations and the resultant instability. Any kind of instability, whether on the "up side" or "down side" is profitable to the few who cause the instability and who know by long experience what direction prices will take.

Contracting the volume of bank money forces a drop in prices. The decrease in the volume of money not only disturbs the balance between the quantity of money and quantity of materials, but also cuts the demand for raw materials, for when the people have less money they can buy less food supplies, etc. Therefore, it is not only the supply of raw materials (wheat, etc.) that counts, it is also the volume of money. The volume of money is, in reality, the important element, because the volume of money (currency and bank credit) determines how much raw materials can be purchased and consumed domestically and, consequently, how much is left for export.

London controlled prices both by fixing the price of an ounce of gold and by manipulating the quantity of deposit money, in the British Colonies and the nations comprising what is called Sterlingaria.

As long as Liverpool controls the situation, it is the price of export wheat which determines the price of the entire amount of wheat, and, therefore, indirectly of all farm products consumed in the United States.

The great fallacy in allowing Liverpool to control the price of raw materials is that the cost of production varies in different parts of the world. Yields differ widely. In some parts the average yield of wheat per acre is two or three times what it is in others. Hence, the growers of wheat in those countries normally have lower costs.

When the world price level is determined at Liverpool, it is very simple to establish price levels which might be adequate for some parts, but be well below the cost of production in others. Few people realize that even in the United States the cost of producing wheat in various areas differs very widely. There is a fallacy in adding up a series of costs, taking a single average, and stating that the general average cost is so much per bushel. Unless the selling price covers the cost of production and a reasonable profit for the great majority of farmers, the all-important wheat growing sections cannot function properly as a part of the economic structure.

Imagine the administrators of the United States Department of Agriculture stating that the average cost of raising a bushel of wheat was 95c; yet the Hoover administration took no steps at all when the average selling prices in 1930-31 and '32 were well below that figure.

The Liverpool market operating as a world clearing house for wheat at times established prices well below the cost of production for the majority of wheat growers throughout the world, even in the areas of lowest production costs.

Also, few Americans realize the influence that Russia has had upon the Liverpool wheat market. Under the present Russian Reign of Terror, Stalin can and does force the Russian people to give up whatever wheat he desires. They can be starved and have been so starved for years. He can use that wheat to glut the Liverpool markets or to sell directly to countries that would otherwise buy in the Liverpool market. That is one of the reasons why those who set out to destroy the economic structure of the world saw the great necessity of first controlling Russia. Russia's condition during the past seventeen years is a warning to the rest of the world — it will meet the same fate if the international money yoke is not cast off.

Russian products have been used as a hammer to strike at the marketing machinery of other nations. In 1929 Russia announced to the world that it was not interested in starting a military war at that time, for a military war was, in her opinion, unnecessary. The Soviet Government proposed to smash the price structure of the capitalistic world which, when accomplished, would produce chaos. This policy had a very far-reaching effect upon the price structure of all countries — including the United States.

One could write volumes showing how easy it is to wreck the price structure by the simple expedient of collapsing the money structure of the nations, thereby curtailing domestic consumption and forcing wheat, which would otherwise be consumed at home, into the export market. When wheat and cotton cannot be consumed in the domestic market, due to the lack of purchasing power, the only "out" for them is the world market, prices for which are controlled at Liverpool. Through this method wheat and cotton can be taken away from people who really need them, and forced on to a weakened market at prices well below the cost of production. America could use much more cotton than we have ever produced if only the money system were honest.

Besides controlling the volume of wheat which will come into the world market, it is very simple to do additional damage through manipulation of the currency price of an ounce of gold in various nations.

Gold brokers, it is reported, meet daily in London at the office of the Rothschilds. The Rothschilds are very conveniently the agents for the Royal Mint. The following firms appear to constitute the assembly of gold brokers:

Samuel Montagu & Company
114 Old Broad Street, London, E.C.2

Mocatta and Goldsmid
7 Throgmorton Ave., London, E.C.2

Pixley and Abell,
Palmerston-house, Old Broad St., London, E.C.2
Sharps and Wilkins
19 Great Winchester Street, London, E.C.2

After England suspended gold payments in 1931 the gold brokers began to change the purely arbitrary price of an ounce of gold in London and in the British Colonies.

The few gold buying firms quietly raised the price of gold. It was raised from its former level of $20.67 per ounce (in terms of American dollars), to, roughly, $28.00 per ounce. When gold was $28.00 per ounce in London, but still $20.67 per ounce in New York, the pound sterling (in terms of dollars) dropped proportionately from $4.86 to approximately $3.50.

It is easy to see what influence that had on American raw material producers.

If an exporter had credit in London which entitled him to one ounce of gold as long as it was in London, his claim on gold could be converted into a purchasing power of $28.00. But when he attempted to bring his money to New York, his credit in London could only be exchanged for $20.67 purchasing power in New York. It is simple to see the great disadvantage which the United States exporters—and that means all raw material producers — suffered under that arrangement. Argentina began to raise the price of gold in December 1929. This accounts for the following fact: "Argentina grain exports are *doubled* over last year" — New Outlook, Oct. 1934—p. 44.

While London was raising the price of gold, from September 1931, she was also raising the currency price of gold in all of the British Colonies. The price of gold in most of the Colonies and in Argentina was raised much higher than the price even in London.

This arrangement made it possible for exporters of raw materials from Argentina, or any of the Colonies, to convert their London credits into the currencies of their own countries and receive even more purchasing power in the Colonies or in Argentina than they had in London.

From the Fall of 1931 until April 18, 1933, the currencies of the British Colonies, Argentina, and Japan were convertible into gold on a more favorable basis than the currency of the United States. In other words, gold commanded a higher price per ounce than in the United States. *This placed the American farmers and all export manufacturers at a great disadvantage, and also forced an enormous drain of gold out of the United States*, thus furthering collapse.

It was the fact that England and the Colonies had raised the price of gold that forced the United States to take the same step. Yet, the controlled newspapers continually shout that England is recovering without a change in her currency, whereas it is being juggled daily.

Always remember that the price of an ounce of gold in terms of the currency of any nation, is *purely arbitrary*: it is fixed either by law, as in so-called fixed-conversion countries (U. S., Holland, France), or by open market bidding by the gold brokers (England, the Colonies, Argentina, etc.). In the latter case, they are "off the gold standard," which, despite the blare of propaganda, means prosperity, not stagnation.

Through connivery and intrigue engineered by the internationalists of foreign countries and their brethren in the United States, the so-called Gold Standard Bill was passed in March 1900. Under this tricky piece of legislation, Congress ostensibly agreed to make U. S. obligations payable in dollars exchangeable for a fixed number of grains of gold for each dollar.

Imagine a sovereignty agreeing to pay its debts, or wanting private individuals to pay debts, in dollars exchangeable for quantities of gold which never did exist. All obligations of the United States Government, or of any private individual should always have been payable in United States legal tender, without any reference whatsoever to any number of grains of gold or any other one commodity into which those dollars were supposedly convertible.

Conversion of United States legal tender dollars into any specified number of ounces of gold always was a physical impossibility. How could Congress legally agree to pay in dollars convertible into a commodity, sufficient volume of which was impossible to provide?

The Gold Clause, on the face of it, is a complete farce. The factual history connected with the legislation involved is contained in a later chapter of this book. It suffices to state here that the so-called Gold Clause is merely another dishonest weapon which internationalists are attempting to use. Do humans *earn* dollars to buy *goods* or gold?

"Reconstruction"

In January 1932, Congress was asked to create the Reconstruction Finance Corporation. Destruction had now reached the stage where even the largest banks in New York City had to seek some place to unload their frozen loans. Via the Reconstruction Finance Corporation the large city banks were able to remove the frozen loans from their own portfolios and put them on to the taxpayers of the United States. Meanwhile, the closing of the smaller banks throughout the country continued ruthlessly. Human suffering and loss of properties went on and on. In June of 1932, just prior to the national political conventions, a large loan to one of the mid-western banks saved the entire banking structure temporarily.

From the time of the elections in 1932 until mid-February 1933, the destruction continued. Every one was waiting for the new President and the promised steps to bring about recovery. In mid-February a large chain of Michigan banks was denied a loan by the Reconstruction Finance Corporation. The closing of those key banks, tied up the biggest industries in the United States, and precipitated bank runs throughout the country. On March 3, 1933, every bank in the United States was closed. The timing was well done by those who were behind the scenes setting the stage for the triumphal entry of the new administration. Americans were terrified, and rightly so. They realized that large cities could not be tied up for more than a few days without causing a social breakdown.

The new President, in his inaugural address, promised "to drive the money changers out of the temple." However, he has yet to carry out his promise. He also said "the only thing we have to fear is fear itself." Can he really be afraid of the private money power? He started well, but faltered after a few months. An old, old, inexpensive remedy for fear is plain courage.

In a very reassuring tone of voice on the eve of reopening the banks, March 15, 1933, President Roosevelt told the people it would take several more days before all of the banks could be prepared for reopening, but no one was to worry if his bank did not open the first day. People believed and waited patiently. After eighteen months many of them are still waiting. Several billion dollars worth of bank deposits, frozen because of the Bank Holiday, are still enjoying a "holiday." The owners of those accounts are also having a holiday from purchasing food and clothing. It is impossible to conceive how the United States Government could go ahead as it has, handing out billions of dollars to socialistic interests, and still pretend it could not open more banks closed on March 3, 1933.

A striking example of inconsistency was the defeat of the McLeod Bill of June 1934 (which would have released one billion in closed banks) upon orders from the President. At the same time he ordered that a one billion dollar housing bill be passed. This money is being spent mainly in the lower East Side of New York, yet the great middle-western farmer cannot have the money that was taken away from him through the closing of the rural banks in the general moratorium on March 3, 1933.

Shortly after the inauguration, the Ministers of Finance of France, Italy and Great Britain rushed to the United States. Each of them had a zealous wish to "honor" the President. Each wanted a promise that the United States would not suspend gold payments. Apparently, the advisers to President Roosevelt agreed that he should grant that request. In mid-April 1933 he changed his mind and announced the suspension of gold payments. Norman Montagu, the Governor of the Bank of England, was on his way to India when the news was flashed. He changed vessels in mid-ocean. Need we wonder why?

As soon as this step was taken the raw commodity markets of the United States began to rise, and in the succeeding three months America had a taste of freedom from European financial strangulation. Our farmers began to buy the products of industry with their newly acquired buying power. We witnessed history's greatest economic recovery in terms of time and percentage. But, simultaneously, the newspapers began to tell the American people that America must settle all difficulties at an "Economic Conference" to be held in London. Of course, informed Americans know that some of the "Adepts" had had their representatives in Europe for some time planning to ensnare America at this Economic Conference.

President Roosevelt refused to agree to the very unfavorable terms demanded from America by the international bankers of Europe at the London conference in June 1933. The President's refusal broke up the conference. On July 3, 1933, the President addressed the people over the radio and told them that he was going to go ahead and raise the price levels, that is, raise the price of gold in the United States to a parity with the price of gold in London and the colonies. This would have enabled the United States to attain a raw commodity price level commensurate with the cost of production and the debt structure of the country.

However, private mysterious forces appear to have thwarted Mr. Roosevelt's plans. In mid-July was a secret agreement made with the Bank of England, with no authority from the United States Congress? The day the news was flashed to the United States all New York banks raised the stock margin requirements simultaneously. The tactics of the crash of October 1929 were repeated. The stock and commodity markets broke wide open. A greater percentage was lost in the value of stocks than had been lost in the initial crash of October 1929. Had America again been betrayed? President Roosevelt and other speakers then notified the people "that the speculators were the cause of the drop." They didn't say which speculators. It would be very enlightening if they would be a little more specific, but informed people drew the correct conclusion. It was not little Mr. Speculator, who had been told by the President to go ahead and make commitments, as he was going to raise the price levels. Mr. Little Speculator believed the words of the President of the United States. Did Mr. Big International Money Speculator force the President of the United States to break faith with the people who had elected him to drive those very big money changers from the Temple?

More Promises

From mid-July 1933 until October 22nd, the President allowed the currency price of gold in the United States to be well below the currency price of gold in London and the Colonies. He took no steps whatever, but the people were showered with a lot of mysterious articles emanating from Washington stating that the President was going to restore the raw commodity price levels. The American people had to be deceived — kept silent by fond but baseless expectations that effective money measures were under way.

On Sunday evening, October 22nd, after the agricultural section had arrived at another real crisis, President Roosevelt made another radio speech. Here he made more definite promises:

"No one who considers the plain facts of our situation believes that commodity prices, especially agricultural prices, are high enough yet. Some people are putting the cart before the horse. They want a permanent revaluation of the dollar first. It is the Government's policy to restore the price level first. I would not know, and no one else could tell, just what the permanent valuation of the dollar will be. To guess at a permanent gold valuation now would certainly require later changes caused by later facts. When we have restored the price level, we shall seek to establish and maintain a dollar which will not change its purchasing and debt paying power during the succeeding generation. I said that in my message to the American delegation in London last July and I say it now once more. Because of the conditions in this country, and because of events beyond our control in other parts of the world, it becomes increasingly important to develop and apply the further measures which may be necessary, from time to time, to control the gold value of our own dollar at home. Our dollar is now altogether too greatly influenced by the accidents of international trade, by the internal policies of other nations, and by political disturbances in other continents. Therefore, the United States must take firmly in its own hands the control of the gold value of our dollar. This is necessary in order to prevent dollar disturbances from swinging us away from our ultimate goal, namely; the continued recovery of our commodity prices.

"As a further effective means to this end, I am going to establish a Government market for gold in the United States. Therefore, under the clearly defined authority of existing law, I am authorizing the Reconstruction Finance Corporation to buy gold newly mined in the United States at prices to be determined from time to time, after consultation with the Secretary of the Treasury and the President. Whenever necessary to the end in view, we shall also buy or sell gold in the world market. My aim in taking this step is to establish and maintain continuous control. This is a policy and not an expedient. It is not to be used merely to offset a temporary fall in prices. We are thus continuing to move toward a managed currency."

In this speech the President promised to go ahead and raise the price of an ounce of gold. *That would have been the right policy.* Had he proceeded, raw material price levels would have increased. Our raw material exporters could have competed with exporters from other countries.

But immediately the newspapers throughout the country released a terrible campaign of terror and intimidation. Mr. Baruch had already favored the United States with a terrifying article on Inflation, in which he wisely warned against repetition of the German inflation. It is so strange "experts" do not explain that raising the price of an ounce of gold is *not* inflation in any sense of the word. Raising the price of an ounce of gold is *revaluation*. Did Mr. Baruch explain that throughout the entire history of money, the only time inflation, as he described it, took place, was when the internationalists wanted to destroy not only the value of the currency but also the government of a country? *Never* has any government itself conducted such an inflation.

A vicious inflation is produced only by printing an enormous amount of paper money and putting it into the money stream of a nation without any regard to the actual amount of money required to conduct the nation's business at price levels which are honest and equitable.

The "German" inflation which "Economists" describe, apparently intending to prejudice the American people against the gold revaluation policy, will be exactly what the American people will suffer if control of the United States money system is not taken out of the hands of the internationalists. *Was it the international bankers, who know no patriotism, who were responsible for the German currency destruction in 1922 and 1923?* It was a private money inflation of Reichsbank Notes perpetrated upon innocent Germans. This was intentionally done to dispossess the great middle class of German people. The same thing will be done to the middle class of American people if they do not arise and restore their money creation powers to the jurisdiction under which it belongs—*the Congress of the United States.*

Mr. Roosevelt raised the price of gold about $2.50 between the latter part of October and the 1st of December. Then suddenly, the propaganda against the gold revaluing policy ceased and raising the price of gold also stopped. People were now told that every Congressman should do exactly what the President wanted done at the next Session of Congress. Mr. James A. Farley, the Postmaster General, as well as many others, took the role of threatening Congressmen with being left at home in the 1934 elections if Mr. Roosevelt were not given dictatorial powers.

Congress convened on January 3, 1934. The President delivered his message personally on the state of the Nation to both the Senate and the House in joint session. But that message lacked frankness and clarity; it was broadly generalized.

The first week of Congress passed uneventfully. At the end of that time several Congressmen who knew that the principal key to the destruction was the money system made speeches demanding that the President set forth his policies. Immediately a secret session was called at the White House on Sunday evening, January 14th. On that occasion the President presented the 1934 Gold Bill. The following day the Congressmen who really had honest United States' money policies at heart, raised their voices in protest. They had asked to have some open hearings on the subject of money and they wanted to understand thoroughly and exactly the nature of any legislation that was passed. But all efforts on the part of members of both the House and the Senate to delay the Bill long enough to learn its contents were thwarted. The Bill was not even printed and circulated in Congress as required by all Congressional precedent. Congressmen voted like marionettes. Only a few sincere men protested. Congressman Beedy of Maine made the following speech:

"I am not going to vote for this Bill. I do not know what is in it. The House has had no benefit of hearings and is without authentic information as to the provisions of the Bill. I cannot be a good legislator and proceed in the darkness of an utter lack of information. Is there a man here who knows what this blanket covers? Is there a man here who knows what act his vote for this Bill containing such a section covers? Is there a man here who could go to his constituents after voting thus blindly and say, 'I knew what I was doing when I voted for the President's Monetary Bill'? I venture to say there are not ten men here who could intelligently explain such a vote. I am not going to vote for this legislation and swallow this thing. I want the chance to sit in committee and question the proper authorities. I want the benefit of regular hearings upon important legislative proposals. Through such procedure are the liberties of the American people secure. Thus, and thus alone, may we as legislators, hope to contribute to the stability of representative government." (January 20, 1934, U. S. Congressional Record, Page 1001.)

For his courage, Mr. Beedy was defeated in the election of September 1934. The high priests of international finance apparently decreed his political crucifixion.

The strange thing about the Gold Bill of 1934 is that no one will claim authorship. After signing it,

President Roosevelt *publicly admitted that he had never read the Bill* and yet he was unwilling to tell sincere Congressmen who the authors were. He signed it on the same day that the American people were tendering all of the birthday parties in his honor. How sad was that spectacle. Sincere Americans paying the President homage and at the same time being given away into subjection to the un-American international bankers.

Before the passage of that Bill several Senators tried to introduce an amendment which would make silver an important part of the monetary base of the United States. They were thwarted.

The reason the international bankers do not want silver a part of the money base is that it would destroy the gold control of the Rothschilds and their fellow international bankers in Germany and France.

The Gold Bill gives the President power to raise the "price" of gold to $41.34 per ounce. It has been $35.00 per ounce since the Bill was signed on January 30, 1934. At the present time, the price or purchasing power of an ounce of gold in the Colonies, Japan and in Argentina, is higher than in the United States. Therefore, all of the raw material producers in those countries have a great advantage over the raw material producers of the United States, where gold is worth only $35.00 in purchasing power. Our gold price being fixed at $35.00, the London gold price jugglers can name their own price at will to the continued destruction of American industry of all kinds.

Revaluation means changing the price of an ounce of gold. It has little effect on general domestic finished goods prices, but does affect the price of raw stuffs and finished goods entering world markets.

One can readily see that the currencies of all the

raw material exporting countries are now "stacked" against the United States.

The parrot newspapers of our country have been used, intentionally, to befuddle the people as to just what revaluation means. They tried to make them believe that changing the gold equivalent of the American dollar and making it correspond with the gold equivalent of the currencies of other countries, was robbing the widows, orphans and bondholders. That was a malicious and deliberate lie. Its back-of-the-scenes perpetrators know better.

Revaluation means changing the number of currency units for which an ounce of gold may be exchanged. It is very simple once the lies and "mystery" are torn away. A specific illustration will help explain.

Prior to December 1929 an ounce of gold could be exchanged in the world market for 21.5 pesos (Argentina money) or 20.67 dollars (U. S. money). In December 1929, the private gold brokers, the super financiers, began quietly to bid more pesos for an ounce of gold.

When the number of pesos was increased from 21.5 to 32.25 per ounce of gold, while the number of currency units per ounce of gold in the United States remained at 20.67, a purchaser of wheat or other raw materials in the world market at Liverpool would have to give up 50% more gold to buy anything in the United States, than in Argentina. (32.25 is 50% greater than 21.5.)

Liverpool importers will not give more gold to buy wheat in America than in Argentina. To meet this artificial condition American farmers must give as much wheat per ounce of gold as the Argentina farmers do.

They must sell their wheat at a serious discount below the natural and fair domestic price. They must sell at a loss which deprives them of any profit or excess of income over outgo, which they must have to buy the products of industrial centers. Thus industry is deprived of the purchasing power of over fifty million people dependent upon farm income.

In considering this colossal fraud upon America, we must always remember that under the existing scheme of things the price of the "surplus" (that which is exported) is the price of the whole crop, despite various efforts to remedy this foolish condition, which efforts mysteriously die aborning.

So wheat, under present conditions, must continue to sell below its natural and fair price, and the farmer obtain less than true value rendered. The very simplicity of the fraud has insured its success, although newspaper blindness or intimidation may have played a part in allowing the fraud to continue. We have been led by lying innuendo to believe that a "drop" in the gold buying power of our currency was bad, if not actually crooked, as though people used currency to buy gold instead of the real needs of life. The cart was put before the horse again, for the exact opposite is true.

Holding "high" the gold buying power of our currency is the real fraud. As shown above, when a skillful play on words (typical un-American deception) has been replaced by ordinary language, the simple truth can be understood by everyone. Beware of those who say their "economics" and monetary systems are too deep and mysterious to be penetrated.

When the United States was raising the price of gold, from April 19th to July 19, 1933, raw material prices were rising.

Over fifty million rural residents had a margin

HOW AND WHY AMERICAN PRODUCERS ARE SHUT OUT OF WORLD MARKETS

How Gold Prices are Juggled Against American Farmers, Laborers and Industrialists

Note: The price of wheat, which governs all farm prices, is set in England, where world "surpluses" go to market. Now, at London, an ounce of gold will buy less U. S. currency than foreign currencies. American farmers are shut out of export markets.

Block A, raw material, originating in U. S. or competing export country, exchanges for Block BC foreign currency, but only Block C in U. S. currency.

Block BC enables foreign producer to buy Block DE finished goods.

American producer can buy only Block E finished goods.

Block F, gold, exchanges for Block BC, foreign currency.

Block F exchanges for Block C U. S. currency.

Foreign buyer will purchase goods where he can get most currency for gold.

Foreign farmers and manufacturers can exchange same volume of commodities for more currency with which to pay overhead and have profit.

The gold price in currency has been adjusted by the "gold crowd" in London to favor Argentina, the British colonies and Japan. The "stabilization" fund is being used to handicap American farmers and manufacturers.

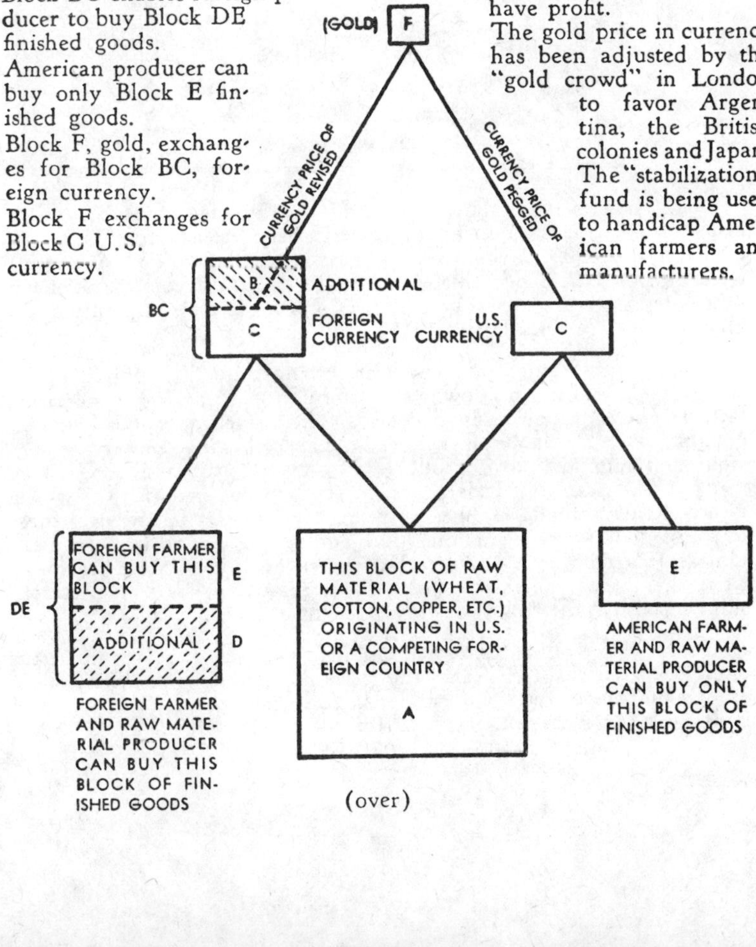

(over)

How Foreign Currencies are "Stacked" Against the United States

Country	Currency Unit	Old parity prior to Dec. 1929	Units exchangeable for an ounce of gold		Increased from Dec. 1929 to Feb. 1933	Units then exchangeable per ounce of gold		Increased to Dec. 1934	Units of currency then exchangeable per ounce of gold
United States	Dollar	1.00	20.67		None	20.67		69%	35
England	£ Ster.	4.8665	85	Shillings	42%	122	Shillings	67%	142
Argentina	Peso	0.9648	21.5		65%	35		117%	47
Australia	£ Ster.	4.8665	85	Shillings	79%	152	Shillings	107%	176
Egypt	£ Ster.	4.8665	85	Shillings	42%	122	Shillings	67%	142
New Zealand	£ Ster.	4.8665	85	Shillings	78%	151	Shillings	106%	175
South Africa	£ Ster.	4.8665	85	Shillings	44%	123	Shillings	66%	141
Canada	Dollar	1.00	20.67		20%	24.80		69%	35
Denmark	Krone	0.2680	77		76%	136		104%	157
Norway	Krone	0.2680	77		53%	117.8		82%	138
Japan	Yen	0.4985	42		140%	101		191%	123

The above figures show that while the number of U. S. dollars exchangeable for an ounce of gold has been raised from 20.67 to 35, which is 69%, the currencies of competing raw material countries, and of Japan, our chief finished goods export competitor, have been increased a greater percentage. For example: Argentina has increased 117% and Japan 191%.

This unfair competition has been arranged by the London "gold crowd." It causes a downward spiral for America. American farmers' buying power is decreased. Less factory goods can be bought. Factory labor is reduced. Labor buying power is cut; labor can buy less farm products and manufactured goods. Farm "surpluses" mount. Farmers are coerced to cut production, which means smaller food supplies and higher prices. Labor can then buy less food — more malnutrition and starvation ensue, etc., etc. Unless this condition is corrected violence is inevitable, which is what the international schemers—the aspirants to World Dictatorship, seek that they may destroy our government.

REMEDY: (1) Renounce gold forever as part of domestic money structure. (2) Raise the price of gold to full parity with other countries to settle international *trade balances.* (3) Give silver important place in settlement of international *trade balances.*

of income over outgo, with which to buy the output of the industrial centers. That accounted for the business acceleration which we had in the Spring of 1933. Finished goods prices were *not* rising, except a few which entered the export markets.

Raising the currency price of an ounce of gold was simply bringing the raw material price levels into line with the previously distorted range of prices for finished goods, so that producers could exchange their raw materials for finished goods on a basis of fair exchange. Every farmer knows only too well that he has been cheated outrageously by the amount of time, labor, etc., which he has had to exchange by way of his products for the manufactured articles which he needed and deserved from civilization for his contribution toward keeping it alive. Many farm leaders know that the price of an ounce of gold in the United States must be on a parity with the price of gold in London and the colonies. However, their voices are, as yet, too weak to overcome the power of those who forced the President's hand in favor of their own money strangulation policies in July 1933. What is needed is a mighty blast from twenty or thirty million farmers and rural workers!!

In July 1934, George L. Harrison, Governor of the Federal Reserve Bank of New York, went on another visit to Europe, this time to the Bank for International Settlements. If he made another private agreement, without knowledge or consent of Congress, we have further proof of the high-handed and unpatriotic methods of international bankers.

The Two Billion Dollar Secret Fund — The "Stabilization Fund"

The Gold Bill of 1934 provided for a stabilization fund of two billion dollars to be managed by the

Secretary of the Treasury. The Congress and the people are not permitted to know anything about the operations of this fund until January 1937, and even the President is not empowered by law to exercise any control or influence. He is entitled to annual audits — *after things have happened.*

When the bill was passed, the American public was fed an enormous amount of false theorizing on the need of a Stabilization Fund. We were told that since England had a great Stabilization Fund, America certainly must also have one.

Before discussing the Stabilization Fund the writer wishes to mention that the American people have been misled as to what was actually done when the so-called nationalization of the gold took place. The people were told that the United States Government actually took control of the gold away from the privately owned Federal Reserve Banks and placed it in the sole possession and control of the Treasury of the United States. That is *not* the case. The Federal Reserve Banks can retake the gold from the United States Treasury under a number of very broad provisions in the 1934 Gold Bill. Of course, these provisions can only be carried out with the sanction of the Secretary of the Treasury.

Under the provision of Section 3 —

> "The Secretary of the Treasury shall, by regulations issued hereunder, with the approval of the President, prescribe the conditions under which gold may be acquired and held, transported, melted or treated, imported, exported or earmarked: . . . (b) by the Federal Reserve Banks for the purpose of settling international balances; and, (c) for such other purposes as in his judgment are not inconsistent with the purposes of this Act."

SECTION 5 — "All gold coin of the United States shall be withdrawn from circulation, and, together with all other gold owned by the United States, shall be formed into bars of such weights and degrees of fineness as the Secretary of the Treasury may direct."

This is exactly what was previously done in England, where, if you had $8,000 in gold demand notes you could get a gold ingot of such value; but which, for ordinary exchange purposes, would be no better than a gold brick. The coin withdrawn from circulation had been remelted into ingots, which cannot circulate.

SECTION 6 — "Provided however, that gold certificates owned by the Federal Reserve Banks shall be redeemed at such times and in such amounts as, in the judgment of the Secretary of the Treasury, are necessary to maintain the equal purchasing power of every kind of currency of the United States . . . No redemptions in gold shall be made except in gold bullion bearing the stamp of a United States mint or assay office in an amount equivalent at the time of redemption to the currency surrendered for such purpose."

You, Mr. Patriotic American Citizen, cannot have gold, but the internationalists can obtain it.

SECTION 10 — "For the purpose of stabilizing the exchange value of the dollar, the Secretary of the Treasury, with the approval of the President, directly or through such agencies as he may designate, is authorized, for the account of the fund established in this section, to deal in gold and foreign exchange and such other instruments of credit and securities as he may deem necessary to carry out the purpose of this section. An annual audit of such fund shall be made and a report thereof submitted to the President."

This annual audit that is submitted to the President shall not be seen by any other officer of the United States. It's a strange thing that such an important audit cannot be examined by other officers of the United States, nor by the Banking and Currency Committee of either the U. S. Senate or of the House of Representatives.

SECTION 17 — "All Acts and parts of Acts inconsistent with any of the provisions of this Act are hereby repealed."

Every American who thinks about the matter, will see that the misnamed "Stabilization Fund" may be a back-handed method of "legalizing" the disappearance of two billion dollars in gold, and Uncle Sam's two billion eight hundred million revaluation "profit" may be largely sunk in frozen foreign credits.

The United States is now a creditor nation. We do not need or want to control the currencies or price levels of any other nation. England has had a stabilization fund because she is a vast importer of raw materials and she wants to control and dominate the financial systems of the colonies.

If the administration were acting for the best interests of the American people, the Secretary of the Treasury would allow *no* foreign exchange transactions except in settlement of actual trade balances or for modest remittances such as travelling expenses or relatives sending small sums to their people in other countries. The remittances of funds to take care of actual importations of goods and reasonable remittances to cover travelling or funds to dependent relatives, should be taken care of, but there should be no export of large amounts of capital permitted.

It is general knowledge that from September

1931, when England suspended gold payments, to April 19, 1933, billions of "wise money" belonging to the internationalists was being used to buy gold bars (which were shipped to Europe) and to buy billions of dollars worth of the currencies of foreign countries. Many unpatriotic Americans bought the currency of Belgium, France, Holland and Switzerland. Those balances cannot be brought back to the United States unless some one is now willing to sell dollar balances.

The foreign exchange market is like any other market. If there is a greater demand for promises-to-pay dollars than there is demand for promises-to-pay pounds, francs, guilders, etc., the dollar will rise. Therefore, when those individuals bring their balances back to New York, some one has to sell dollar balances, otherwise, the price of New York exchange would rise very high in relation to the price of the pound, franc or guilder, promises-to-pay. Unless some one supplies American dollar balances, either gold must be shipped from those European countries or the price of the dollar in terms of them must rise.

Under the "Stabilization Fund," Uncle Sam is the victim. With the taxpayers' money he must now buy foreign currency balances to let these internationalists bring their credits back to New York from various foreign countries. Why should the American taxpayers' money be frozen in sterling, francs, guilders and lira? — only because the operation of this fund permits this. Once these balances are back in New York, the owners of them can send them back to Europe again in the form of gold. The provisions of the Bill permit this.

It is strange that the Treasury Department was never interested in learning the names of those who brought gold back to the United States, particularly in the few weeks following the passage of the Gold Bill in 1934. These people received $35.00 per ounce, while the American who had $100 in gold, and the poor people who had a few gold coins, were threatened by the President if they did not bring back their gold and get $20.67 per ounce. It certainly pays to be an internationalist.

THE MYSTERY OF THE GOLD BILL OF JANUARY 1934

The Chief Executive was very careful, when signing this bill, to make it clear to those standing around, including the newspaper reporters, that he had nothing to do with writing it, and had not read it before signing; that he was taking it on faith from the Secretary of the Treasury. The Secretary of the Treasury, in turn, also stated that he had not read it but that it was what the "experts" wanted.

Well may we wonder why the Chief Executive and his cabineteer, the Secretary of the Treasury, have not been willing to tell who wrote this bill. Of course, it could be that a bill of this nature could have originated in New York, because it so favors the money creators there who have, since its passage, been taking advantage of its generous provisions for dealers in foreign currencies: but that would be a violation of the Chief Executive's promise "to drive the money changers from the temple."

If the President learned, for instance, that the Gold Bill of January 1934 was written by a man who had become rich on advice and arbitrage—fractional point scalping of international money transfers, the intricacies of which only the money creators are familiar with—it should be reasonable to suppose that the President would be fired to intense ire.

And if it were announced to the patient and

trusting American people that the Gold Bill of 1934 was written by a money changer and that the preparation of it took place at this man's office in Wall Street, it is reasonable to suppose that the patient American people would begin to get an insight into the money creators' skullduggery. They would certainly demand a real investigation, as well as an explanation as to why the most important pieces of legislation were jammed through Congress without reading or debate; signed by the President in ignorance of what the bills contained, and advised by the Secretary of the Treasury who acknowledged similar ignorance of the contents.

Just suppose, for instance, that the people learned that when the money changers were thrown out of the temple they took the temple's "precious" contents with them! Just suppose that the man who actually wrote the Gold Bill of 1934 sits in the councils of other individuals who are honestly trying to fight the money creators, and who do not recognize the dual role of certain individual players. He sits in the councils of the money creators and then in the councils of men who are trying to fight the money creators and give the American people an honest deal. Such insincerity and duplicity is common among money creators.

"Presto-Chango Allimagesto"
Say the slick money "mystery" men —
The money bookkeeping is ours,
The people pay in lovely showers!

Abracadabra, my gold dollar,
When they took it I did not holler:
Shipped to Europe, bought for a song,
They brought it back, *near twice* as long.

Tomorrow it will leave again
On a sea of rolling green,
Then the People will be told —
"The trouble is, we have no gold!"

Then some Rothgeld will demand
We recognize his mighty hand —
Clack our foreheads on his stoop,
Each one stamped "A Nincompoop."

CHAPTER IX

UNDER THE SEARCHLIGHT

AN ANALYSIS OF THE NATURE OF WEALTH, MONEY, AND DEBT

Historians tell us that Egypt lived and prospered for over 2500 years *without money*, because money was unnecessary in that kind of social organization, where each family was self-sufficient as to its needs for food, clothing, shelter, etc.

We are further told that the Roman Empire had and used money, because in that stage of material civilization each family was not self-sufficient and thus had to exchange its surplus products for its own needs. The Romans did not *understand* the function of money, and this lack of understanding of the necessary mechanism of civilization known as "money," resulted in the downfall of Rome.

It is all too apparent that what is missing today is a means by which *Surpluses* can be distributed to the "*Jobless,*" and the Jobless put to work earning the "Surpluses." Every intelligent person knows that money, properly speaking, is but a medium of exchange. Understanding an honest, scientific money system *must* become general, if we, as a nation, are to throw off the shackles by which unconstitutional private money practices have kept us so long in subjection.

The continued existence of our present civilization — the highest the world has ever known — depends exclusively upon whether or not we shall, as a people, bestir ourselves into setting up a money system such as provided for by the Constitution of the

United States, and such as existed for only a few years after this nation was founded.

The first violation of the Constitution of the United States was accomplished by those responsible for chartering the misnamed "Bank of the United States" in 1791. (Note how the name corresponded to the "Bank of England," "Bank of France," "Bank of Italy" — all being private instrumentalities.) "The Bank of the United States" was privately owned and, in violation of the United States Constitution, had the privilege of issuing (creating) money. The history of the Bank of the United States is covered in another chapter.

A few statesmen have courageously fought the dishonest and unconstitutional money system. But their voices and sound arguments have never reached the nation via the press except in a way which did not state the truth; lending itself to ridicule and derision — the standard weapon of the enemy, used on all fronts.

Understanding a money system requires consideration of several simple fundamental facts:

WEALTH — The wealth of this nation consists of its physical things — its lands, minerals, factories, homes, public buildings, railroads, utilities, food and clothing supplies, etc. Money is a convenient medium or reckoner used in bringing about exchanges of actual wealth. Wealth has physical properties which classify into two sections:

1 — Consumer goods, or perishable goods.

2 — Capital assets, or instruments used in the production of consumer goods.

Consumer goods, or perishable goods, are all of those physical things which are consumed directly in living, and the destruction of which actually motivates human life. The food we eat, the clothing we wear, the coal we burn in heating our homes, are destroyed in motivating life itself. Consumer goods are all of the perishable goods which, in final form, are ready for human consumption and are actually destroyed in sustaining human life.

Capital assets do not motivate life itself. For example: we do not eat a railroad car or a farmer's plow, but both are used in the process of producing and distributing the things we do eat. They are the necessary instruments to facilitate production and distribution. These assets wear out and become obsolete.

All physical goods, whether consumer goods or capital goods, follow the laws of physics. They are actually destroyed in human consumption or, as instruments of further production, they wear out and grow obsolete.

A financial system which is honestly and properly set up must recognize the physical qualities of both consumer and capital goods, for its deals solely with the *physical* things. It is the introduction of non-physical or metaphysical elements (such as confidence) which permits manipulators to throw things out of gear periodically.

MONEY—Money is not wealth. Money is merely a convenient medium used to reckon the relative values of actual wealth which individuals exchange with each other. A money system is a mechanical means set up to facilitate production of goods and their distribution to individuals. To give money anything but an exchange function permits perversion.

We are dishonestly told that a money system depends upon "Confidence." This is the case under the existing scheme; but it is perversion brought down on us from centuries-old deceptive practices.

Money is a *demand* claim of an individual for wealth (the physical thing). All members of society engaged in work, contribute toward and help produce the store of physical goods which society needs to live. When an individual produces something which he does not consume himself, but which he turns over to the society to consume, he receives money. Money is a *demand* claim upon the general supply of goods (wealth). A gardener grows potatoes. He and his family do not consume all of the potatoes. He, therefore, turns over the potatoes to the total stock in the nation. In return, he receives money. He has produced and contributed into the wholesale "hopper," physical goods which human beings need for living. Upon turning it into the hopper, he received demand claims upon the total physical goods in the hopper. Money is the individual's ticket or *demand* claim given to him, because he has contributed wealth which has been made available for the society. He spends his demand claim (money) on clothing, house rent, food, automobiles, education, etc., or invests it in capital assets (buys a bond, shares of stock, a home, a farm, etc.)

The total money in a community or a nation, that is, the total demand claims, should bear a scientific relation to the total consumer goods which the members of that community or nation have produced and have in the hopper ready for human consumption at any particular time. Remember, money is a *demand* claim.

The quantity of money in a nation should not increase or decrease excepting as the physical consumer wealth increases or decreases. As producers grow more efficient and produce more physical goods available for human consumption, then of course, there should be a bigger money supply, because money is the only practical medium known to our civilization by which goods available for use may be moved from producers to consumers. This theory is so simple that it has taken innumerable lies, propagated through ostensibly respectable channels — such as business schools, text books, "Economic Research Bureaus," newspapers, etc. — to conceal the fundamental truth. The misinformation was originated and propagated by the few — for selfish ulterior purposes — to keep the American people steeped in the falsehood that the trouble with our economic system is something "mysterious"; too deep for any but the erudite few to understand.

It is all-important to remember that money now takes various forms. The functions are one, but the forms differ. In the United States the two principal forms of money are bank deposits (created by bankers lending their promises-to-pay which are subject to checking), and paper currency, which is tangible. Gold and Silver tokens also exist but they play a very minor part in the actual conduct of every day business. People commonly use silver coins, but gold coins, under the present law, cannot be held by ordinary private American citizens.

The power to periodically wreck our economic structure lies exclusively in the special and unconstitutional privilege held by private parties (banks) to create or cancel money (bank deposits via loans) at will. So long as these special privileges continue in private hands we shall inevitably have periodic trouble. The signers of our United States Constitution foresaw this and attempted to save the nation from it. Their plans were forestalled when the misnamed Bank of the United States, having private money issue powers, was chartered.

Over 95% of the business in the United States is conducted through the use of bank checks or intangible bank deposit "money," as contrasted with actual paper currency. Currency is the actual money you carry around in your billfold. The amount of that in use in the United States for many years has been relatively small, the reason being, the less actual currency in use as money the more private bank created money can be expanded and contracted. Practically all of our deposits are banker created "money." They are created by bankers making loans (promises-to-pay). Interest is charged on every single dollar of their promises-to-pay.

Bankers have absolute control over this "money." They can increase or cancel the amount of it at will, and they force eternal tribute in interest. That is why it is so difficult to correct the abuses; the profit is too enticing.

To mislead American people, there have appeared in newspapers frequent inspired discussions stating that there is more currency in existence than there was in 1929. This is a true statement, but it is misleading, and is intended to be misleading. Pocket money (currency) commonly occupies the center of our mental stage when speaking of money, but it has been relatively unimportant in the total business picture. For example:

June 30	Pocket Money (Currency)	Bank Deposits (Loans) (Bank Manufactured Money)	Total Money
1929	4.7 Billions	53 Billions	58 Billions
1933	5 Billions	35 Billions	40 Billions

Our thesis is that actual currency — constitutional government-created money — should replace every dollar of bankers' credit money; so that every dollar carried as a deposit by a bank must be matched by a dollar in currency in the bank vaults or by actual loans (real money) which were made to borrowers. This is the only way to place the *volume* of money, the life blood of all industry, beyond the control of unsocial interests where it now resides.

As was stated, more than 95% of the business in the United States is conducted through the shifting of bank deposits by the use of checks. The reader has noted from the table above that there has been an enormous collapse in the amount of bank deposits in existence. This has been brought about by bankers calling in their promises-to-pay (loans), bankers' credit "money." In reality, collapsing the bank deposits to the extent shown, has resulted in destroying the demand claims of individuals—in cancelling money—and in distorting the relationship which should exist between the demand claims (money) in the hands of individuals and the actual physical consumer goods available for distribution, and which the people need if they are to maintain decent living standards.

Since 1929 this country has not lost any population, or have any farms or factories been destroyed (we did destroy some hogs and cotton upon the mistaken or perverted advice of the Department of Agriculture). The people have not suddenly changed all of their wants. They still want food, clothing, etc. What has happened? The human wants are there, and the physical supplies and factories are in existence through which those human wants could be satisfied, but something has happened to destroy the relationship that should exist. Approximately eighteen billion dollars worth of demand claims (money) have been cancelled. The bankers called in their promises-to-pay which they had loaned out at interest, so that they are no longer owned or available or even exist for use by human beings. Therefore, the demand claims (money) are now not sufficient to move the physical volume of consumer goods (both raw materials and finished goods) at equitable price levels, which would have to be produced and moved if the people were to have the food and clothing which they did produce and exchange their services for in 1929.

If the people can no longer command the same volume of food and clothing, the producers of these things have to curtail. Therefore, unemployment exists and it will continue to exist until the proper ratio is restored between the physical consumer goods which the people want, and are capable of producing and need to maintain life, and the amount of demand claims in their possession obtained for labor or service which they may use at will.

Could anything be more stupid than a situation wherein we have people who want to work and need the products; we have the farms, raw materials and factories with which to produce, yet people cannot work but must endure privation of all kinds; even starvation in many instances? Men whose sincerity is open to serious question keep telling the people that there is nothing the matter with the money system of the United States. They write books filled with palpable falsehoods. No more vicious untruths could possibly be uttered than those by which whole nations of people have been induced to submit the quantity of their economic life blood — money creation and cancellation powers — to the control of certain individuals. The control over the American supply of domestic money and raw material price levels has been operated from London since the close of the Civil War.

Banking — There is no business in this country or in any other country which uses the Continental system of banking, which is not dependent upon a knowledge of price movements. (Caused by changes in bank money supply.)

"Of all the discoveries and inventions by which

we live and die, this totally improbable helix of bank credit" (bankers' promises-to-pay) "is the most cunning, the most liable, the least comprehended, and next to high explosives, the most dangerous. All that bankers themselves really know about it is how it works from day to day. Beyond that, it is a gift from Pandora." — *A Bubble that Broke the World.* (Writer inserted parenthesis.) Domestic bankers, too, have been deceived by the overwhelming false propaganda emanating from high and powerful sources which they believe merited respect; they have been cowed by the incessant shouts of false leaders who insisted that the money system had become a sacred thing, "traditional," if you please, and that it was outside of the scope of the people to make any changes, however sensible. "Thou shalt not 'tinker' with the money system," has become the guiding commandment governing bankers.

If *domestic* bankers in general, excepting a few conspiring leaders, had ever critically examined and therefore had really understood the system whose machinery they operate, they would not have been parties to such a destructive conspiracy against society. Many bankers realize and admit, after they study and really understand the present system, that it is unscientific and dishonest and has contributed more toward human suffering than all the plagues and pestilences known to mankind.

Too, the present system has had its fleshpots for its devotees; its sycophant worshippers who found that the Pandora's box mentioned above yielded profits which, while mysterious, were sweet — too sweet to give up without a struggle.

There is reason to believe, however, that honest bankers in general will welcome a frontal attack upon the system by which so many honest bankers have been year after year deprived of their banks — approximately 15,000 banks have failed since 1920.

Imagine a system, whose purported function is to provide the means for exchanging the physical goods of the nation, permitting those private individuals operating that system to be vested with the power to create and cancel promises-to-pay (bankers' money) at will; besides having the system so arranged that foreign financial manipulators can force an expansion or contraction of the quantity of money without the concurrence of the community American banker. In other words, to perform a sleight-of-hand trick on money, causing it to disappear while human beings and the physical goods they can produce exist.

Our banking system today is a collapsible structure. Practically all of the money supply must, under the present system, inevitably consist of bankers' promises-to-pay; that is, the money under our present system must be created through banks lending promises-to-pay.

When a thing is loaned, it may be recalled. Therefore, a nation, whose money is principally made up of bankers' promises-to-pay (loaned to individuals), is at the mercy of the lenders. Calling the loans and cancelling the promises-to-pay destroys the supply of money. Curtailing the supply of money faster than the physical volume of goods decreases causes prices to drop (deflation), because money is scarce while goods are plentiful, so that each dollar will buy more goods. Every one knows this. What chicanery has been used by the unsocial few to perpetuate the abuse will never be fully known!

Under this system, all business men must continue to be *good hard-working borrowers*. They must never be allowed to understand that by calling in loans, at will, the price levels can be changed and businesses can be placed on the skids, with the end of the slide visible only to the innermost insiders.

The United States is now, not only granting unconstitutional and dishonest money creation and cancellation powers to private individuals, but it is going a great deal farther. *Private individuals now have power to issue their unsecured promises-to-pay in exchange for Government Bonds, which are taxpayers' promises-to-pay secured by a general mortgage on all of the properties in the country and a first claim on all national income due to the fact that Congress has the power to tax private individuals.* Imagine a nation allowing private individuals to exchange their puny unsecured promises-to-pay for taxpayers' promises-to-pay (Government bonds) and calling these unsecured private individuals' promises-to-pay (their "credit") "money," then lending that money to the taxpayers themselves (nation).

Under this deceptive method taxpayers (the nation) must pay interest to private individuals — pay on the nation's borrowings of private promises-to-pay. For instead of issuing their own national notes as money (national currency), they have allowed private individuals to issue their promises-to-pay and exchange them for Government bonds which are secured by a prior claim on all properties and national income; which in reality are taxpayers' promises-to-pay (the Nation's promises-to-pay). The promises-to-pay which private individuals issue to the United States Government are unsecured.

When private individuals (bankers) need currency, they take part of the Government bonds in their portfolio and send them to the United States Treasury. They receive from the Bureau of Engraving (operated at the expense of the United States) currency (pocket money). Private individual bankers pay no interest for the use of this currency but the bankers continue to collect interest on the bonds which they have deposited with the United States Treasury. These bankers, private individuals, must keep only a 5% cash reserve with the Treasurer of the United States to pay for the redemption of any currency that might be presented to the Secretary of the Treasury.

The Federal Reserve Notes which bankers obtain in this way have printed on their face that the United States of America will pay *on demand* so many dollars. Americans are led to believe that they are issued by and are an obligation of the United States Treasury. They are *not*. They are issued by private individuals. In reality, the taxpayers are responsible but the private individuals collect the profits (interest).

Banking, as it is conducted in the United States today, is actually a conspiracy operating against society. It is operated to periodically destroy property values, and disastrously curtail income, wages and profits; under control of the "Federal" Banks, loading upon the people the maximum possible burden of tribute in the way of interest, both public and private. The maxim is, "Make the nation carry the maximum amount of interest possible. Keep the masses paying interest to the privileged few." Interest is simply the overwhelming tribute which all of the producers of real wealth in the nation are paying to a few who enjoy the unconstitutional and dishonest privilege of creating money.

Note carefully that the original issuance or creation of money, *paid* into circulation, should always be interest free. Carefully distinguish this original issuance of money upon its creation with the *lending* of *real* money, which has been obtained by those who have *earned* it by rendering personal services or real goods in exchange for that money. In actually lending real money so earned, one may properly expect a fair interest rate. This important point will doubtless be deliberately obscured and misrepresented by the privileged few, skilled in using deceptive terms and erecting smoke screens.

INFLATION — The word "inflation" is intentionally misused to create terror in the minds of the people. Inflating is the act of increasing the money (demand claims) of a nation faster than the volume of consumer goods available for distribution can be increased. Bankers can and do cause inflation every time they create their own promises-to-pay at a faster rate than consumer goods can be produced. This is credit inflation or bankers' money inflation.

There are two kinds of inflation: one by expansion of bankers' credit; the other by expanding the currency (billfold money). The latter may be an expansion which will be scientific and adequate and no more; or the kind of expansion as was carried on by the private international bankers, during the "French" Revolution, after the "Russian" Revolution of 1917, and in Germany after the War, etc. This destruction of the value of currency (making it actually worthless) has never been brought about by politicians, but always by the international bankers themselves. It has never been the statesmen-politicians, but always the *international bankers* who have caused unjustified inflation *wherever it has occurred in the past 150 years*. There is not one example of a government which mis-used its national currency.

The statement which indicates that bankers themselves suffer from inflation, seems unreasonable at first thought. Domestic bankers do suffer. They lose everything. Their banks are destroyed. Also, all insurance policies and mortgages become worthless, because the money paid to discharge them has no purchasing power, but the international money manipulators gain possession of the Nation's real wealth through honest bankers' losses.

The fact is that *only* international bankers profit by this procedure. During the last 150 years, whenever the currency of a country has been destroyed, the Government of that country has also been destroyed, and the country has been taken over in toto by the international bankers. They take possession and control of the entire country; loyal citizens lose everything, including their property and their rights. It is certain people who are now decrying an honest money system in the United States; shouting "inflation" to terrify people whenever honest recommendations are made, *who will destroy the currency which we now use when they are ready to act.*

According to a banker's definition, *sound money* is money that is convertible into gold at a fixed number of dollars per ounce, at the will of the holder. In reality, convertibility into gold is a myth and a fetish. It has never been possible at any time, in any nation, after a so-called modern banking system had been set in operation.

In 1929, there existed in the United States less than five billion dollars worth of currency (pocket money), and about fifty-three billion dollars worth of bank money (deposits—bankers' promises-to-pay). In other words, there was approximately fifty-eight billion dollars in money. That was about twelve times the total amount of gold in the country. Yet, bankers told us at that time we had "sound money." Besides the fifty-eight billion dollars in money, there existed in the United States approximately two hundred twenty-five billion dollars worth of bonds. Many of these carried a gold payment clause. In other words, the investment bankers had enlarged the already stupendous myth by stating that these bonds were also convertible into gold. Imagine, nearly three hundred billion dollars of obligations and money to be converted, and approximately five billion dollars worth of gold into which to convert. It was an obvious fraud. Yet, that was called *sound* financing and no comments were permitted. There is perhaps no convention or fetish ever put over on modern civilized nations that compares with the intentional deception contained in the so-called gold convertibility of money and bonds. Money and bonds never were and never could be convertible into gold—except in a very small percentage, even if we had all the gold in the world!

The only reason internationalists ever placed the gold conversion clause in force was to enable them to convert money belonging to themselves into gold and export that gold to collapse the banking structure of the Nation. In order to conceal the deception, it was stated that *all* money was convertible into gold. If international bankers in Europe or in New York betimes wanted to convert their New York balances into gold, they could do so and then ship the gold out of the country. Every dollar's worth of gold they took out of the system cancelled a maximum potential $30.00 worth of bank money (deposits), bankers' promises-to-pay. One can readily understand why they continue to cry for gold convertibility. They *had* to have it so they could pull gold out and collapse our economic structure and reap a harvest thereby. It was no grave concern for the well being or the happiness of Mr. American Citizen, or for the widows and orphans, that prompted the determined interest in gold convertibility. Mr. Internationalist may weep bitter tears for the good old "traditional" gold standard. We note that his "grieved" predecessors did not weep over the good old traditional silver standard when it was dishonestly removed as a part of our legal money base in 1873, after having been equally important with gold since the founding of this country. Who ever heard of an international banker shedding genuine tears over American widows and orphans? We also note the failure to advocate a resumption by Congress of the power which belongs to it under the Constitution of the United States.

It is one thing for a nation itself to issue sufficient currency, bearing its own imprint, to effect the volume of exchanges necessary to feed, clothe and shelter its people, and it's quite another thing for a group of predatory internationalists to print money by the bale and inject it into the currency stream of a nation. That is exactly what was done when the French money system was destroyed at the time of the French Revolution. The money was really printed in England, and was injected into the French money system by paying it over to the conspirators to be used in bribing the "adepts" and the "dupes." It has been reliably chronicled that seventeen printing presses and 400 men were employed in England at that time to manufacture and carry on the traffic in this counterfeit money. By this means the French Government money (Assignats) was destroyed, and later the same private individuals gained control of the new money system after they had acquired possession of most of the property in France.

When the Russian currency was destroyed in 1917, the international money powers ordered a foreign warship to sail for Kronstadt, the naval station of St. Petersburg, carrying printing presses, which at once began to emit fake money, which was injected into the Russian currency stream and finally destroyed the entire money system of Russia.

If the money system of this nation were honestly managed, those entrusted with the power to issue currency bearing the imprint of this nation, would issue it only as the people increased their stock of consumer goods available for distribution and consumption. If the emissions of currency were made scientifically, currency would be injected into the system as the flow of consumer goods increased; price levels would be maintained at approximately stable levels, and there would be no such thing as gyrations in the price structure excepting as weather influenced farm supplies and, hence, no business depressions.

The inspired statements about "fluctuations in the value of a commodity dollar" are falsehoods. A commodity dollar really means that 100 cents would always buy about the same amount of food, clothing, services, etc. We now have a truly "rubber" dollar. Under our present system, wherein a few private individuals can control the volume of our medium of exchange, they can and do determine whether a dollar will buy one bushel of wheat or three bushels, or whether two dollars or six dollars will be necessary to buy a pair of laborer's shoes.

Increasing the money supplies, whether it be currency or bank deposit money, out of all reasonable proportion to the consumer goods available to be exchanged, produces sharp price increases. Vice versa, decreasing money supplies, either currency or bank deposits (bankers' promises-to-pay), out of all proportion to consumer goods available for distribution, causes a disastrous decline in the price of raw materials. If the decline is of sufficient proportion, it can cause a complete breakdown of the system.

Who will deny that the decline in prices of raw materials was preceded by a decline in the amount of bankers' credit outstanding? The great raw commodity decline preceding our crash of 1929 started in raw material prices in Europe, following a drop in the volume of European bank money (private bankers' promises-to-pay). Since London was determining our price levels, as soon as raw materials began backing up in Europe, our price structure began to collapse.

Raw material prices respond very readily to decreases in the supply of either real money (currency), or of bank credit money, called bank deposit money. They are not controlled by trade association price fixing policies, such as prevail in many classes of finished goods.

Inflation in regard to money has exactly the same meaning as when used in regard to forcing gas into a balloon. A balloon can stand a certain amount of gas, but if more gas is forced into the balloon than the walls can support, the balloon will burst. The time to stop filling is easy to see.

Inflation used in connection with money means increasing the medium of exchange, that is, the demand claims, without correspondingly increasing the actual physical volume of consumer goods (perishable goods) to be exchanged. If consumer goods and the flow of money increase simultaneously in direct proportions, inflation does not occur, just as a balloon would not become inflated if one kept increasing the dimensions of the wall as rapidly as gas was forced into it.

If physical goods are produced as rapidly as money is paid into the currency stream, more goods can be distributed, but no appreciable price rise will take place. This is the desirable situation for, after all, the object of all business is to manufacture and distribute goods—the things human beings need to live. An honest money system would have and perform that function and *that function alone*. What the United States must have is an enormous increase in the production and distribution of physical units of *finished* goods, but not a price increase in finished goods. Our finished goods factories need volume, and human beings need the distribution of finished goods in enormous volume.

Prices — The price of an article is the number of dollars or cents which it will command in exchange. A laboring man may command $6.00 a day for his work, that is, the price of his labor. With his $6.00 he may command a pair of shoes, that is the price of shoes. Labor and shoes are both expressed in terms of dollars, although one day's work equals one pair of shoes.

Under a scientifically correct money system, prices of raw materials and those of finished goods must be in proper alignment with each other, and they must not vary widely over any period of time. For example: If the price of wheat, corn, cotton, iron ore, and other basic raw materials collapses, a given amount of money will command a larger amount of those physical products. If a decline or a rise in raw material prices is of substantial proportion, the relationship between the demand claims (money) and the time claims (bonds) becomes distorted in a manner that prevents proper working of the system. For example: If six bushels of wheat bring $6.00 in one year, and it has cost $4.00 to produce it, the farmer has $2.00 in net purchasing power. If the price of wheat drops so that six bushels will command only $3.00, while his costs remain practically the same—he will, in reality, have no purchasing power, for his costs of

$4.00 exceed his proceeds of $3.00 by $1.00. He is then in a position where he is unable to meet his own overhead, interest and taxes, and has no purchasing power in the industrial world.

The significance of prices is not understood by the average person who has not had an opportunity to examine this indicator—for that is what "prices" are.

Practically every effort of the Federal Government to "aid" the farmer during the past many years of artificial stress—"Federal" "Reserve" system-created (Secret meeting, May 18, 1920)—has been toward the rebuilding of prices.

Every effort has been directed toward effecting some change upon the total volume of real wealth in the nation, the product whose "price" was the subject of examination, or of manipulation.

The McNary-Haugen bill was designed to help the farmer.

The "Federal" (another misnomer) Farm Board Act likewise was said to have the same purpose.

> The Bankhead bill aimed to raise the price of cotton. Millions of pigs and cattle were destroyed to raise the price of pork and beef on the hoof.
> Every third row of cotton was plowed under, over the protest of the all too sensible mules, to raise the price of cotton.
> Etc., etc., etc., etc., ad infinitum et ad nauseam.
> But intentionally *not one* glance was directed at the other side of the scales, the indicator of which names the *price* of things, the other side being the monetary supply and the international valuation of the price of an ounce of gold.
> *Why?* Simply because the money power had decreed: *Thou shalt not make honest the money system!*

Until George F. Warren, farm authority of the New York College of Agriculture at Cornell University, Ithica, New York, informed several farm organizations how other currencies were "stacked" against the American farmer, and these farm organizations persuaded the President to listen to Warren, nothing was done toward changing the price of an ounce of gold in New York. London, the British Colonies and Argentina had raised the price of an ounce of Gold. Argentina started to raise the price of gold in December of 1929. London and the British Colonies were raising it from September, 1931, on. Yet, when America started to do the same thing for the sole reason that we were forced to do exactly what other raw material exporting countries had done, the uninformed and paid "economists" decried the policy and called it "inflation." They had not the common honesty to say that we were forced to raise the price of gold or compel our farmers to suffer a terrific price disadvantage in world raw material export markets, especially at Liverpool and Manchester. They deliberately obscured the plain fact that changing the currency price of an ounce of gold is not changing the domestic monetary quantity, hence, not inflation in any sense of the word. It is in converting the proceeds of export sales, particularly of our raw commodities, into our own currency (dollars) that the price of an ounce of gold is important. If gold is lower in New York than it is in London or in the British Colonies, the American farmer suffers.

Until the farmers, in their good sense, saw that Warren was right, no one dared to challenge the international bankers' right to voice and rigidly enforce the above commandment.

The Warren "experiment" (so-called) *worked*, but the cohorts of the Money Power, rulers of the duped Brain Trusters, got to work immediately and before three months' benefit had been experienced in 1933 from the operation of the farmer-endorsed Warren monetary policy, and before gold had been raised to a full parity—they had maneuvered things so that the President was mysteriously forced to throw the farmers out, again to be devoured financially by the disparity between farm and city prices, the difference between what the farmer gets for his products and what he has to pay for the products of the city.

"Prices," remember, reflect the balance between the supply of things people need, and the *purely artificial supply* of what people use to buy what they need, namely, money.

BONDS (Debts) — We have seen clearly that money is a *demand* claim for wealth. That demand claim may be exchanged for physical consumer goods at the will of the holder. But if an individual does not wish to exchange his money for some form of consumer goods, he may exchange his demand claim (money) for a time claim (bond). He may buy a time claim entitling him to wealth at some future time. In usual language, he may buy a bond.

If the money which he turned over, that is, the demand claim, was used to create capital goods (instruments of further production) to be honestly used in further production—a factory, railroad, etc., etc. — that bond is a *sound* claim, provided the contract stipulates that the bond shall be repaid out of profits of the business earned during the useful life of the asset itself.

No bond should be outstanding after a given capital asset (instrument of production) has passed out of use through depreciation or obsolescence. The annual payment on a bond should include a small amount of interest and a partial return of the principal.

Any *bond outstanding beyond the period* in which the *assets against* which it was *issued* are in *actual use* in the processes of *production*, is *unsound*.

Bonds bear interest. Interest follows the law of mathematics. If a bond were issued and allowed to run beyond the useful life of the asset upon which it is a claim, the interest claim would run on after the asset had ceased to exist. This, of course, is a fundamental fallacy. However, we have some striking examples of bonds being issued against assets, the useful life of which could not conceivably endure until the maturity of the bond. Imagine! there are outstanding in the United States, numerous Railroad and Public Utility bonds which do not mature within 100 years: Chicago & North Western First and Refunding 5s due May 1, 2037; Kansas Gas & Electric 6s due September 1, 2022. There are numerous such examples in the country.

If the money spent in exchange for a bond were spent on consumer goods which were used or destroyed, that bond also is an *unsound* claim, and its existence vitiates the economic system. This is the status of our War Bonds.

We have seen that a financial system is based upon demand claims and time claims. The demand claims must bear a scientific direct relationship to the total amount of physical consumer goods ready for distribution, and the time claims must be based only upon the actual amount of capital assets which are in existence and being used as instruments of further production. As long as these two fundamental factors are honestly observed, the money system could be operated and the flow of money increased as the nation increases its ability to produce more of the physical things which men and women want and need to live and enjoy some of the comforts of life. There could be no such thing as a collapse in the total amount of demand and time claims unless, of course, a nation had suffered some enormous physical destruction of capital assets and consumer goods, such as the destruction of properties by a war or earthquake, or the exhaustion of food reserve supplies because of a severe crop failure. Otherwise, a money system should move along and be expanded as population grows, and as scientific advances make production in increasing volume possible.

In contrast to that kind of a system, we have in the United States today a collapsible money system, based upon changeable gold reserves and private bankers' promises-to-pay. The whole structure can be collapsed at the will of international bankers by their converting credits into gold; pulling the gold out of the monetary base, by shipping it abroad and juggling the rediscount rate.

If I bought a bond in 1927 which matured in 1933, I would have received in 1933 demand claims on a larger volume of physical goods than I actually gave up in 1927 when I turned over my demand claim for a time claim. See Debts. Therefore, in reality, I am asking the individual who borrowed my money to pay back more actual purchasing power than I gave to that individual. Because secret forces had diminished the number of demand claims in the money system, raw material price levels dropped. As they dropped, the entire money system became distorted because all of the time claims (bonds) called for a definite number of dollars, and the purchasing power of each of those dollars increased as the price levels dropped. In that case, the payment of money to meet bond maturities involves the payment of greater purchasing power than the money originally borrowed.

A money system can operate with stability and

fairness only when raw material price levels approximate those prevailing at the time the major part of the bond structure of the country was created. As soon as distortions in the price structure make it impossible to meet bond interest and the principal when due, the whole economic system cannot articulate. All phases of business begin to back up, that is, production, transportation and distribution cannot be carried on efficiently. Hence, unemployment arises. Unemployment in the face of intense want and suffering, and the availability of raw materials, is prima facie evidence that the system has had some of the cogwheels maliciously removed.

To remove a part of the demand claims in a money system, and by that act to distort the time claims, has about the same effect upon the mechanical money system of a nation as the removal of a considerable portion of the blood stream and interference with parts of the body which create blood corpuscles would have upon a healthy human body. A money system is really a circulatory system in a nation's economy. If it is maliciously tampered with—restricted or throttled—the whole economy withers. That is exactly what has happened so often during the past 70 years and is the cause of the situation that prevails in the United States today.

War Debts—One of the major fallacies and most vicious elements in the financial structure of the United States today (1935) is the existence of an enormous amount of War Bonds. In 1912 the United States had a national debt of slightly over one billion dollars. The major part of that debt structure represented money which the Government had borrowed to pay for the purchase of capital assets. In strict accounting practice, if the Government were keeping books accurately upon a proper accounting basis, the retirement of those bonds would have been provided for through the revenues derived by the Government from the people in exchange for the services which were being performed for the people by means of those particular buildings.

In 1913 Congress passed the "Federal" Reserve Act. It was loudly advertised as a glorious achievement. The Congress was told that it was the last word in modern banking practice. Undoubtedly it was for those who inserted trick clauses and removed essential protective mandates. Congressmen were told that it was modeled after the Bank of England, the Bank of France, and the Reichsbank of Germany, so that it could not fail to be well nigh perfect.

What the American people were not told was that all of these European banks are *not* governmental institutions as their names were intended to infer, *but are private banks,* whose charters were the result of legislative trickery and have for centuries enslaved the people of their respective nations. Our people were *not* told that the New Federal Reserve System was modeled upon the system exemplified by the Rothschild European Central Banks with their misleading names.

So we accepted the mis-statements of 1913, and our text books in high-schools, colleges and universities were re-written to proclaim the glories of the Federal Reserve System. We were told that we would never again have banking collapses, and that business depressions could now be avoided due to the elasticity of the system. These were grave falsehoods because the Federal Reserve System simply turned over to agents of the international bankers still greater powers to create a collapsible banking structure than they had previously possessed.

The fact that we were told that our Federal Reserve System was modeled upon the continental or international system, such as the Bank of England, should have been a warning. England, in the course of her history, has had more severe and longer business depressions than any other country. Why? Because the controllers had collapsed her economic structure more frequently. Yet, we were told and made to believe that our banking system, modeled after that pattern and upon the same principles, would prevent business depressions. How simple was our faith! And, of course, the re-writing of our text books was directed by international interests.

President Roosevelt issued the following statement in February, 1934. It was contained in a letter to Governor Black of the Federal Reserve Board. It stated that the Gold Reserve Act in no way interferes with Credit, Currency or Responsibilities of Reserve Banks which, according to the President "have simply exchanged their gold for gold certificates issued by the Treasury and collateralled by 100% of gold." The President's letter as made public by the Board follows:

"My dear Governor:

"Several days ago I approved the Gold Reserve Act of 1934. The law itself in no way impairs the strength of the Federal Reserve Banks. They have simply exchanged their gold for gold certificates issued by the Treasury and collateralled by 100% of gold. These gold certificates so collateralled with gold supply all Reserve requirements of the Reserve Act. This bill interferes in no way with the credit, currency or supervisory responsibilities of the Reserve Banks. Their powers will continue to be exercised in the interest of Agriculture, Commerce and Industry, just as they have been for the past twenty years.

"It gives me pleasure at this time to express my appreciation of the splendid services that the Federal Reserve System has rendered in connection with our efforts to bring about recovery. It has been an institution of incalculable value throughout the twenty years of its existence; soon after its organization it was an important factor in enabling this country to aid in winning the war, and more recently it has given firm support to the Government's efforts in fighting the depression. It has stood loyally by the interests of the people by supplying them with a sound currency, by placing at the disposal of member banks a large volume of reserves available to finance recovery, by exerting a powerful influence toward the rehabilitation of the commercial banking structure and by co-operating in every way with the Government's financial program.

"Very sincerely yours,
(Signed) FRANKLIN D. ROOSEVELT."

In this statement on the Federal Reserve System one sees that President Roosevelt does not comprehend the exact nature and operations of the Federal Reserve System. Apparently, he does not realize that the Federal Reserve System is one of the most destructive economic instruments ever placed in the hands of private individuals and has been used as such. In this letter President Roosevelt has extolled its glories for war financing—its aid in "winning the war." We really wonder whether we won the war. Let the reader decide as to the honesty of the methods used to finance the war.

In August of 1914 the World War started. The story of that financing is a long one. Touching upon the major parts will show the terrific fallacies in the method through which that financing was done.

The war had not long been in progress when England and the Allies began to draw upon us for supplies—food, clothing, ammunition, etc. To finance the purchase of these supplies from our own citizens, England and the Allies borrowed money in the United States. The American people bought British bonds, French bonds, etc.

However, very shortly it was no longer possible to sell British bonds and French bonds to the American people, the single reason being that these bonds soon absorbed more bank deposit money than the people had. Then, the international bankers advanced private credits to Europe. They advanced their credits (loans) to pay for the food supplies, ammunition, clothing, etc., that were being produced here by our people but sent out of the country to the Allies, and they took the notes of the various governments as security for their private advances.

Woodrow Wilson was elected to his second term on the plea that he had "kept America out of the World War." In the early months of 1917 Lord Balfour began to send hysterical notes to Woodrow Wilson telling him that unless the United States came into the conflict, England and the Allies would lose.

On the floor of the United States Senate the day we decided to join the Allies, the principal reason advanced as to why we should get into the war was *that it would enable us to obtain "our" claims at the inevitable subsequent peace table*. In other words, we had to enter the war principally to protect the mysterious dollars which the internationalists had already advanced and had caused our country to advance, to the Allies.

Once the United States entered the World War, we began financing operations on a huge scale. The

Government began to buy from the people food supplies, clothing supplies, ammunition, etc., to equip and maintain an army and navy. Remember our definition of consumer goods, or, rather, perishable wealth. The food, the ammunition, the clothing supplies, etc., were all being destroyed daily.

How did we finance the purchase of those gigantic amounts of perishable goods which were destroyed in the conduct of the World War? We financed them by allowing the Federal Reserve System (a privately owned and controlled central banking institution) to create its own private promises-to-pay and our national Government borrowed these privately owned banks' promises-to-pay.

Let that be repeated: The war Bonds of the United States Government were "bought" by the Federal Reserve Banks *not* with money or other real assets given over to the Government, but with private banks' unsecured promises-to-pay, which were called *money*—bank deposit credits. The System *did not have* the assets with which to buy the bonds so it "paid" for them with private promises-to-pay, as was the actual intention of the Act. These private promises-to-pay ("credit") against which the Government wrote checks, paid for the war materials. The Government exchanged interest bearing bonds secured by all of the property of all of the people for the unsecured promises-to-pay of the private Federal Reserve Banks. The Federal Reserve Act, as well as the National Banking Act, placed the promises-to-pay of private bankers *above* that of all of the people (the Nation). Do good sensible citizens realize that fact? Would they have permitted it if they had been told the plain truth? Ask any banker or economist if it is true or not. Never mind the "explanations"—just get the *truth*; and then apply common sense.

Why didn't the Government issue non-interest bearing United States currency to pay for the war materials?

A war is a communal affair! If a nation is called upon to defend itself or the principles for which it stands, the ensuing war is the responsibility of *every* man, woman and child within the nation. The only honest way to pay for domestic purchases used in conducting a war is for the government to issue non-cancellable United States currency in direct proportion as production of consumer goods is increased. That process would be fair to every individual in the nation. But here is the perverse method the privately owned Federal Reserve System used to shift the burden from the privileged few on to the masses.

In pointing out the dishonest principles involved the following quotation is forceful:

"It is clearly absurd for the King to borrow for the normal expenses of Government. It is only more absurd for him to borrow from his own subjects for the abnormal expenses, such as those of a war."—*The Breakdown of Money*, by Christopher Hollis.

The United States Government printed government bonds which were signed by the Secretary of the Treasury. These Government bonds are taxpayers' promises-to-pay. They are secured by mortgage on all of the properties within the nation and are a prior claim on all national income, due to the fact that Congress has the power to levy taxes. The member banks of the Federal Reserve System took these interest bearing Government bonds (taxpayers' promises-to-pay) — in other words, the privately owned Federal Reserve Banks *created* deposits payable to the United States Government. The Federal Reserve Banks turned over to the United States

Treasury a 5% reserve of real money against the total amount of bonds which the Government issued to them in exchange for their private promises-to-pay (which they called money and which was spent by the United States Government). These manufactured deposits became immediately available for checking purposes by the United States Government. This was credit, or bank deposit inflation, the most dangerous possible, because it could be collapsed at will by secret private interests; which was done in 1920, when suddenly, the "bottom fell out" of our economic structure.

We borrowed the privately owned banks' promises-to-pay, spent them on consumer goods (perishable goods used in conducting the war) and agreed to pay interest. It was the creation and release of money faster than the volume of perishable goods could be increased and the spending of these enormous amounts of "bank created money" by the National Government for perishable goods that caused the spectacular rise in prices. We had a credit inflation, a bank deposit money (bankers' promises-to-pay) inflation.

At the time of the credit inflation of the World War, consumer goods were needed by the National Government in huge volume. However, the money supplies—in that case bank deposit credits—were created at a faster rate and in larger volume than the consumer goods could be produced and made available for consumption. This caused a tremendous rise in the price levels. We were, therefore, inflating money in relation to the physical consumer goods available.

Increasing the volume of money becomes unsound only when it is done in volume entirely out of proportion to the physical volume of consumer goods available for exchange.

Once these enormous amounts of Government bonds had been placed in the system, they gave the Central Banks a tremendous leverage. By buying Government bonds from community banks, the Central Banks can increase the community banks' reserves and, hence, enable the community banks to increase their promises-to-pay enormously. Vice versa, they can sell huge amounts of Government bonds to the community banks and, hence, decrease the reserves of the community banks and force them to call in their promises-to-pay, thereby collapsing the money structure.

When the Federal Reserve Act was passed, we were promised that this power over money would be used to "stabilize" our economic affairs, but the record clearly proves that this tremendous power, placed in private hands by the Federal Reserve Act, has actually been used exclusively *to aggravate the fluctuations!*

Not only are those War Bonds unsound because they were issued in payment of goods which were destroyed in the World War, but they also put the most dangerous possible weapon into the hands of the Central Bankers—a gigantic volume of Government bonds—which can be used to increase or decrease the reserves and lending power of the member banks at will.

The people of the United States are still paying interest on those War Bonds. The cost of the war is running into millions and millions every day. If these bonds are allowed to exist much longer, they will cause a complete destruction of the natural private property system of this country, because they are forcing the payment of interest upon these gigantic sums, to a privileged few, resulting in the further concentration of income.

From the beginning of the World War until its close, the national debt was increased from slightly over one billion dollars to approximately twenty-six billion dollars. Most of those War Bonds are still outstanding. They are unsound and dishonest, and are vitiating our economic system, which recognizes every individual's right to enjoy the fruits of honest private effort and, hence, to own, use and control private property.

There is no more justification for a nation having war bonds outstanding than there is to a belief that the consumer goods consumed or destroyed in conducting that war could be reconsumed. They should be recalled and paid for in United States currency, issued dollar for dollar, just as rapidly as the people are able to increase physical production of consumer goods, so that we can inject that much currency into the money stream (demand claims), without causing raw material prices to rise beyond the levels which we want them to attain, and which they must attain if the so-called "business depression" is to be overcome. It could be overcome and the country put on its feet within a few months if only those in power took this step. Is continuance of the "business depression" intentional? Is the inability to increase the world's interest-bearing indebtedness by war to be accomplished by doles, or employment on unnecessary projects?

Government Bonds

The United States has outstanding total Government bonds in the amount of about twenty-seven billion dollars. A large part of these were issued to pay the cost of consumer goods which have been destroyed, or to pay operating expenses of the Government. With the appropriations made by the last Congress, that amount will soon be over thirty billion dollars; over $240 per capita; over $1,000 per family. Each laboring man is thus being secretly but actually bled for interest and principal payments upon that amount, which represents not a real loan of real assets, but a loan of privately created imaginary credit money. The banking system "risked" its private credit — and *at once* (not merely in prospect) received mortgages (Government Bonds) on 125,000,000 people in payment for the "risk." "Risk"— forsooth!

The stock of the Federal Reserve Banks is not owned by the Government of the United States. It is owned by private banks exclusively. They do not pay one cent for the use of the great privilege of lending to the United States the nation's own credit. Instead the nation pays them. The United States does not, in any way, participate in the profits of the Federal Reserve System. When the Act was originally passed, an inducement was offered the people in that the United States Government was to participate in the profits after the surplus account had reached a certain percent of the total capital invested. But later on so-called "perfecting amendments" were added to the act so that today the United States is not entitled to one single cent from the operations of the Federal Reserve Banks.

Examine a Federal Reserve Note issued by any one of the twelve Central Federal Reserve Banks. You will note that the Federal Reserve Banks do not agree to redeem them. The Federal Reserve Notes read: "The United States of America will pay to the bearer on demand." The United States guarantees all of the paper money that is issued by the Federal Reserve Banks. The Federal Reserve Banks do not issue this paper money upon their own financial responsibility, yet they collect interest on it.

Do the Federal Reserve Banks pay for the privilege of issuing these Federal Reserve Notes (paper currency)? No, they do not. The Federal Reserve Act, Section 16, provided that they would pay an interest charge fixed by the Federal Reserve Board. The Federal Reserve Board has always fixed that rate at zero. Therefore, these twelve Central Banks and the member banks use the nation's credit to the extent of many, many billions and never pay for it. Practically all of the currency (pocket money) we have in circulation today is currency issued by the Federal Reserve Banks. They use the nation's credit free, but the nation itself is paying interest on it every day it is outstanding. Under the present Federal Reserve Laws the people can expand their currency only by going deeper into debt and paying more interest.

Under our present arrangements, if the United States Government needs a million dollars, it issues bonds for that amount to the Federal Reserve Banks. The Federal Reserve Banks "buy" the million dollars in bonds. They can then redeposit those same bonds with the Government and receive a million dollars in new currency printed at the Bureau of Engraving and Printing (owned and operated by the United States Government). While these Federal Reserve Banks use and loan the currency, they will also get interest on the Government bonds which they have deposited. They are required to keep only 5% cash on deposit with the Treasury and to pay ½ of 1% tax which is supposed to cover the cost of printing and replacing worn out currency. No intelligent person can give any good reasons (excepting that the system is thoroughly dishonest), as to why the United States Government should not issue the currency in the first place, rather than issue tax exempt interest bearing bonds, and then permit the holders of those bonds, the bankers, to use the bonds as security for the issuance of currency.

However, when honest Congressmen demand that the United States Government stop this dishonest practice, and print sufficient money itself to carry out the constitutional mandates, the holders of this great privilege (the powers to create money) and their congressional satellites and sycophants repeat like parrots such phrases as "printing press money," "rag money," "rubber money," "fiat money," "baloney money," and "greenbacks." They do not tell the people that it is the same kind of money that is now printed for private banks, and that it would be backed by the same security, which is the wealth of the nation. They do not tell the American people that they are paying over one billion dollars in interest per year because they allow these private individuals to do exactly the same thing they tell the Government (the people) it cannot do. If the money were issued directly by the Government instead of through subterfuge, the only difference would be that the people (the Nation) would not be paying interest to private individuals for issuing its own money.

The issuance and *control of the volume* of currency should be a Governmental function. It should never have been placed in the hands of private corporations. Our slogan should be: "Get the Government out of private business and private corporations out of the Government's business." That means that the duty to create and control the actual amount of money in this nation be resumed by Congress. The Constitution so provides.

A few years ago Mr. Thomas A. Edison was asked if he favored the Government borrowing to develop a project then being considered. Mr. Edison's reply was: "Any Government that can issue a dollar bond, interest bearing, that is good, can issue a dollar bill non-interest bearing, that is good. The only difference is that the bill . . . does not draw interest."

The Government, as we have already seen, should issue currency as the people's ability to produce more consumer goods increases. The amount in circulation should be dependent entirely upon the stock of physical consumer goods which the people have produced and have ready for distribution. The amount of money in the country should not be dependent upon the pleasure of those controlling the privately owned Federal Reserve Banks.

Further, the age-old private bank privilege of creating bank deposit money must be uprooted and forever destroyed. It is the base of our monetary abuses. Congress should issue currency to meet the monetary requirements of the Nation. That currency should bear the imprint of the United States Government. Banks should deal in that currency which would be real money non-cancellable and having no vanishing possibilities.

How many Americans have been taught the difference between the Federal Reserve Agent and the Governor of the Federal Reserve Board? The truth is, as the Act was originally passed, Congress was led to believe that these two functions would be performed by two individuals, each of whom had exactly opposite interests at heart. In other words, one would be a watchdog over the other. The Federal Reserve Agent was supposed to really look after the interests of the people. His function was to protect them. How many Americans know that one man occupies both of these positions? Of course, he has two offices, one is across the hall from the other in the great Central Federal Reserve Bank of New York.

This one man, who occupies both places, while he is in one office is the Federal Reserve Agent. There he looks after the interests of the people. When he crosses the hall he becomes Chairman of the Board of Directors of the Federal Reserve Board and there he must vigorously look after the interests of the Federal Reserve Banks.

The point is this: suppose the Federal Reserve Agent wants new currency — that is, Federal Reserve Notes. He wires the Bureau of Engraving and Printing, which is operated by the United States Treasury and says: "Print the bank ten million dollars of new currency." They print it because he represents the Government. The law says that when this currency is printed (which is being secured by taxpayers' promises-to-pay taxes at future dates, and a blanket mortgage upon all of the property and incomes of the people), and delivered by the Federal Reserve Agent to the Chairman of the Federal Reserve Board, an interest rate shall be charged. The truth is that the interest rate never has been charged. Being left to the discretion of the Federal Reserve Agent, the rate was always placed at zero. The Federal Reserve Banks are using the credit of the nation free.

There is no reason why the United States should pay a billion dollars a year interest to these private individuals who, for their own profit, use our country's money powers as they choose. The power to issue money and to regulate the value of money, according to the Constitution of the United States, should be vested in Congress alone.

Do Americans Want a "German" Currency Destruction in the United States?

Today the United States needs an increase in the volume of money. The volume of money should be increased until price levels of raw materials have risen to the point where they cover the cost of production and leave an honest margin of profit to the producers of raw materials; until national income is sufficient to carry the legitimate private bond structure outstanding and provide employment for those who want to work. After that level has been reached, the flow of money can be increased only as actual physical production of wealth is increased. Once the price level has reached the point necessary, further emissions of money must come only as physical production is increased, otherwise, undesirable price rises would take place.

The financial system of the United States could be adjusted within a very few months to bring about the required price rises in raw materials and to absorb the unemployed.

Here is the story of what happened in Germany and what probably *will happen in the United States* if the American people do not awaken and take control of their money system out of the hands of unpatriotic internationalists.

The World War ended in 1918. As of March 31, 1919 (just before the "Peace" Conference was called and the Versailles Treaty signed), the price levels of Germany were only 117% higher than they were before the World War began. This was a smaller price rise than had actually taken place in the United States. The public debt of Germany from the beginning of the World War until March 31, 1919, had increased one hundred thirty billion Marks. In terms of dollars that would be, roughly, thirty billion dollars. The United States had increased its own public debt to a similar amount.

The German financial structure was in no condition whatever to warrant the destruction of the currency, *if that had not been the planned intention of the international money lenders.*

Under the terms of the Versailles Treaty, practically all of Germany's gold was taken away from her, together with 75% of her iron ore deposits and mines. All of her colonies were taken away and about 25% of her other physical property. The terms of this Treaty were diabolical. They were directed to destroy the real German people. From the time of the signing of the Treaty in June 1919 until the beginning of 1922, the international money powers who were in control of the Reichsbank and the German Government, were manipulating to gain control of actual physical property in Germany. They went so far as to get the banking laws of Germany drastically changed, so that they could borrow unlimited amounts from the Reichsbank and purchase physical property with the knowledge that the loans could later be repaid with worthless currency.

To give one some idea of the volume of currency that was turned out in Germany, one has only to note what happened to the price levels of Germany. Remember that during the war the German price levels had not increased as much as they had in the United States. In 1920 the price level in Germany increased 1500% over the pre-war level; in 1921 it reached 3500% over the pre-war level; in 1922 it was 147,000% over the pre-war level, and by October 23rd, when the currency became worthless, it was 709 billion percent over the pre-war level. In other words, predatory internationalists had printed private marks and forced them into the money stream with the avowed purpose of destroying the money system of Germany. That meant the destruction of all insurance policies and mortgages owned by the real German people.

The international bankers had prepared themselves. They had obtained control of the physical properties and could later pay loans, many of which had been manipulated through the privately owned Reichsbank, with worthless money.

The inflation in Germany was misnamed. It was not a German inflation. It was a private money issue inflation, perpetrated by international schemers.

The inflation was not a government money inflation. It was an inflation of private Reichsbank notes. The officers of the Reichsbank — a privately owned institution — were responsible for issuing money in sufficient volume to destroy the entire banking structure and make all of the money of Germany worthless.

The same thing will undoubtedly happen to the United States if the people continue to allow their money system to be manipulated by those who have been in complete control for the last twenty years. They will profit, just as they did in Germany, by gaining possession of the physical properties. With the destruction of the money system will go the Government of the United States — the only protection the individual has for his property, civil and religious rights.

Any one who cares to investigate the "German" Currency Destruction, or the French and Italian revaluation in the 1920's, should read "Foreign Currency and Exchange Investigation Conducted by Gold and Silver Inquiry of the United States Senate," pursuant to Resolution 469 — 67th Congress. This document is now out of print, but is obtainable in some libraries.

CHAPTER X

THE "MYSTERIOUS" ACCORDION-LIKE PROMISES-TO-PAY SYSTEM EXPLAINED

THE UNITED STATES MONETARY SYSTEM OF TODAY (1935)

Today, when the reader sees in the newspapers that the banks are stuffed with money which they can not lend, only careful reading informs him that this is not money, but money creating power, which is unused.

When we read about billions in "excess" reserves lying "idle" in the Federal Reserve Bank, that in truth, means that the member banks (community) have not loaned as many promises-to-pay (bank deposit money) as are possible under the law, with the deposits (reserves) the member banks have on the books of the Central Bank. In other words, they are not loaning as many promises-to-pay as they might, without themselves borrowing at the Central Bank.

Generally speaking, the money actually *does not exist* until it is *created* by the making of a loan. The doubting reader may verify this at any bank.

The reason for the deception in terms lies in the fact that if the American people had ever been told the plain truth, that more than 95% of all the nation's money is based upon its debt instead of its wealth, their common sense would never have permitted the erection of such a blood-letting system as the one which forces every man to pay interest to the banking system for manufacturing the nation's money.

How many honest Americans have ever been permitted to learn that if one obtains a "dollar" for his labor, and spends his dollar for food, that dollar has been paying tribute to the banking system for its very existence? Would they permit it if they knew? Would they countenance collection of interest on practically every dollar in the money stream which changes hands in the nation, *if they knew?*

Why should John Smith, carpenter, who has worked 8 hours for James Jones, home owner, have to pay tribute to Charles Allen, banker, for the privilege of receiving as pay, not physical goods from Jones, but purchasing power in the form of dollars?

Yet *that* is exactly what happens, for *practically* every dollar which stands to Jones' credit at Allen's bank has been created by a loan from Allen's bank (or some other bank) to some one, and this dollar eventually found its way into Jones' bank account.

And any banker will verify this also, even if he has never thought of it in just this way or has never visualized the fact that under present "law," money can not exist without somebody being charged interest upon it by certain highly privileged private entities called "banks." (Only a few hundred millions out of the 40 billions in the money stream today is non-interest bearing money.)

It must be repeated and emphasized that the Main Street banker, and for that matter, probably the LaSalle Street, and even some Wall Street bankers, had little to do with the origination of this vicious system by which money can be created only by some one going into debt and paying tribute in the way of interest until that particular money is withdrawn from the money stream (by retirement of the bank loan). True, some of the leaders may have been willing cats-paws for the power behind the scenes, but the real manipulation was conceived and executed by the foreign money power, which always held in its hands the secret reins by which the amount of money could be expanded or contracted through the operations of the twelve central Federal Reserve Banks, by arbitrary import or export of gold.

Kinds of Money

That old necessity called "money" is nothing but a counter or reckoner used in *the exchange* of goods and services. It has heretofore been hard to get, harder to keep, and hardest to understand. It is proposed to make it easy to keep, easier to earn and easiest to understand.

That domestic money must be synonymous with "gold" is a fiction which must be uprooted from the popular mind if our civilization is to endure.

A careful distinction must be made between tangible money (coins or paper billfold money) and bank credit money created by a bank making a loan (crediting a deposit on its books to the borrower). This is subject to checking. All of the deposit money so created cannot be taken out of the banking system in the form of currency. This was well demonstrated prior to the closing of the banks in 1933. Every one could not obtain currency for the amount his bank deposit called for, for the reason that that much currency could not be provided "under the rules of the game."

The following outline will enable the reader to distinguish between the two:

I. Tangible Money:

1. Coins—Silver and copper tokens. Before April 18, 1933, gold coin could be obtained, but it was not used in daily transactions.
2. Currency—Billfold paper money which you get from the bank and carry out in

your pocket. At the bank you may receive a variety of currency:

(a) Federal Reserve Notes
(b) National Bank Notes
(c) Silver Certificates
(d) United States Notes
(e) Gold Certificates

II. Bank Credit Money:

Not represented by tangible money, but by bankers' promises-to-pay created by banks making loans, crediting the amounts to the deposit accounts of the borrowers.

The following is a detailed explanation of the different kinds of currency.

(a) *Federal Reserve Notes.* Look at one (assuming "they" have left you one). It says the United States Government will pay you so many dollars, but that particular one you possess was issued by one of the twelve privately owned Federal Reserve Banks. Prior to March 1933, they all stated that you might convert them into gold by presentation at one of the privately owned Central Federal Reserve Banks. That was what was called good old *hard sound* money. "Hard" meant convertible into gold if you got there first and "sound" meant convertible at the arbitrary, legally fixed rate of $20.67 for one ounce of gold.

It was never explained that "hard" as a legitimate adjective was really a myth, because there always existed many times more money (pocket billfold money and bank deposits) than gold.

You were never told that that gold convertibility did not exist for your benefit and protection, but only for the international bankers who, when they wanted to collapse the money structure (cause business depressions) of the nation, began converting their balances into gold and shipping gold bars out of the country.

Just how sincere that desire to "protect" you actually was, can be well demonstrated. Prior to March 5, 1933, many citizens, in well-founded terror, obtained gold coins and "hoarded" them. But international bankers got gold bars and shipped them *out of the country*. The individual who kept his gold coins within the country was commanded by the President to bring them back and obtain $20.67 per ounce. But the internationalists may now bring their exported bars back and receive $35.00 per ounce. Evidently it pays to be an internationalist.

It was right to raise the price of an ounce of gold, but it certainly was wrong not to treat all owners of gold alike. If the United States citizen who kept his gold in this country received only $20.67 per ounce when he was commanded by the President to return it to the Treasury, the international banker should have received only $20.67 when he transferred gold back to the United States from European vaults.

The argument that raising the price of an ounce of gold is destroying part of the value of the dollars in savings accounts; is impairing the value of insurance policies and trust funds, and constitutes a 41% capital levy; is a malicious lie foisted upon the American people by the international bankers and the *parrot section of the press,* to prevent their understanding the necessity of our having the price of an ounce of gold the same as it is in other countries which are also entering the raw material world export markets.

If gold has a lower price per ounce in New York than it has in London or raw material exporting countries, the farmer who has shipped wheat from the United States will receive fewer dollars than he would if the price of an ounce of gold were the same as in London. Changing the price of an ounce of gold is *revaluation,* sometimes misnamed devaluation. It has *nothing whatever* to do with the correct use of the word inflation.

Federal Reserve Notes are obtained by the ordinary "member" banks from the Central Federal Reserve Banks. They are obtained by the member bank borrowing at the Central Bank and depositing Government Bonds as collateral, or by the member bank selling Government bonds or some of its customers' promises-to-pay (commercial paper) to the Central Bank. Remember, Government bonds are taxpayers' promises-to-pay secured by all of the property in the nation and the taxing power of Congress. These secured Government bonds are turned over by the Government to private bankers, in exchange for their *unsecured* promises-to-pay. When the Central Banks need Federal Reserve Notes (currency), they turn Government bonds over to the United States Treasury and in return receive currency (Federal Reserve Notes). They continue to collect interest on the Government bonds deposited with the Treasury, but they pay no interest for the currency which the Treasury Department turns over to them.

The Federal Reserve member Banks were required to keep only a 5% gold reserve with the Treasury prior to the Gold Act of 1934. This fund was intended to take care of whatever Federal Reserve Notes (currency) might be presented at the United States Treasury for redemption. However, the Gold Act of 1934 gives the Secretary of the Treasury authority to redeem in gold Federal Reserve Notes (currency) which are presented by owners in foreign countries. *But the American citizen cannot get gold to use as domestic money.* This privilege given to foreigners and unpatriotic Americans to get gold is but one of the subterfuge methods used by internationalists to take gold out of the United States.

Is it any wonder to thinking Americans that the private individuals who now enjoy power to create money spend hundreds of millions upon false teaching and propaganda to prevent the American people from understanding the gross dishonesty in the system now operated?

The real joker in this is that the people are paying interest on all currency outstanding in the form of Federal Reserve Notes, as well as all "credit" or "deposit" money in the banking system.

Honesty demands that the Government issue currency directly to the people as provided by the Constitution. Why should it issue its nationally secured interest bearing tax-exempt bonds to private individuals in exchange for those private individuals' unsecured promises-to-pay, and then issue currency, upon which no interest is collected, to those same private individuals upon their re-depositing with the United States Treasury those same Government Bonds?

Before the Glass-Steagall Amendment to the Federal Reserve Act in February 1932, the Federal Reserve Notes outstanding in any one of the twelve Federal Reserve Districts were backed by a 40% gold reserve and 60% commercial paper. Commercial paper is sixty to ninety-day notes of individual manufacturers and merchants; merchants who borrow for these short periods to finance the movement of inventories pledge those inventories as security on their notes. Here we have another classic example of one-way security. Bankers accept from merchants their well-secured promises-to-pay. They give the merchant in exchange, their own unsecured promises-to-pay, which are called *money*. The money is nothing but the manufactured credit which the banker has created.

This meant that for every million dollars worth of currency (Federal Reserve Notes outstanding in the District), the Central Federal Reserve Bank possessed a 40% reserve in gold and a 60% commercial paper reserve. This provision gave the banks strict control over the volume of currency and "credit" money because they could regulate the amount of commercial paper outstanding by refusing loans to manufacturers; in other words, not accept their short-term notes. Also, the international bankers, by moving gold out of the country, could force a rapid contraction in the volume of Federal Reserve Notes outstanding.

After February 1932, however, Federal Reserve Notes (pocket money) were backed by 40% gold and 60% Government Bonds. The reason for this change was that practically no commercial paper existed because of stagnation of business. Business men were not borrowing to move inventories for the simple reason that inventories were not salable. The people had no purchasing power because many billions of bankers' promises-to-pay had been cancelled. Until the law was changed, in the absence of an adequate volume of commercial paper, a 100% gold reserve was required against the outstanding Federal Reserve Notes. This gold reserve had to be maintained at whichever one of the twelve Central Banks had issued the Federal Reserve Notes.

From 1930 on, gold was being shipped out of the United States in large amounts by the international bankers. While this went on, it became necessary to substitute 60% Government Bonds instead of commercial paper. Later, when still more gold was removed (because gold was lower in New York than it was in London and because the international bankers were drawing it out of this country to collapse the credit structure), it became necessary to use Government Bonds as 100% of the backing for Federal Reserve Notes. Thus, the Gold Standard completely evaporated, since Government Bonds are nothing but taxpayers' promises-to-pay taxes.

Under the unsound, dishonest system in existence today, we allow the Federal Reserve Banks to issue their puny promises-to-pay, for which the Government exchanges with them the nation's (taxpayers') promises-to-pay. The people are charged interest on the bonds and also on the currency.

(b) *National Bank Notes.* The National Bank Act passed February 25, 1863, gave private banks the right to deposit certain issues of Government Bonds and receive National Bank Notes. National Bank Notes can be issued by any National Bank upon meeting the following requirements: Designated issues of Government Bonds are deposited with the United States Treasury; the Bureau of Engraving then engraves National Bank Notes bearing the name of the issuing bank. The National Bank collects interest on the bonds deposited with the United States Treasury and is required to keep only a 5% gold reserve. The Treasury Department gets no interest on the currency it issues. An honest monetary system would require that the National Bank Act be changed so that such an unintelligent practice could not be continued. The National Bank Act is discussed in another part of this book.

(c) *Silver Certificates.* These are outstanding in small denominations. They are warehouse receipts for silver, but the value of the commodity silver, for which one could be exchanged, is less than the face value (purchasing power) of the silver certificate. These are issued by the United States Government. They are non-interest bearing and an honest form of money. What possible pardon can there be for a nation to pay interest on money of its own issue; especially when issued for the benefit of those who loan it back to the people again *at interest?*

(d) *United States Notes.* During the Civil War honest Abraham Lincoln saw that the important but undisclosed purpose of the war was to get the United States heavily in debt to London bankers. Abraham Lincoln had good common sense, backed up with honesty and courage. He knew that the Constitution of the United States provided that Congress should have the sole right to issue money. He determined that the United States Government would issue currency to pay for domestic purchases of war materials and also pay the soldiers.

The Act of February 28, 1862, authorized the issue of one hundred and fifty million of such money. The first issue was full legal tender, acceptable in the payment of all debts. This was "Lincoln money" and is the kind of money which the people will demand that the Government issue and *pay* (not loan) into circulation, when enough of them learn the whole truth, — and nothing but the truth.

The second issue of United States Notes was authorized by an Act of July 11, 1862. In the passage of this Act, Congress restricted the legal tender quality of these Notes. The restriction clause was that they were not acceptable in payment of interest on the public debt, and import duties. A third issue of one hundred and fifty million was authorized by Act of March 3, 1863. There are outstanding at the present time $346,000,000 of these Notes. There is on deposit with the United States Treasury a reserve fund of one hundred and fifty million dollars in gold. This was placed there during the Administration of Cleveland, when the internationalists were deceiving the people into accepting the false idea that a gold backing was necessary for domestic currency. This was a part of the high pressure salesmanship.

United States Notes are the kind of money for which the private banker is *not* charging the taxpayers interest. They are real money and pass today as full legal tender, despite the vicious "exception clause." If all of the money in use in this country were issued by the United States, we would not have periods in which the volume of money suddenly diminished for some "mysterious" reason.

The internationalists (called "bullion brokers" in those days) contemptuously called the United States Notes "greenbacks" to mislead the people and discredit issuance of money by the government.

(e) *Gold Certificates*, sometimes piously called "yellow backs." These are warehouse receipts for gold. The Federal Reserve Banks (Central Banks) were given Gold Certificates when the Government pretended to actually nationalize the gold in January 1934. The international bankers put up a sham fight at that time to make the public believe that the gold was actually taken out of their control. It was *not*.

Not only have they full legal control over the "Treasury's" gold today, but they also have a two billion dollar secret fund misnamed a Stabilization Fund.

The foreign exchange market is a place where promises-to-pay dollars are exchanged for promises-to-pay pounds sterling, francs, guilders, etc. The

United States is a creditor nation. The imports are negligible. Hence, there is no large demand in the United States for promises-to-pay francs, pounds sterling, guilders, etc. To allow the international bankers to exchange their promises-to-pay pounds sterling, francs, guilders, etc., for promises-to-pay dollars, some one has to supply promises-to-pay dollars. That supply does not exist because of the scarcity of legitimate trade transactions. Therefore, the privileged interests had Congress blindly establish a two billion dollar secret fund.

With that fund, the international bankers will be supplied with promises-to-pay dollars by Uncle Sam, which means the American taxpayers. When Uncle Sam gives up promises-to-pay dollars in exchange for promises-to-pay francs, sterling, guilders, etc., the international bankers get the promises-to-pay dollars and Uncle Sam gets the promises-to-pay foreign currencies. Since Uncle Sam has no occasion to make purchases in foreign countries, his balances will remain frozen in various foreign countries. The international bankers, who have gotten dollar balances by having Uncle Sam exchange his dollar balances for balances in foreign countries, can use their dollar balances in the United States. They can convert them into gold and ship more gold out of the country to the vaults under the Seine River in France.

Is it any wonder that the so-called "Stabilization Fund" is a dark secret and that not even the President of the United States will know what goes on until a year after the transactions take place; Congress will not know until 1937? Is it any wonder that the authors of the Gold Bill of 1934 have never had the courage to disclose their names?

Americans may some day awaken to the fact that our gold has been shipped out of the country, probably, to the Bank for International Settlements—which Americans have repeatedly denounced—or perhaps, to the $2\frac{1}{2}$ acre gold vaults of the "Bank of France" under the Seine River.

Bank Created Money or Check Money

We now approach the discussion of bank money, or bankers' promises-to-pay. These promises-to-pay (bankers' credit money) can amount to from ten to fifteen times the total of cash on hand and reserves at the Central Bank. This type of money is used daily in the form of bank checks to buy goods and services, and to pay debts. It comprised about 88% of America's total money in 1934, and comprised approximately 95% in 1929. *This is the secret of all depressions.* Bank deposit money may be *forced* into oblivion by manipulations of relatively small quantities of real money.

These private individuals' promises-to-pay are issued only as loans repayable with interest. They can be recalled at the will of the private individuals. Actually, privately owned banks have the power to call in and cancel all but a small percentage of the money supply of this and all other nations.

Even relatively small fluctuations in the volume of their outstanding promises-to-pay cause prices to rise or fall. This power which controls domestic price levels is the power to control all businesses and workers. Declines in the price levels cause loss of business profits, unemployment, and foreclosures.

Bankers do not lend real money. They lend their private promises-to-pay money. The borrower, in over 90% of all cases, does not carry his loan from the bank in cash, but leaves it "on deposit" in a checking account. Banks lend from 10 to 15 times the amount of legal tender money they possess and collect interest on this money. That is how the many 18% to 25% dividends are paid, although people naively believe that banks earn their way by paying 3% on bona fide deposits and charging 6% on loans of those real deposits. No wonder so many banks have been started which never should have been given a charter.

Deposits of a member bank (community bank) at the Central Reserve Bank (misnamed Federal Reserve) are counted as cash, although they are only imaginary money. They are the credit "reserves" (on the books of the Central Reserve Banks — any one of the twelve Federal Reserve Banks).

Banks may lend at interest from 10 to 15 times the amount of "reserves" they have on the books of the Central Banks. These reserves on the books of a Central Bank have been created in most cases by the Central Bank making a loan to the member bank, or by "buying" Government Bonds from the member bank.

The member bank generally keeps its total loans (promises-to-pay) from 10 to 15 times the number of dollars the owners of the bank have invested in the bank (the amount of the capital plus the surplus of the community bank). In the case of National Banks, the Comptroller of the Currency watches the expansion of each bank and can command each to stay within the limits of ten to fifteen times the amount of capital and surplus. State Banks which are not part of the Federal Reserve System are controlled in the same way.

Deceptive Terms Used in Bank Balance Sheets

A *Banker's Balance Sheet* shows under the heading "Cash on Hand and Due from Banks" how much cash and deposits at the Central Bank (one of the twelve Federal Reserve Banks) he possesses. Cash is the legal tender money in his own vaults. Deposits at the Central Bank are counted as cash. They are his credit (reserves) on the books of the Central Bank. Banks may lend at interest a sum agreed to from 10 to 15 times the amount of credit (reserve) they have on the books of the Central Bank.

These credits have been *created* by loans from the Central Banks. If the Central Banks force member banks to buy Government Bonds, they absorb part of the member banks' reserves on the books of the Central Banks. This forces the member banks to call in some of their promises-to-pay outstanding with business men (to control the volume of money).

Example:

A private Bank has Cash—currency	$1,000,000
"Deposits" Central Bank	1,000,000
Total Reserves	$2,000,000

This bank could lend promises-to-pay up to 20,000,000 to 30,000,000 dollars. This is one of the "legalized" fictions which must be exposed in its true light.

If the Central Bank forces the member bank to use $500,000 to buy Government Bonds, then the member bank's reserve is only $1,500,000 and its promises-to-pay (credit money) must be cut down accordingly to $15,000,000 to $22,500,000.

The people have too long been fooled by the deception represented by the customary item in bank statements called "cash and due from banks." The cash should be shown separately for it is actual money. The "due from banks" is not actual cash, but credit money.

Also, the attractiveness of the Federal Reserve Act to bankers lies in this astonishing fact: if a bank has $100,000 real money, it may lend its credit up to $1,000,000 to $1,500,000. However, if this bank borrows another $100,000 at a Federal Reserve Bank and leaves this deposit on "Reserve" (what a fake!) at the Federal Reserve, it can then "legally" lend out another $1,000,000 to $1,500,000 of bank created money.

The bank, when borrowing at the Central Federal Reserve Bank, must post as collateral either Government Bonds or "commercial paper"; the latter being highly liquid notes of business men, secured primarily by actual goods in stock, in process, or in transit, and secondarily by their businesses also. Consider this, therefore: a business man borrows $1,000 of banker's credit, paying interest and depositing the world's best collateral. The bank may deposit that $1,000 note at the Federal Reserve (re-discount it) and thereby obtain a "reserve" deposit of $1,000 less the discount, which then "legally" permits it to lend *another* $10,000 to $15,000—all on his customer's credit. This was the "credit" balloon of infinite expansibility used by the internationalists to "finance" America's gigantic share in the legalized murder of about 40,000,000 in the World War and "Russian" Revolution!

In accepting this plan, bankers were intrigued by the extra but actually sub-rosa profits: but they overlooked the enforceable *collapsibility* of the system, which has been designed and used to ruin thousands upon thousands of banks since the World War—and ruin their depositors.

By increasing or decreasing the rediscount rate (rate charged by the Central Banks to the member banks for advancing cash credits to the member banks in exchange for some of the member banks' customers' short-term promises-to-pay) the Central Banks can influence the volume of total credit outstanding. In other words, when a member bank wishes to increase its deposits on the books of the Central Bank, it has only to sell to the Central Bank some of the promises-to-pay of its own customers. The Central Bank charges the member bank a rate of interest on the unmatured note of the member bank's customer. This rediscount rate also controls the rate on Government Bonds.

Too often the rediscount rate has been influenced by foreign internationalists, as in 1927 by Montagu Norman, Governor of the Bank of England.

By increasing or decreasing the rediscount rate drastically, the value of the Government Bonds held in the portfolios of the member banks can be effectually cut down. This cuts down the member banks' reserves.

Thus the system by which member banks borrow from Central Banks or are forced to buy Government Bonds, enables the Central Banks to control the member banks (and the Nation's monetary supply — influencing prices) by increasing or decreasing their "reserves" on the books of the Central Banks.

Gold — The Weapon

The twelve Central Banks of the United States are largely controlled as to their lending power by the movements of gold which are manipulated by the Internationalists. When gold is withdrawn from the country both the volume of currency (pocket money) and promises-to-pay (deposits) must be curtailed. The Central Reserve Banks, that is, each one of the twelve Central Banks, must maintain, under the law, a 35% gold reserve against the deposits (reserves) which the member banks have on the books of the Central Banks. In other words, if a member bank—that is, one of the community banks—has a million dollar reserve on the books of the Central Bank, the Central Bank would have to have a 35% gold reserve against that million dollar deposit of the member bank on the books of the Central Bank. The 35% gold reserve would amount to $350,000.00. Formerly 40% gold reserve was maintained by the Central Banks against the Federal Reserve Notes (currency outstanding).

One can readily see the tremendous effect moving gold in or out of the country has on the size of the nation's monetary supply. Each gold dollar controls (100/35) 2.86 member banks' reserve dollars at the Central Federal Reserve Bank, and each dollar of Central Bank deposits of a member bank (community) allows the member bank to lend ten to fifteen of its own created dollars. Each gold dollar, therefore controls 28.60 to 43.10 credit dollars of member banks. When a gold dollar leaves the country, if the system is expanded to the limit, 2.86 Federal Reserve dollars (member bank deposits) must be curtailed—collapsing, destroying (potentially) 43.10 bank money dollars. Federal Reserve Notes formerly required a 40% gold coverage. Every gold dollar that left the country forced the retirement of $2.50 in paper money outstanding. The reader may decide if this "great" system has produced results favoring civilization.

Movements of gold are determined at the pleasure of the International Bankers. Before the War they bore some semblance to the relationship existing between the value of imports and exports. If imports exceeded exports, gold moved out of the country to settle the difference (to pay the bill). This is the only proper use for monetary gold today. When the nations learn how to use clearing house certificates as between nations, however, gold will be used only to fill teeth and garnish the arts and vain people.

Since the War, International Bankers have maintained several billion dollars (some estimate around eight billions) in liquid balances and have transferred a substantial part of them into gold and taken it in or out of countries at will—hence, expanding or collapsing the money structure at pleasure and without any warning to their victims—the citizens of any country they choose to wreck for profit.

It appears they chose to wreck the United States. They first moved gold into this country in the early 1920's and then pulled it out ruthlessly from 1930 to 1933. The *International Bankers* therefore, really control the movements of gold and, hence, our country, under the Federal Reserve System, is at their mercy for;

(a) Employment and prices depend upon the price level.

(b) The domestic price level depends upon the total quantity of money in the nation.

(c) The quantity of money depends upon private bankers' promises-to-pay outstanding (loans).

(d) Private bankers' outstanding promises-to-pay depend upon Deposits in the Central Federal Reserve Banks.

(e) Deposits (Reserves of Member Banks) at the Central Banks depend upon the "Open Market Operations of the Central Banks" (either they are buying Government bonds from or selling Government bonds to the member banks). They also depend upon the

"Rediscount Rate," the rate charged by the Central Banks for advancing to the member banks credits in exchange for some of their customers' promises-to-pay. (Commercial Paper.) This rate also determines the price of Government bonds. If the rediscount rate is raised from 4% to 8%, Government 4% bonds, due in ten years, will drop in price from around 100 to around 70. This also cuts down the market value of the member banks' entire list of bonds.

(f) Central Banks' Reserves against member banks' deposits and also the amount of currency (Federal Reserve Notes) outstanding depend upon the movements of gold.

(g) Movements of gold depend upon the *pleasure* and desires of the International Bankers, who know no patriotism or social justice.

(The writer wishes to state also that the attitude and orders of the bank examiners have a tremendous influence on the reserves of the member banks. The bank examiners can arbitrarily throw out some of the member banks' paper and by so doing, force the member bank to curtail. Since 1920 the member banks have been at the mercy of a corps of bank examiners who operate under orders from "the Chiefs" of the United States Treasury. They were very arrogant and unfair in many of their decisions; ruthlessly forcing the closing of banks which could easily have been saved if the certain known officials had not been willing to allow the destruction of the economic fabric of the United States.)

There are several Federal agencies with bank examination powers. Some of these have been added during the "emergency." Loans approved by some are thrown out by others. The local banker who really wants to lend to his solid neighbor business men has indeed a precarious path to tread! Need we ask why bank credit is "plentiful" but unused? Need we ask if this is all an "accidental" condition? The President has acknowledged it.

Deposits of member banks are of two classes — Demand and Time. Demand deposits are practically all created by the banker making loans — issuing his promises-to-pay to industrialists. Most banks require that the borrowers maintain a balance of 20% of the loan. Hence, the *borrowers* pay interest on the deposits (reserves) which the *banker* must keep with the Central Bank.

Time deposits are savings accounts. They require a very small reserve on the books of the Central Banks (3% or slightly more, dependent upon the size of the City). Hence, savings accounts help maintain the entire "reserves" of the member banks on the books of the Central Banks. Hence also, the desire to obtain savings accounts is explained.

If bankers' promises-to-pay are curtailed, money becomes scarce (a given amount purchases more physical goods) and prices fall. If the price level falls, all debts require the payment of dollars which have a greater purchasing power. If price levels drop drastically, debts cannot be paid.

Under a correct and constitutional money system, time deposits and demand deposits would be very carefully segregated. All deposits would be of *real* money but the parts played in the banking structure would differ. Each demand dollar would be a real dollar. All demand accounts would be handled by the banker in return for a *fee*, to which he would be entitled for services rendered. Checks could be used as they are today but each check would represent the transfer of real money. Bankers would settle balances in real money. Demand deposits would be *demand* deposits. Time deposits would be classified strictly as to short time or long time. Short time deposits, that is from six months to a year, could be loaned by the banker on strictly short term loans for commercial purposes. Long time deposits would be invested in bonds extending only over the period for which the long time deposits were made. Bonds of varying maturities could be bought. Demand deposits would be genuine demand claims on consumer goods. Such a scientific arrangement would be almost 100% insurance against loss of money deposited in banks. Bank failures would become very rare. Domestic bankers would really be able to serve the customers of their own communities. They would not be the victims of control systems which have, in the past, prevented them from serving their own communities in the manner they desired.

How the Gold Standard "Is Worked"
The "Federal" "Reserve" System

BLOCK "C"

DEMAND DEPOSITS

Manufactured by the member banks. This "credit"-money is *created* by debiting "Loans and Discounts" and crediting "Deposits." For each dollar so manufactured a member bank must have 13¢ "on deposit" at the Central Bank.

There are 12 Central "Reserve" Banks. Member banks are the town and city local banks.

BLOCK "D"

TIME DEPOSITS

These credits are also bank manufactured. But, in a given bank they are deposited there largely as transfers of "deposits" created by other member banks.

For each dollar of "time" deposits a member bank must have 3¢ to its credit on the books of the Central Bank.

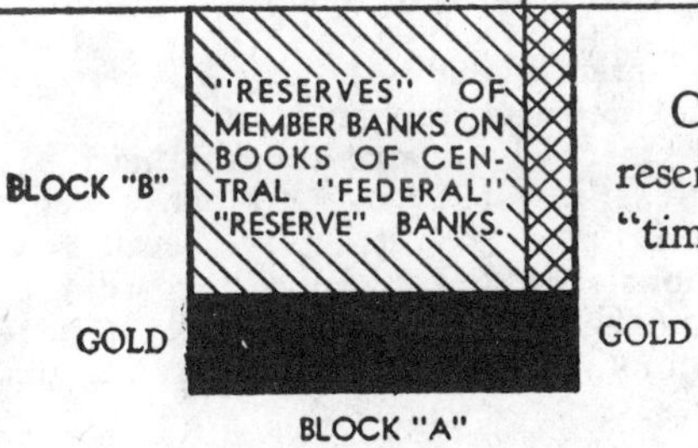

Criss-cross section represents "reserves" against "time" deposits.

Block "A," which is gold, must be 35% of Block "B." Block "B" are "reserves" which are nothing more than credits on the books of the Central Banks. These credits must be 3% of time deposits and 13% of demand deposits of the member banks.

(over)

How the Gold "Standard" Evaporated

Prior to the "Moratorium" of March 1933, both "time" and "demand" "deposits" were supposedly convertible into currency, and the currency into gold. Now one sees why "confidence" is necessary. How could Blocks "C" and "D" be converted into Block "A"? Block "A" represents the entire gold supply.

In addition to this so-called conversion of bank deposits, there existed, prior to March 1933, so-called conversion privileges for all Federal Reserve currency (pocket money outstanding).

Federal Reserve Notes (currency money) could be issued by a Central Bank to the extent of 2½ times its actual gold, after deducting the amount of gold necessary to constitute a 35% reserve against the "deposits" of member banks on the books of the Central Bank.

Pocket currency, normally is equivalent to about 5% of the total bank "deposits." Prior to the Glass-Steagall Bill of February 1932, each dollar of pocket currency was "backed" by 40c in gold in the vaults of a Central Federal Reserve Bank and 60c in commercial paper. If "confidence" were "lost" the conversion of currency into gold would absorb the gold base very quickly, and cause the entire banking structure to collapse. Confidence was *lost*. In February 1932, it became necessary to back the currency with 40c in gold and 60c in Government Bonds. In March 1933, still more "confidence" was "lost." The Federal Reserve Act was then amended so that Government Bonds, not gold, now constitute the *entire* "reserves" against currency.

Banks buy United States bonds from the United States Treasury with the manufactured money, which they create and "lend" to Uncle Sam. Uncle Sam gives them currency (Federal Reserve Notes) in exchange for those same bonds.

The inner few (internationalists) may convert a very small fraction of their bank deposits into gold, and by either "earmarking" or exporting it, force the banks to call their loans—collapse the monetary structure. From 1929 to 1933 banks were thus forced to collapse the nation's monetary structure, because gold was exported for "international banking accounts" according to the New York Trust Company's bulletin, September 1934, pages 197-201. Today *Americans* cannot obtain gold, but internationalists may still obtain it at their pleasure.

This is the so-called "sound" money system predicated upon "confidence" and "mystery." Is the reader satisfied that such a "sound money" system should be maintained or does he wish a non-collapsible, honest money structure which will permit the exchange of goods to take place at equitable price levels at all times? Such a system could not be manipulated by the chosen few,

The "Mystery" of Foreign Exchange

The market where promises-to-pay dollars are sold for promises-to-pay foreign currency, is called the Foreign Exchange Market. The value is determined by the demand. If there is a big demand for promises-to-pay dollars by those who hold bankers' promises-to-pay pounds, francs, or any other foreign currency, the dollar will rise in relation to the pound, franc, etc. In other words, more promises-to-pay pounds, francs, etc., will be required to buy a given number of promises-to-pay dollars. (This is what happens when the dollar is "unpegged.") When the United States was on a "so-called" gold basis; when promises-to-pay dollars were demanded in greater volume than promises-to-pay dollars were offered, the cost of obtaining promises-to-pay dollars would rise. If it rose so that it required more than $4.90 to buy a pound sterling, gold would be shipped. The old parity was 4.8667 dollars for one pound sterling. At 4.90, the cost of shipping, insurance, etc., on the gold itself would be covered. Hence, at above 4.90, gold would be shipped out of the United States.

The international bankers bought large amounts of foreign currencies before the United States suspended gold payments in 1933, and during the few weeks ensuing. When those promises-to-pay pounds, francs, guilders, etc., were returned to the United States, after the Gold Bill of 1934 was passed and the two billion dollar fund was handed to Secretary Morgenthau, Uncle Sam bought pound, franc, guilder, etc., promises-to-pay and gave up dollar promises-to-pay. The international bankers got dollar promises-to-pay, and Uncle Sam got pound, franc and guilder promises-to-pay *which must stay frozen in Europe.*

If Uncle Sam brought his now-frozen balances

home, the dollar would rise rapidly. *The only honest way to have treated the American international bankers who bought foreign currencies was to have refused to sell dollar promises-to-pay,* excepting to individuals who could show actual bills rendered for the purchase of foreign goods, and modest transfers of capital for travel, etc. *No other foreign exchange transaction should have been allowed.*

The Kind of Money Structure Each Nation Should Have: the Only Kind the International Bankers Cannot Juggle at Will

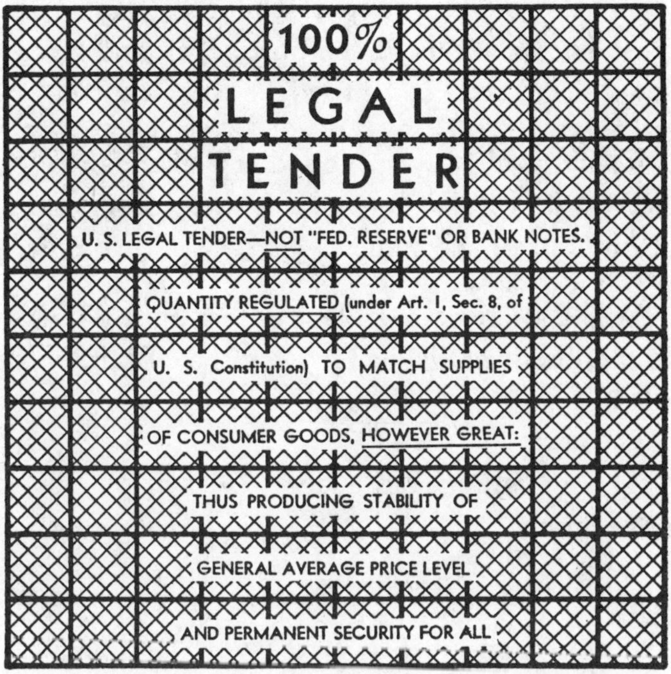

U. S. legal tender created by the U. S. Monetary Trusteeship to match national productiveness.

Quantity *regulated* by Monetary Trustees answerable to the United States Congress.

This legal tender will be owned by individual citizens, and deposited in *privately* owned banks.

The National Government should have *no* control over banks. Banks should be state chartered, custodians and lenders of real money.

Silver should be given an important place in the settlement of international *trade* balances.

Gold and silver currency prices should *not* be fixed (pegged). With a free gold and silver market raw materials entering world markets could reach equitable and fair price levels.

What would a group of children, playing store, say, if one should hold the button-bag and refuse to allow the contents to be used?

They would say: "You don't play fair." And what would they *do?* — take it away from him and put him out of the game.

What do we, so-called grown-ups, do? Mope and wonder; but thank God for the "Brain" Trust.

There is an age-old adage, "God helps him who helps himself."

Said his Lordship (1630): "Well, God mend all." "Nay, by God, Donald, we must help Him to mend it," said Sir David Ramsay.

We have been told that the Supreme Court of the United States must have laws *submitted* to it before it can act. How long shall we wait to demand that it be asked to *pass* upon the constitutionality of our present banking laws?

CHAPTER XI

THE HISTORICAL FACTS

Pretended vs Real Reasons

History should tell us how we arrived where we are and who were responsible. In explaining our present predicament, it is necessary to give historical facts, which may be readily verified by consulting original sources.

It is emphasized that what we are about to state has not appeared in the text books from which we "learned" history. The complete omission of rational reasons for events accounts for the dryness of history. When we investigate the facts and place upon them the only interpretations permitted by common sense, history becomes intensely alive. Our patience is lost with the tommy-rot taught, the pretended reasons which caused peoples and nations to take strong action.

Our Untaught Colonial History

The War ending in 1604, resulting in Spain's loss of the region included in the Virginia grant, left England free to extend her occupation in America. The Crown was glad to have private citizens undertake settlements and granted them charters at their own terms. Each Colony could make its own laws, so long as they were not inconsistent with the laws of England; each had its own Assembly, and was a separate part of the British Empire. The English Parliament had no power over the Colonies originally, and did not try to stretch out its deadening hand until prompted to do so by the Bank "of England," chartered in 1694.

The first charter of Virginia, 1606, contained the following explicit words:

> "X. And that they shall, or lawfully may, establish and cause to be made a coin, to pass current there between the People of those several Colonies, *for the more ease of traffic and bargaining* amongst them and the natives there, of such metal and in such manner and form, as the said Councils shall there limit and appoint."

The Crown thus specifically renounced its power over the money of the Colonies.

The following, taken from the first charter of Massachusetts, 1628, is typical of the manner in which the American governments were given the full right to make their own laws:

"And we do ordain that once in the year . . . the governor, deputy governor and assistants and all other officers of the said company, shall be assembled to make, ordain or establish all manner of wholesome and reasonable orders, laws, statutes, ordinances, directions and instructions, not contrary to the laws of this our realm of England."

All changes or amendments to charters enlarged the earlier granted powers. The Colonial constitutions were *never* restricted. If they had been, the Colonists would have resisted as the citizens at home did whenever the Crown attempted to encroach upon their hard-earned rights. The Americans did resist successfully, and with finality, over 100 years later.

The main principle under which paper money may correctly be created by a government may be illustrated by the following wording of one of the early State notes issued by Massachusetts:

"This indented bill for ten shillings, due from the Massachusetts Colony to the Possessor, shall be in value equal to money, and shall be accordingly accepted by the Treasurer, and Receivers subordinate to him, in all public payments, and for any stock at any time in the Treasury. Boston in New England, December the 10th, 1690. By order of the General Court."

Here "money" plainly meant "legal tender."

Since our facts concern money, it is necessary to state that for 500 years before the first charter to American Colonists was granted, the English tallies had been in full use as legal tender. Therefore, when the American charters extended to them all powers not inconsistent with English laws, the power to create money — legal tender — was included. In the first charter granted it was specifically mentioned. In others, it was sometimes omitted as superfluous.

Paper money now coming into use in various parts of the world — having long since been invented in China — the Colonies began utilizing this convenient form of money. The American Colonies created their own money, and paid it into use via public expenditures until there was enough in circulation to effect necessary exchanges without restraint. The quality which made money legal tender was its acceptance by the government for taxes, and its recognition as a lawful medium for settling all indebtedness between the government and private individuals.

In 1672, during the Dutch War, Charles II of England tried to introduce government-issued paper money in place of the inconvenient tallies. Strangely, he ran into secret opposition which effectively blocked him. However, his attempt gave the precious metal custodians, the multiplicate receipt lenders, a bad scare. Success of his plan would have meant that their sub-rosa scheme of lending what they did not own, in reality, claims to metal which did not exist, would have been exposed and the mysterious power of gold destroyed.

Aside from inconvenience, the only trouble with the wooden tallies was that their quantity was regulated, not by the great needs of commerce but by the small needs of the Crown. Hence, in order to carry on business, it was necessary to borrow from the strong room keepers to meet the deficiency.

It took a revolution in England to lay the foundation for the Bank "of England." This took place in 1688. Six years later the bank received its special privileges. Soon afterwards, a Board of Trade was set up, with John Locke as a member. This bank lost no time in getting busy to accomplish the purposes for which it had been established.

In 1694, under the guise of a disputed succession to the throne of England, the gold gang forced William III to legalize their previous sub-rosa practice, thereby legalizing the system by means of which the gold worshippers could periodically despoil all producers and workers.

In order to emphasize the facts, we quote from *The Breakdown of Money,* by Christopher Hollis:

"In 1694 the Government of William III was in sore straits for money. A company of rich men under the leadership of one William Paterson offered to lend William £1,200,000 at 8 per cent on the condition that 'the Governor and Company of the Bank of England,' as they called themselves, should have the right to issue notes to the full extent of its capital. That is to say, the Bank got the right to collect £1,200,000 in gold and silver and to turn it into £2,400,000, lending £1,200,000, the gold and silver, to the Government, and using the other £1,200,000, the bank-notes, themselves. *Paterson was quite frank about it that this privilege which had been given to the Bank was a privilege to make up money.* 'If the proprietors of the Bank,' he wrote, 'can circulate their own fundation of twelve hundred thousand pounds without having more than two or three hundred thousand pounds lying dead at one time with another, this Bank will be in effect as nine hundred thousand pounds or a million of fresh money brought into the nation.' In practice they did not keep a cash reserve of nearly two or three hundred thousand pounds. By 1696 we find them circulating £1,750,000 worth of notes against a cash reserve of £36,000.

"Intelligent critics saw that the experiment had proved that it was perfectly possible to manufacture money without any metallic backing but that it was dangerous and iniquitous to allow the privilege of that manufacture to be in private hands. For instance Bishop Berkeley, the idealist philosopher, writing in 1735 his Queries Proposed to the Consideration of the Public, asked 'Whether it be not a mighty privilege for a private person to create a hundred pounds with a dash of his pen,' and 'Whether it be not evident that we may maintain a much greater outward and inward commerce, and be five times richer than we are, and our bills abroad be of far greater credit, though we had not one ounce of gold or silver in the whole island.' "

Not long after the Bank "of England" began to create its private money, the rapid growth of the American Colonies attracted attention at home. Not satisfied with the profits they made through regular commerce with the Colonists, the "merchants" wanted more; so began an insidious campaign to exploit the industrious Colonists.

Benjamin Franklin — Advocate of Scientific and Honest Money

Benjamin Franklin was born in 1706, the youngest son of the youngest son for five generations past. He came of long-lived people and grew up in a sturdy and industrious atmosphere.

Unfortunately, his autobiography, in our time, has lost popular ground amid the swirl of senseless printed matter. His writings would be extremely useful in our daily life. His letters written on matters of public business from 1757 to 1790 are most revealing as to the true motives that actuated the British in their economic war upon America. Strangely, they are omitted in current biographies. No doubt the reason for this is that Franklin discusses honest money too frequently for the comfort of our present day money creators. Were it not for his writings there would be little reference available to the public concerning the basic cause of the American War for Independence. The text books which are commonly used in our day, as well as that of our parents, carefully omit the causes which Franklin — the great statesman and philosopher — describes.

After reviewing the monetary legislation of the early Colonies, Dewey, in *The Financial History of the United States,* tells how the Colonial issues were suppressed: "The English government showed its disapprobation of the reckless monetary issues by suppressing the Land Bank in Massachusetts in 1741: and finally in 1751, Parliament *exercised its prerogative* and enacted a law forbidding any further issue of legal tender or bills of credit by the New England Colony, and in 1764 this earlier prohibition was extended to all other Colonies."

Mr. Dewey, in speaking of Parliamentary prerogatives, is in direct opposition with Franklin, as well as with the Colonial charters under which the Colonies were free states. Dewey goes on: "The interference of home government in prohibiting paper issues had more than immediate results; it provoked opposition; was regarded as an unjustifiable interference, and helped to develop the growing discontent with government by England."

On Page 30 of the same book Dewey states: "Franklin in 1766 told England that one of the reasons for the ill feeling in America toward her authority was the prohibition of paper money."

On February 17, 1768, Franklin, in London, wrote the following letter to Joseph Galloway:

"In mine of January 9th, I wrote to you that I believed, notwithstanding the clamor against America had been greatly increased by the Boston proceedings, we should attempt this session to obtain the repeal of the restraining act relating to paper money.

"It had been previously concluded among us, that, if the repeal was to be obtained at all, it must be proposed in the light of a favor to the merchants of this country, and asked for by them, not by the agents as a favor to America.

"We entered into the subject, and had a long conversation upon it, in which all the arguments he used, against the legal tender of paper money, were intended to demonstrate, that it was for the benefit of the people themselves to have no such money current among them; and it was strongly his opinion, that after the experience of being without it for a few years, we should all be convinced of this truth."

In a previous letter to Joseph Galloway, dated June 13, 1767, Franklin detailed a meeting of the British Parliament:

"But in the House, when the chancellor of the

exchequer had gone through his proposed American revenue, viz. by duties on glass, china ware, paper, pasteboard, colors, tea, etc., Grenville stood up and undervalued them all as trifles; and, says he, 'I will tell the honorable gentleman of a revenue, that will produce something valuable in America; *make paper money* for the Colonies, issue it upon loan there, take the interest, and apply it as you think proper.' A Mr. Townsend stood up and assured the House that a bill was prepared for that purpose and that it would be brought before them."

Abuses and errors in creating the paper money of the various Colonies may be summarized in the words of Dewey:

"There were interest-bearing notes, some of which were legal tender, while others were not; there were non-interest bearing notes, some of which were legal tender for future obligations but not for past debts; some were legal tender for all purposes, and others not legal tender between private persons, but receivable for all public payments. In some instances funds arising from certain sources of taxation were pledged for the redemption of the notes, in others not. In some cases they were payable on demand; in others, at some future time. Sometimes they were issued by committees, and sometimes by a specially designated official." — *Financial History of the United States.*

Undoubtedly, some of the Colonies had made errors and had suffered the results of them. Yet, the people *went* to *war* to retain their sovereign privilege of creating their own money. We can learn, from past errors, what has to be done to make a money system work properly so as to be neither explosive nor collapsible. These are twin evils which can be avoided if we will it so, and demand such a system as is in accordance with honesty and common sense.

Our early history books strangely omit the facts that for some years prior to 1773 the British Parliament had busied itself annulling the laws under which the American Colonies had exercised their fundamental right to create and issue their own money. Much is said of Taxation without Representation, but what underlies that phrase is omitted. The fact is that the Bank "of England" manipulators, having gained control over British industry through frequent depressions, cast their greedy eyes on the commerce and industry of America, and set to work to lay hold of the money of the Colonies and, hence, the industry of the Colonists.

Due to the intrigue carried on by the private money powers, the American Revolution was, according to some historians, unwittingly financed by King George III himself.

Meyer Amschel, of Frankfort-on-the-Main, entered the scene. He conceived the idea of enlisting young men as mercenary troops, painting to them the glories of military service, etc. When King George III was unable to secure British soldiers to fight their cousins across the Atlantic, he went to the Landgrave of Hesse Cassel, at Hanau, near Frankfort. George III paid \$20,000,000 to the Landgrave for approximately 16,800 Hessian mercenaries (\$1,200 per head) who had been organized and trained by Meyer Amschel. The Landgrave loaned this \$20,000,000 to Meyer Amschel at a low rate of interest for ten years.

It is well known that the foreign borrowing of funds for the American Revolution was accomplished through the efforts of Robert Morris. It is not so well known (although it is boasted of by some historians) that Robert Morris secured his funds from Haym Solamon. It is furthermore stated that although Solamon "gave" everything he had to the American Revolution, he still remained the richest man in America! That is real genius.

Those who know anything of international banker solidarity will appreciate immediately that Meyer Amschel (whose family of five sons and five daughters took the name of Rothschild from the Red Shield which hung in front of Meyer's shop in Frankfort-on-the-Main as his trade-mark) loaned the money to Solamon, which was in turn loaned through Robert Morris to the American Colonies. Thus, George III paid for the American Revolution and the international financiers played both ends against the middle; no matter who lost, they won, and lives were sacrificed on both sides.

The greed of the "English" financiers had brought on the American Revolution, and it was money changers in other quarters who facilitated the financing. We see how the international money power was expanded in the American Revolution. This is related not to disparage the American Colonists. They were forced to revolt against the tyranny of "London" bankers. These facts are stated to show that the greed of international money was rampant then, as now. They created the trouble between the Colonies and the British Empire by their greed, and then profited from the trouble created.

The entire attempt to usurp the rights of the Colonists was laid along such lines as would serve the banking interests, by at last bringing the Americans economically to their knees.

High prices were placed upon British manufactures sent to the Colonists, though there was "overproduction" at home. This drained the Colonists of the specie (coins) obtained by trade with other nations.

An embargo was laid upon commerce with other nations than England, which then made it impossible for the Americans to obtain the specie with which to pay English manufacturers, who were already by this time mere factory managers for the bankers, as many of our "princes of industry" are in the present day. This forced American borrowing from the bank overseas, and the building up of bonds and interest in acknowledgment thereof.

The money of the Colonial Governments was abolished by laws passed in violation of the American charters by the English Parliament. The bankers did not even want the Colonists to be able to trade among themselves without paying tribute across the Atlantic in interest on the promises of the Bank "of England," which they were thus forcing the Americans to borrow for home use in trading.

The Stamp Act of March 22, 1765, was not only taxation without representation, which the Colonists *could* have borne with nothing but a loss of dignity; but its terms demanded that stamps must be paid for in *specie,* which they did not have and were not allowed to obtain by trading with alien nations. The trap was set so that they would have to borrow from the Bank "of England" at interest in order to pay the tax. Do our school histories explain this?

The objective was to force tribute by the Americans on the Bank "of England's" ficticious and dishonest money creations. Franklin shows how it required 20 years to corrupt sufficiently the House of Commons to cause the passage of the laws desired by the Bank "of England," which were a direct usurpation of the rights granted by the Crown to the Colonial assemblies. Willing Kings had granted those rights a hundred years before — several generations before the money creators usurped money powers in England.

The first attempt to "slip over" a clause which

would pave the way for later aggression, failed. This failure made it necessary to change the complexion of the House of Commons. The House of Lords was already on the side of the money creators, all the Lords being wealthy men, or having formerly been wealthy but now indebted to the Bank "of England" for the maintenance of their own positions.

Franklin's writings indicate the existence of corruption in the British Parliament:

To Joseph Galloway, Dated London, Feb. 17, 1768:

"Mr. Beckford has brought in a bill for preventing bribery and corruption in elections, wherein was a clause to oblige every member to swear, on his admission into the House, that he had not directly or indirectly given any bribe to any elector; but this was so universally exclaimed against, as answering no end but perjuring the members, that he has been obliged to withdraw that clause. It was indeed a cruel contrivance of his, worse than the gunpowder plot; for that was only to blow the Parliament up to heaven, this to sink them all down to ———. Mr. Thurlow opposed his bill by a long speech. Beckford, in reply, gave a dry hit to the House, that is repeated everywhere. 'The honorable gentleman,' says he, 'in his learned discourse, gave us first one definition of corruption, then he gave us another definition of corruption, and I think he was about to give us a third. Pray does that gentleman imagine there is any member of this House that does not *know* what corruption is?' which occasioned only a roar of laughter, for they are so hardened in the practice, that they are very little ashamed of it."

To Wm. Franklin, dated London, March 13, 1768:

"The Parliament is up, and the nation in a ferment with the new elections. Great complaints are made that the natural interests of country gentlemen in their neighboring boroughs is overborne by the moneyed interests of the new people, who have got sudden fortunes in the Indies, or as contractors. *Four thousand pounds* is now the market price for a borough. In short, this whole venal nation is now at market, will be sold for about two millions, and might be bought out of the hands of the present bidders (if he would offer half a million more) by the very Devil himself."

The American Confederacy Period

The first Continental Congress convened September 5, 1774. In October the delegates agreed upon a Declaration of Resolutions and the Association of the various Colonies was agreed to for the purpose of boycotting Great Britain. England then forbade trade with her own Colonies.

On July 6, 1775, the Continental Congress agreed upon the "Declaration of the Causes and Necessity of Taking Up Arms." On July 31, Lord North's Conciliatory Resolution was declared ridiculous. On August 23, King George III issued his Proclamation of Rebellion, and events rapidly led to the Declaration of Independence on July 4, 1776. As an important aside, it should be noted well that on May 1, of the same year, Adam Weishaupt in Bavaria had issued his Manifesto on the Order of the Illuminati; setting in motion a political force designed to bring about the direct opposite of what the Americans were determined to accomplish.

On June 11, 1776, the Continental Congress set up a committee "to prepare and digest the form of confederation to be entered into between the Colonies." On November 15, 1777, the Articles of Confederation were agreed to. The first Congress met on

March 2, 1781. From then until the Constitution of the United States was ratified in 1789, that document formed the basis of the government.

The Articles of Confederation did not give the Continental Congress the power of taxation. The Continental Congress did *not* issue legal tender because it could not under the Articles of Confederation. It could not levy taxes, hence, could not make good its issues by taking them back at face value. It could not even enact its own laws for the punishment of counterfeiters. None of these conditions exist today with our sovereign government, yet the money creators hold up the Continental currency as a terrible example. Are they sincere? Are we to assume that "experts" do not know these historic facts? The following quotation is taken from Dewey:

"The issues were made in so wholesale a fashion, the responsibility of maintaining their credit was so largely divided, the tie between the issue and redemption was so weak, that the lesson learned is little applicable to modern conditions, and we cannot get much practical help for sound finance out of a general denunciation of the Continental currency."

In this resume Mr. Dewey inadvertently omitted the most important part, which he mentioned previously, as follows: "Much disorder was introduced by the counterfeiting of notes both by English and Americans, and many efforts were made to prevent it by altering plates, calling in certain issues, and *requesting individual States* to pass severe laws for the punishment of counterfeiters."

Going further, Dewey quotes "a vigorous commentator" as follows: "The Articles gave to the Confederation the power of contracting debts, and at the same time withheld the power of paying them . . . It provided the mode in which its treasury should be supplied for the reimbursement of the public credit, but over the sources of that supply, it gave the government contracting the debt no power whatever. Thirteen independent legislatures granted or withheld the means according to their own convenience."

The currency of the Continental Congress became worthless *primarily* because it was illegitimate. It was born of necessity, but was unsupported by law, by popular consent, or by taxing power.

To assert that over-issues are an inseparable characteristic of government-created money, is to assert that the people will not support the same through taxes which, as Benjamin Franklin frequently stated, is absurd. We must have a government, and it must be supported. It is always well supported when the people are permitted to work, permission for which is freely granted by the gold crowd whenever there is a war. *Then*, there is always enough money for the simple reason that they create the money to conduct the war, just as they cause the war itself.

Benjamin Franklin was well aware of the abuses to which government-created money can be subjected. If he were alive today, he could witness that the privilege of private bank created money, called bank "credit," has been abused to such extent that millions upon millions of our people have been robbed of their life savings and are in want and sorrow. Franklin knew that all human institutions had to be *managed* properly. With all of his first hand knowledge of abuses of government money during the Colonial period, he did not swerve from his conviction that a government-issued currency was a public benefit and *could* be properly managed if the people only demanded it, as they did in his own State, Pennsylvania.

Plain common sense immediately cuts a clear distinction between the conditions under which the powerless Continental Congress issued its currency, and the conditions now: for the powerful Constitution adopted in 1789 because of the weakness of the Articles of Confederation, gave our present Congress the sole power to create money; to make it full and unrestricted legal tender; to use the original purchasing power attending issue for the common benefit; to levy and collect taxes which establish the inevitable redeemability of the money; and last but by no means least, to punish directly counterfeiters by its own authority. Furthermore, the present Congress is mandated to regulate the value of money for the people, which can be done only by regulating its quantity.

Alexander Hamilton — Stepfather of Our Country

To understand how it was possible for the monetary swindle to be fastened anew upon the young nation, it is necessary to understand Hamilton himself.

Hamilton was born in the West Indies. For at least two years after his birth, his mother, Rachel, was married to one Levine, a wealthy planter. Hamilton claimed that he was born January 11, 1757, but even a friendly biographer states that this may be doubted on the ground that this date would credit him with impossible precocity.

His mother, Rachel, was unfaithful, and Levine divorced her in 1759. Rachel then went to James Hamilton; and her son, Alexander, changed his name, a common practice among money changers. He grew up crowned with ability, but cursed with an inferiority complex, which accounted for his savage determination to rule. Yearning for figures and accounts, at the age of "13," he went to work for Henry Cruger, largest merchant in the Caribbees. Within two years, he was left in complete charge of this large business, while Cruger was absent on an extended voyage. In September of 1772, at the age of "17," he left for New York, which was his home until his death in the duel with his business and political rival, Aaron Burr, July 12, 1804.

Coming to New York armed with letters from business friends, he entered grammar school and boarded with a friend of Cruger's. He transferred to King's College, now known as Columbia University, the home seat of much that reflects the effects of the economic doctrines Hamilton fastened upon the country. Columbia is also recognized as the point of origination of much of the "Redism" with which we are now surfeited.

Here he met many influential men, including William Livingston. By temperament Hamilton was an admirer of "English" business methods and industrial policies, so much so that throughout his adult life, he was charged with being a British sympathizer. This charge was justified, if by a British sympathizer we mean that his ideas of a private central bank were identical with those upon which the all-powerful Bank "of England" was fashioned.

Through his powerful friends, two years after the War for Independence began, at the age of "20," he obtained an appointment as Lieutenant Colonel and an assignment as Secretary to General George Washington. He was a long-range schemer. During his services under Washington, he constantly studied money, coin, gold, silver, foreign exchange, etc., all of which seemed to run in his very blood. He obtained one of the first copies of Adam Smith's *The Wealth of Nations*, and the influence of this perverted economic doctrine was witnessed in his engineering the debt system of money into existence in the United States.

From 1777 to February 1781, Alexander Hamilton was on General Washington's staff handling commissary affairs. During this time he was studying *The Wealth of Nations,* by Adam Smith, which had been given to him by his mysterious "discoverer," whose identity has never been disclosed.

In February of 1781 he broke with George Washington over a trivial matter. Washington gave him every opportunity to return, even requesting a conciliatory interview, but the arrogant Hamilton refused. The character of Washington is attested by the fact that he never, in after years, allowed this act of Hamilton, when Washington needed him in a crisis, to affect his attitude.

During the time when Hamilton was in General Washington's service, he was writing letters to influential men discussing economics. Even at that time, he was preparing to inject his (that is, Adam Smith's) ideas of government and finance into the new nation which was being born in the struggle with England. He already had formed definite ideas for a privately owned central bank. He based his plan on the Bank "of England," the great private privileges of which he so admired, and on the doctrines of Adam Smith, the father of "classical orthodox economics."

During the war period the Continental Congress had issued paper money, although it was *without power to do so*. Neither did it have the power to tax — the necessary twin of the power to create money. In addition to the lack of authority, there was the activity of the private money creators and lenders. These people dared not permit honest public money to gain a foothold. They controlled trade and supplies and refused to accept any but their own issues of money in payment. Consequently, the money issued by the Continental Congress fell in value.

Hamilton's study of finance was stimulated. He wanted to learn how the private money creators had been able to destroy the government-created money. He wanted to get on the right side from a personal standpoint, for it would never do to make enemies of those so powerful as to be able to destroy public money. His natural leanings toward a central private money creation system were strengthened when he realized that such a system could be put over on an uninformed public. Accordingly, he wrote to a powerful member of Congress stating that the only plan for preserving the currency was such as would make it to the interests of the moneyed men to "cooperate" with the government. In 1780 he had suggested a bank with a capital of ten million dollars from *foreign* sources and two million from domestic, the latter to be guaranteed by the government!

The Bank of North America

Immediately upon the ratification of the Articles of Confederation in 1781, Alexander Hamilton, then "24," wrote to Robert Morris outlining a plan for a private bank modeled after the Bank "of England." No time was to be lost in setting up a permanent gravestone over honest public money.

Though the Articles were only a loose agreement between entirely independent States, chiefly, for protection against a common aggressor, Hamilton, Morris, *et alii,* began plans immediately to take the money power away from each of the Colonies and centralize it in private hands, which would then become supreme over the citizens of the various independent States. He was, in effect, planning to set up an international bank for these independent States. He planned to place this bank under control of European capital. Those who controlled such liquid capital were internationally allied in a plunderbund that was hundreds of years old.

On April 30, 1781, Hamilton wrote to Robert Morris: "*A national debt, if it is not excessive, will be a national blessing; a powerful cement of union; a necessity for keeping up taxation, and a spur to industry.*" He then recommended a "National" bank with a capital of ten or fifteen million dollars, to be paid 2/6ths in specie, 1/6th in securities on good European funds, and 3/6ths in good landed security. It was to be erected into a legal corporation for thirty years, during which no other bank, public or private, was to be permitted. Its capital and deposits were to be exempt from taxation, and the United States collectively, individually and conjointly with the private proprietors were to be responsible for all of its transactions.

Its sources of profit were to be the sole right of issuing currency for the United States equal in amount to the whole capital of the bank. Loans were to be made at a rate not exceeding 8%. It was to discount bills of exchange, and contract with the French government for the supply of its fleets and armies in America, and with the United States for the cost of supplies of their army. Dealings in real estate were to be permitted, to buy at favorable opportunities the real estate of men who, having rendered themselves odious, would be obliged to leave the country.

This was the proposal of Hamilton, then "24" years old, made three months after he had insolently quit General George Washington on a pretext. "This letter led to the closest relations between Hamilton and Robert Morris, but vehement as was the character of Morris, his schemes fell far short of the daring suggestions of his young counselor."—Bancroft's *History of the Formation of the Constitution.*

Robert Morris did not go so far, and limited the capital to $400,000 in gold and silver, to be increased at the bank's discretion. Note that this project had to be ratified by every State, as the Articles of Confederation had not given Congress the right to incorporate legal bodies. Robert Morris calmly asked Congress to ask from the States this power, together with the power to prohibit every other bank.

Subscriptions languished and Morris applied to John Jay, Ambassador to Spain, for funds from that government, saying: "I am determined that the bank shall be well supported until it can support itself, and then it will support *us.*" This was written by Robert Morris, held out to us as a great patriot.

John Adams wrote of Morris, "He has vast designs in the mercantile way, and no doubt pursues mercantile ends which are always gain."

"Because of Morris' knowledge of . . . banking connections abroad he knew how to bring about more orderly dealings in foreign exchange in the execution of foreign loans." — Dewey.

During 1781, about the time Cornwallis surrendered at Yorktown on October 19, a remittance of $500,000 had been received at Philadelphia from the King of France. This came under the custody of Morris as Superintendent of Finance for the Continental Congress, for, supposedly, the King of France was lending the money to the United States. Bancroft says the following: "In January, 1782, Morris, with no clear warrant, subscribed all the sum that remained in the Treasury, being about $254,000, to the stock of the bank, which was thus nursed into life with public money"—three months after the virtual end of the war!

Thus was born the Bank of North America, the legal establishment of which was supported by a charter from the State of Massachusetts in 1782. "The bank was then practically founded on government funds, but managed by officials of its own selection." — Dewey's *The Financial History of the United States.*

Fortunately, the Bank of North America was never recognized by most of the States. This was Hamilton's reason for advocating a stronger union. When that was later accomplished, he tried again for his central bank, with greater success.

Alexander Hamilton is held up to us as the purely "patriotic" advocate of a strong central government. It is strange that this turn in his peculiar patriotism was not evident until after the Morris-Hamilton Bank of North America had failed to obtain the coveted exclusive right to create the money required by the people. The Articles of Confederation had met no objection from Hamilton until the States had rejected the North American Bank.

Morris had quietly put the $254,000 of public specie into the bank's capital in January, 1782. It had taken two months to wheedle the first charter from one of the States, Massachusetts. Despite the universally acknowledged financial crisis of the War for Independence, evidently the people wanted *independence*—not Hamiltonian "independence."

Pennsylvania recognized the bank in March and granted a charter on April 1. Ten days later New York did likewise. Pennsylvania, significantly, repealed its act in 1785, but Delaware replaced part of this lost ground by its charter granted in 1786. All of the other States "sat tight."

Thus, it required no clairvoyancy on Hamilton's part to realize, in 1782, that the States did not intend to give up the better half of their sovereignty to a private internationally controlled money creating bank. They realized that such a bank would receive the privilege of controlling the entire country.

Therefore, "In obedience to instructions . . . he went to work . . . for he believed that 'very little could be done till the entire change of the present system.' "—Bancroft.

Hamilton—Father of Our National Debt

As stated previously, the United States government was founded after engraving processes had been perfected and paper money had begun to be used. Benjamin Franklin indicates very clearly in his writings that the founders of this nation were determined that the right to create the money of the nation and pay it into use should belong to the government.

Before the formation of the first Cabinet, Washington had asked Robert Morris to take the portfolio of Secretary of the Treasury. He declined, and to Washington's complete astonishment, recommended Alexander Hamilton. In the light of the past connections between Hamilton and Morris, the purpose of the recommendation is evident. The great George Washington made the one mistake of his career. He took the advice of Robert Morris and almost undid the splendid possibilities of the seven-year war he had just won. We may still retrieve that error if enough people become informed *in time*.

In 1790 the foreign debt of the United States was about $12,000,000, having been borrowed from Spain, France and private capitalists in Holland and Germany. The domestic debt owing to the various citizens was $42,000,000. A part of this debt is believed to have been money that was transferred to private individuals from Frankfort on the Main to be loaned to the colonists.

The total debt of all of the states was about $21,500,000, being their expenditures on behalf of the war for independence. It is incorrect to call our struggle for independence a revolution, inasmuch as that term has now come to mean the direct opposite of the objective sought by the colonists in the war from 1775 to 1783. The war of independence in the United States was the exact opposite in purpose to the "French" Revolution, which dethroned a monarchy and enthroned first a murderous tyranny and then an emperor.

In spite of the provisions of the Constitution under which the government should create the amount of money necessary to conduct the nation's business, Hamilton in 1790, after the death of Franklin, proposed that the public debt, then amounting to approximately $75,000,000, be converted into interest bearing bonds. The certificates of indebtedness had fallen to 15% of their face value by the same bearish operations of speculators of the same type that later raided the United States notes which Lincoln issued during the Civil War.

It is obvious that the citizens of the new nation could not conduct their business without a medium of exchange. The utter propriety of vesting the sole right to create money in the popular government had been recognized and congealed in the Constitution. What would have been more proper than for the new United States government, which had been adopted by a vote of the people, to create the actual money necessary to discharge the public debt and pay off the creditors with United States money? Paper money had been in use in Europe so that counterfeiting had long since ceased to be a problem; means having been found to control it. The private "Bank of England" had been printing and lending its own paper money for 100 years.

The government had a debt to pay and the citizens needed money as a medium of exchange. Instead of creating the money and paying the debt, the debt was funded into bonds. If that is what Hamilton stood for, and we know he did, he was far from being the sort of Secretary of the Treasury we have been taught he was, for he was in there serving the apostles of debt rather than the people whose Constitution he had sworn to uphold and defend.

Hamilton brought in his report on the public debt, as requested by the new Congress. The all-important point must be constantly kept in mind that the new Congress had the power "to coin money and regulate its value." Hamilton must, therefore, find a way to set aside this power, if his coveted central money-creating bank, patterned after the Bank "of England" was to come into being. He worked on Congressmen to support his plan for converting the public obligations into *interest-bearing bonds*. He passed out hints to key men regarding recommendations in his report, which should have been properly an official secret. As the result, these certain Congressmen scrambled to pick up, at enormous discounts, the paper which they were told would be converted into interest-bearing bonds.

The great agricultural population fought Hamilton under the leadership of Thomas Jefferson. He called the bank a "prostitution of laws which constitute the pillars of our whole system of jurisprudence." Hamilton said: "It shall be under a private and *not* a public direction—under the guidance of individual interest and not of public policy." Benjamin Franklin died in 1790. Despite Jefferson's efforts, Hamilton was able to put his bank plan into action, for he had the ability to cause men to act against their own best long-range interests.

Communications were slow. The uninformed rural regions gave up their paper for 15c on the dollar. One member of the House actually sent two fast vessels to the South to purchase paper. How Hamilton was able to carry his point, that is, sell out the new nation, is understood by the fact that 45% of the members of the House bought this paper on his advance information. There is nothing new about the "art" of using Judases.

"Hamilton proposed that the doors of congress should be thrown wide open whenever the finances were under discussion, though the proposal, had it been accepted, would have filled the galleries with holders of certificates of public debt." —Bancroft. The meetings were naturally held in cities, where the money class was strong, and the voice of the rural backbone of the nation, which Franklin and Jefferson recognized as all-important, could not be heard because of the slowness of communications.

In our day, however, that would be an excellent suggestion, provided that the meetings were actually broadcast on the radio, so that the people would *not* have to rely upon abridged and censored newspaper accounts, shaded to reflect what the money creators dictate. The people's voice in response to skullduggery would quickly reach the capital.

Hamilton's debt proposals won. The debt certificates held by "speculators" who had beaten them down to 15% of their face value and bought large amounts of them at such discounts, were converted into interest bearing bonds with a 6% coupon rate, to be paid off from the sales of government lands in the west, the chief part of the public revenues.

At the time of the chartering of the Bank of the United States the population was slightly under four million. Converting this public debt into actual money would have created a debt free circulation of legal tender money of about $19.00 per capita. This money was required for the people of this nation in order to get to work in producing and exchanging the fruits which the vast resources of the new nation provided.

Having saddled this philosophy of debt upon the young nation in violation of the plain requirements and common sense of the situation, Hamilton's next move in 1791 was to bring forth his proposal for a privately owned Central Bank for the creation and lending of money. This was a direct violation of the new Constitution. The untimely death of the great apostle of common sense, scientific government and honest money — Benjamin Franklin — had made it possible for Hamilton's debt philosophy to win.

Debts instead of legal tender were used to discharge the government's obligations. The money which the citizenry was to be forced to use was now to be created out of debt—that is, by the lending out by private individuals of their own private promises-to-pay. These private promises-to-pay were to constitute the money in use in the nation.

Thus, Alexander Hamilton, held out to us as the greatest Secretary of the Treasury, was actually the greatest public apostle of public debt, which is a gross perversion of the essence of scientific government. Oh, Debt and Interest! What falsehoods have been perpetrated in thy names!

Immediately upon Franklin's death the public obligation was converted into these interest bearing bonds. This move made not only a burden out of an opportunity and an obligation to create the medium of exchange which the people needed but, what is more important, left the need for a medium of exchange unfilled. The necessity continued and helped to make the people feel the pinch that was required in order to have them accept the Bank "of the United States." The need for a medium of exchange was then satisfied by chartering another "national" bank. This private bank was then permitted to create the money the people required for their business transactions, by printing its promises-to-pay, which it loaned to those who were able to pay interest and who had assets to pledge.

Thus was the present system in its original essence saddled anew upon the young Republic. How this rebirth of European abuse ever escaped the veto of intelligent George Washington, no one can tell. We had just fought a seven year war for independence from exactly the kind of financial domination with which we were now allowing ourselves to be shackled.

Hamilton's Bank "of the United States"

The Constitutional Convention convened in 1787. If space permitted, the writer would quote Benjamin Franklin extensively, to show the caliber, character and intentions of most of the men who drafted that immortal document. Benjamin Franklin was then past 80, but the part he played in the convention has left an immortal heritage to all Western civilization.

He repeatedly indicates the firm belief of most of the men in that group; that *Christian* honor and justice must be practiced by any man or nations who would build worthily. Many Americans have the general impression that Alexander Hamilton was really a contemporary of most of the signers of the Constitution. He was not, for he was relatively an infant compared to the other venerable statesmen. Is it any wonder that the schemer Hamilton's practices contrasted to the wisdom and integrity of the others who constructed what has been well termed "the key to the science of government"?

The new Constitution recognized the basic fault and the failure of the Confederation — due to its lack of taxing power by which alone it could perform its first function, self-preservation. The writers of the Constitution saw to it that Congress was given the power to *create* money, to *regulate* money, and *to tax.*

The power to coin (create money) has never been exercised except as to the metal coins. The same power as it applies to other kinds of money, i.e., paper, was never exercised until Abraham Lincoln determined to free the whites from economic slavery as he had freed the blacks from chattel slavery.

The money creators have not objected to the public authority exercising its right so far as the subsidiary coins are concerned, because even before the Bank "of England" had been chartered, paper money had come into use in many parts of the world, so that specie was already largely obsolete. The money creators needed only to have the paper money franchise, and the privilege to deal in imaginary money, to accomplish their purpose. The minor coins became merely as so many toy blocks with which the people and their Congress and Mint were permitted to play on the pretense that these were all the money there was, and that the power over subsidiary money was the power over *all money*.

Hamilton had learned the use of deception. He

knew that many people could be fooled by a name, as is the case of the Bank "of England," which was then nearly 100 years old. In that country the people had begun to forget and new generations had never been informed, that the Bank "of England" was nothing but a private mint, where imaginary money was created and loaned for private profit. Few knew that it had been established practically at the point of a gun aimed at a throne.

Hamilton represented the "mercantile" group in politics, which group was opposed to the people at large. He influenced Congressmen by revealing his plans to them, which included appeals to their greed. He thereby, in 1791, through the first violation of the Constitution of the United States, got an exclusive charter for his bank. He believed in the centralization of monetary power in the "mercantile" interests. Consistently, throughout his life, he opposed the productive and agricultural elements of the population, whom he termed "ground-grubbers," who produced the goods which enlightened men turned into gold by following Adam Smith.

Hamilton said: "The emitting of paper money *by the authority of government* is wisely prohibited to the individual states by the national constitution; and the spirit of that prohibition ought not to be disregarded by the government of the United States. The wisdom of the government will be shown in never trusting itself with the use of so dangerous and seductive an expedient." — Dewey, page 69.

No, this would never do: far better, in Hamilton's opinion, for this "dangerous and seductive expedient" to be placed in the hands of private bankers for their special privilege and private profit, together with the privilege of restricting the quantity of the same at such times as would result in the widest possible destruction of price levels and consequent loss of the fruits of their labor by the producing class! And Hamilton set to work with the aid of the money lenders to see that the people's bookkeeping (money) would never be free: that they would never have the use of any money that was not paying tribute to private creators.

The constitution definitely gave the Congress certain very explicit powers: and stated that all those not so given were reserved to the states and the people. But Hamilton, the skilled user of words, invented the idea that other powers not stated were implied. He was almost alone among the men we know best, in advocating this measure, for Randolph, Jefferson, Madison, Maclay, Adams, etc., did their best to beat it.

Hamilton was without effective opposition in the Senate, as that body at that time represented the moneyed interests, the aristocracy. The fight was confined to the House, where Jefferson led the forces against granting this sovereign power over the nation's coin to private and specially privileged parties, on the grounds of its being rankly unconstitutional.

Hamilton, the schemer, brought up for the first time that omnibus of legislative perversion, the doctrine of implied powers.

The President, not being convinced that the vote in the house told the real story, and fearing the dangerous precedent which would be set by the doctrine of implied powers *(how real those fears have proved!)* asked Madison to prepare a veto for the bill. But he wavered before the persuasive eloquence of the purring voice of Hamilton, and signed. Washington, the Virginian planter, was fooled by young Hamilton, the financial "expert."

And Hamilton rushed off to be the honor guest at a special reception given by the Chamber of Commerce of New York City, in honor of their victory over the producers of the nation.

Hamilton was not in office for the benefit of any one but himself. When development of his original plan was complete, he retired from office, again leaving George Washington without respect to the latter's wishes. This was in January, 1795.

But things did not work out as he had planned. Aaron Burr, the hated financial and political rival, had just tricked the New York legislature out of a "water company" charter which actually conferred banking privileges, thus breaking the strangle hold which Hamilton's bank had had on banking in New York State for about ten years.

Running true to ancient form, the forces that had used Hamilton to effect the legalization of their "set-up" now cast him aside. His power waned. His enemies, who had fought for the people for so many years (Jefferson, Madison, Adams, etc.), gained in strength. Hamilton did not derive the expected benefits from the debt system which he had just saddled upon the young nation. He saw that the Bank "of the United States" was in hands that wanted to push him aside.

Accordingly, he repented his efforts to have the circulation completely controlled by a privileged few, and wrote the following letter to Oliver Wolcott, the new Secretary of the Treasury:

"New York, August 22, 1798.

"My Dear Sir:

"No one knows better than yourself how difficult and oppressive is the collection even of taxes very moderate in amount, *if there be a defective circula-*

tion. According to all the phenomena which fell under my notice, this is our case in the interior parts of the country . . .

"For these and *other reasons* which I have thought well of, I have come to a conclusion that our *Treasury ought to raise up a circulation of its own*. I mean, by the issuing of Treasury notes . . .

"This appears to me an expedient equally necessary *to keep the circulation full* . . . it will be easy to enlarge without hazard to credit.

ALEXANDER HAMILTON."

Thus did our "greatest" Secretary of the Treasury, our original financial Judas—"patriot," show repentance *after* he was cast aside by his high priests of private money creation.

In passing, the writer wishes to note that since the appearance of *The Wealth of Nations*, by Adam Smith, a group of medicine men, Houdini worshipers and cabalistic artists have been employed at very remunerative salaries to beguile the unsuspecting public.

"Economist" is the learned term still applied to those who write unintelligible discussions of money, prices, public finance, and so-called political science.

A strange but true fact is that many of the people drawing high salaries in this "profession" are totally innocent of the part they play in propagating false principles and in enslaving their fellow human beings. However, their very innocence tends to discredit their promulgations.

Many financial institutions employ professional economists and the officers of these institutions, feeling their own inadequacy to cope with "mysteries" follow the enunciations and writings of these "experts."

Adam Smith and Adam Weishaupt devoted their talents to writing perversions of the truth. Adam Weishaupt is the father of Socialism, now commonly known as Bolshevism, and Adam Smith is the father of modern economics, ex-ethics.

As the years have passed, those whose interests were served by the false principles enunciated by Adam Smith, have willingly paid other adepts to enlarge upon the original false principles. Dupes in the field of economics have copied the false principles and handed them out under the guise of learned discussions. Since the days of Adam Smith, it has required the subsidizing of a few smart men; the rest have accepted the doctrines without question because they had been previously accepted. The fact that they did not make sense made no difference to those who were dazzled by the false principles accepted in so-called high intellectual and financial quarters.

Dr. John Robison, who published in England in 1797 *Proofs of a Conspiracy Against All Religions and Governments of Europe*, has given us the origin of the word "economist." In describing those who were engaged to inculcate false doctrines during the period prior to the French Revolution he said the following:

"They took the name of Economists and affected to be continually occupied with plans for improving Commerce, Manufactures, Agriculture, Finance, etc., and published from time to time respectable performances on those subjects. But their darling project was to destroy Christianity and Religion and to bring about the total change of government."

Was it mere coincidence that Adam Weishaupt worked five years perfecting his plan for the destruction of society *from below*, and gave it to the world in 1776, and that Adam Smith also completed his plan for the destruction of society *from above* in 1776, when *The Wealth of Nations* was published?

Weishaupt was frankly anti-Christian. Smith, according to the International Encyclopedia, "was the first economist to divorce political economy from ethics." Is this mere coincidence?

The evidence at hand today creates a grave suspicion that the two Adams (Weishaupt and Smith) were financed by the same international money. It becomes clear how Hamilton was serving those who favored slavery and not the champions of genuine freedom, such as was Benjamin Franklin. There can be no lasting freedom of any kind without economic freedom, which cannot exist without monetary freedom.

Our European "Model" Bank

The Alexander Hamilton chosen name of the "Bank of the United States" is misleading, just as is the "Bank of England," "Bank of France," "Bank of Italy," the "Reichsbank," etc. They are all privately owned banks, named to convey the idea to the uninformed that they are Government institutions endowed with the privilege of issuing money.

The Bank of the United States established branches in various cities. During the first twenty years of its existence a number of States, unwilling to accede to having one Central Bank endowed with unconstitutional money creating power, had chartered State Banks. At the time of the expiration of the "Bank of the United States" charter in 1811, there were nearly ninety State charter banks in existence. These State banks vigorously opposed the existence of one Central Bank given the power to create and cancel money.

The charter of the "Bank of the United States" expired in 1811 and, rightfully, was not renewed. It was held that one *private* Central Bank enjoying the unconstitutional privilege of creating money and destroying money at pleasure would, through its branches, soon become a gigantic octopus that would stifle competition and quickly concentrate ownership of all physical property in the hands of a few. It was wisely decided that if private money creation powers were granted at all, it would be far less hazardous and more equitable to permit a number of independent banks to be chartered. There would be less danger of a few individuals manipulating the whole economic structure for their own aggrandizement, in wealth and power. This was sound reasoning and produced relatively beneficial results, although still a violation of the Constitution. It was a case of accepting the lesser of two evils.

The second war with England—the war of 1812—was primarily the result of alien efforts to destroy thriving businesses and create chaos to force those in charge of the National Government to submit to the tyranny of internationalists—to grant another charter to the Bank "of the United States."

Of course, the second war with England brought grave uncertainty to all of the States. This brought trouble to many of the small institutions. In 1816, after a bitter struggle, a second misnamed "United States Bank," also privately owned, was chartered. This bank, in violation of the Constitution, also had power to issue paper money. The violation was in granting that privately owned bank the power to create money — a prerogative which only Congress had under the provisions of the Constitution. Then, as today (1935), banks should have all been privately owned, but they should have been custodians and lenders of real money. Only Congress should have the power to place its imprint on a piece of paper and call it money—full legal tender in the transaction of all business.

This second "Bank of the United States" was also chartered for twenty years. Its capital was $35,000,000, of which only $7,000,000 was held by the United States Government. This bank issued its paper money in amounts of not less than $5.00, payable in specie, and transacted a general banking business. It established branches in all of the important cities throughout the country. In 1830 there were thirty-seven of these branches.

The Bank of the United States (misnamed) was acting under the same money creating principles which our present day unconstitutional central banks enjoy. A demand arose throughout the States that money creation privileges should not be granted to private individuals. General Jackson was elected to the Presidency as a candidate who would oppose the rechartering of the bank. In 1832 he vetoed the Bill which would have renewed the charter of the misnamed "Bank of the United States."

After the Second "Bank of the United States"

When this illicit control institution was denied a charter, only the State banks chartered by the several States remained. In 1837 there were 637 State banks in the country, having an aggregate capital of $291,000,000.

During the entire time in which the United States did not have a Central Bank granting powers to private individuals to create money, foreign bankers were constantly trying to create trouble for all of the independent State banks. The independent State banks should never have enjoyed the privilege of creating money but, even though unconstitutional, it was less dangerous to grant that power to a number of institutions than to grant it to one bank misnamed the "United States Bank."

From that time until the passage of the National Banking Act in 1863, the international money powers waged a constant battle to gain, through a central bank, control of the money creation powers in the United States. The basic error involved in the banking situation from 1791 onward, was the delegation of the privilege of issue to privately owned banks. Banks then, as now, should have been privately owned, but lenders of *real* money. The power to create money is a constitutional mandate to Congress, which it should fulfill; and the delegation of which to others is a violation of our basic law, and of the fundamental principles of political science.

The Real Cause and Purposes of the Civil War

The international bankers had been unsuccessful in their efforts to establish a *private* Central Bank in America. They were, therefore, unable to manipulate the entire money system of this country. The then-existing large number of State banks, while they did have their own power to create money, had the saving grace of being practically all independent units. Therefore, no small group could meet and decide financial policies for the whole nation.

The American Civil War was planned in London in 1857. Certain bankers made an agreement that the Paris branch of one group would support and finance the South, and the British branch of the same group would take the similar role for the North.

Through clever propaganda they fostered the "Slavery Issue." The real issue was to divide the United States against itself and so weaken the Republic that it could eventually be divided among the internationalists for exploitation.

Few Americans realize that the American Union escaped destruction at the time of the Civil War, only through the assistance given Abraham Lincoln by Tsar Alexander II of Russia. The Tsar of Russia had for many years known the methods of the internationalists. Alexander II understood the intrigue behind the Civil War. He came to Lincoln's aid.

The internationalists of London and Paris had caused the landing of troops from five European countries in Mexico. They were preparing to march into the United States in aid of the South when the Tsar of Russia gave notice to the five powers that if any one of them dared to put a single soldier on American soil, it must consider itself immediately at war with Russia. On September 8, 1863, the Russian squadron of Admiral S. Lesowsky came to San Francisco, and on September 11, 1863, the first battleship of the Russian Atlantic squadron of Admiral A. A. Popoff reached the New York Harbor. Both Admirals had orders from the Tsar: "*Be ready to fight any power and take your orders from Abraham Lincoln.*"

It is a sorry commentary that so few Americans have ever had an opportunity to learn by their own research the true history of the United States, particularly what Abraham Lincoln faced in his fight to preserve the American Union. Civil War veterans knew the part that Russia played in helping Lincoln but, strangely enough, the school books have withheld the truth. The story of the Civil War is also bound up with the sad fate of the internationalists' puppet, Maximilian in Mexico.

The Efforts of President Abraham Lincoln to Enforce Laws For an Honest Money System

In July, 1862, aroused by Abraham Lincoln's courageous and honest efforts, the infamous Hazard circular was written by an agent of London bankers and very judiciously distributed among the professional money lenders of America, not forgetting as a matter of course the Senators and Congressmen of the United States. That infamous circular favored the abolition of chattel slavery in America, but only to pave the way for a more subtle form of slavery. We quote the exact phraseology:

> "Slavery is likely to be abolished by the war power and chattel slavery destroyed. This I and my European friends are in favor of, for slavery is but the owning of labor and carries with it the care of the laborers, while the European plan, led by England, is that capital (money lenders) shall control labor by *controlling wages*." (Banishing purchasing power at will and making the laborers victims of unemployment).

The same document states further:

> "This can be done by controlling the money. The great debt (national) that capitalists (money lenders) will see to it is made out of the war, must be used as a means to control the volume of money. To accomplish this the bonds (debts created in conducting the war) must be used as a banking basis. We are now waiting for the Secretary of the Treasury to make this recommendation to Congress."

It fell to the lot of Mr. Jay Cooke, the great war financier, fiscal agent of the Government and general spokesman for the debt beneficiaries, to assume the somewhat difficult role of restating Hamilton's falsehood so as to fool the people again on the "blessings of public debts." Mr. Cooke said:

> "We lay down the proposition that our national debt made permanent and rightly managed will be a national blessing. The funded debt of the United States is the addition of $3,000,000,000 to the previously realized wealth of the nation. It is $3,000,000,000 added to the available actual capital. To pay this debt would be to extinguish this capital and lose this wealth."

Imagine the deception and audacity of Mr. Cooke. Wealth is a physical thing—resources, houses, farms, etc. He tried to tell the American people and did make some of them believe that debts of the tax payers (government bonds) are wealth. They are not. Mr. Cooke received $25,000 per year for repeating the lie and making it stick. But Jay Cooke was not the sage his theorizing purported. His company failed in 1873, unrescued by those who hired him to deceive the public.

The "National" Banking Act was enacted on February 25, 1863. It was then and is now known to be outrageous. The Act was misnamed "National" to deceive the people. It was national only to the extent of using the nation's money issuance powers dishonestly. It gave national banks the power to issue the nation's currency. National banks under that act could and still have power to issue currency (paper money) by simply depositing certain issues of government bonds with the United States Treasury and obtaining currency. Therefore, the privately owned national banks collect interest on the bonds deposited with the Treasury but they pay no interest for the currency which is released to them. They keep only a 5% gold certificate reserve with the Treasury to take care of whatever currency might be presented for payment at the Treasury. Think this fallacious proposition through! Government bonds are tax payers' promises-to-pay, secured by a first lien on all physical property within the nation and a first lien on national income, because Congress has the power to tax. These fully secured interest-bearing tax payers' promises-to-pay are created by the Government and exchanged for privately owned banks' promises-to-pay which are unsecured. These unsecured promises-to-pay of private individuals are *borrowed* by the United States Government. These private individuals' promises-to-pay are called money. Imagine a banking system which permits tax payers' promises-to-pay to be exchanged for private individuals' promises-to-pay.

At the time the "National" Bank Act was passed President Abraham Lincoln was honestly teaching the people to understand that non-convertible paper money created on the authority of the United States Government was *the only kind of currency that should be allowed.*

Bismarck knew the truth and revealed it in 1876 to a German, Conrad Siem. His statement was published in *La Vieille France,* Page 216, March, 1921. Bismarck said:

"The division of the United States into federations of equal force was decided long before the Civil War by the high financial powers of Europe. These bankers were afraid that the United States, if they remained in one block and as one nation, would attain economic and financial independence, which would upset their financial domination over the world. The voice of the Rothschilds predominated. They foresaw tremendous booty if they could substitute two feeble democracies, indebted to the financiers, for the vigorous Republic, which was practically self providing. Therefore, they started their emissaries in order to exploit the question of slavery and thus to dig an abyss between the two parts of the Republic. *Lincoln never suspected these underground machinations.* He was against slavery, and he was elected as such. His character prevented him from being the man of one party. When he had affairs in his hands, he perceived that these sinister financiers of Europe wished to make him the executor of their designs. *They made the rupture between the North and the South imminent.* The masters of finance in Europe made the rupture to exploit. Lincoln's personality surprised them. His being a candidate had not troubled them; they thought to easily dupe the wood-cutter. But Lincoln read their plots and understood, that the South was not the worst foe, but the financiers."

Lincoln did not confide his apprehensions but he watched the gestures—He decided to eliminate the secret money power by establishing a system of money such as the Constitution had provided. He had not studied "finance," but his robust common sense revealed to him that the source of any nation's wealth resides in the natural resources and the work carried on in the nation.

Lincoln knew that the way to finance the Civil War was to have the United States Government itself issue non-cancellable United States currency but to issue it only in such amounts as corresponded with the nation's ability to produce the actual physical things needed to conduct the war. Lincoln made one issue of $150,000,000 of United States currency. But when the time came to issue more, to pay for war materials, the international financiers had succeeded in ruling Congress. The new issue of United

States currency carried a restricting clause; "it was not legal tender for the payment of taxes or import duties." This restricted these United States notes and since they were not good for all purposes for which money was used, it was not in reality full legal tender. This move prevented Lincoln from financing the Civil War in an honest constitutional manner.

After the War, Lincoln was determined to set up a Constitutional Money System; for he realized the ultimate fate of the Nation if foreign bankers were permitted to dominate the country. Bismarck made the following statement regarding the death of Lincoln:

"The death of Lincoln was a disaster for Christendom. There was no man in the United States great enough to wear his boots, and . . . (money creators) went anew to grab the riches of the world. I fear that foreign bankers with their craftiness and tortuous tricks will entirely control the exuberant riches of America, and use it to systematically corrupt modern civilization. They will not hesitate to plunge the whole of Christendom into wars and chaos in order that the earth should become their inheritance."

Horace Greeley wrote in 1872 his opinion of the National Bank Act. These are his words:

"We have stricken the shackles from four million human beings and brought all laborers to a common level, not so much by the elevation of the former slaves as by practically reducing the whole working population, white and black, to a condition of serfdom. While boasting of our noble deeds, we are careful to conceal the ugly fact that by our iniquitous money system we have nationalized a system of oppression which, though more refined, is not less cruel than the old system of chattel slavery."

London Bankers Expressed Fear That United States Would Establish a Constitutional Money System

At the time Abraham Lincoln was struggling to thwart the vicious schemes of foreign bankers and set up a money system, as the Constitution of the United States provided, London international banker-controlled newspapers were expressing great fear. The fear was that the United States would establish an honest money system and be forever free from the clutches of the International Bankers. The following is taken from the London Times:

"If that mischievous financial policy, which had its origin in the North American Republic during the late war in that country, should become indurated down to a fixture, then that Government will furnish its own money without cost. It will pay off its debts and be without a debt. It will have all the money necessary to carry on its commerce. *It will become prosperous beyond precedent in the history of the civilized governments of the world.* The brains and the wealth of all countries will go to North America. That government must be destroyed or it will destroy every monarchy on the globe."

Please note their clever appeal to the monarchs, their debtors.

The fear of London bankers was that the United States Government would "furnish its own money without cost." That policy would enable the people of the United States "to carry on their own commerce" and "become prosperous beyond precedent in the history of the civilized governments of the world." Think of the sagacity and wisdom of the founders of this nation to provide for a really scientific and honest money system! London had to admit its value to America. Then think of the incautious, nay foolish confession of the British Bankers, through the London Times in the previous paragraph. Could we wish for a better testimonial to the efficacy of the "greenback" ("Fiat money," "Printing Press money") than that furnished by its very enemies?

This was the financial policy, the *effect* of which the London Times pointed out so forcefully, so accurately, and so correctly, that was advocated by Abraham Lincoln. Abraham Lincoln was determined to set up an honest money system and allow the people of the United States, particularly the workers, to enjoy the great benefits which this Nation is capable of offering to every sincere individual.

Had the money system which Lincoln demanded, and which was provided for in the Constitution of the United States, been established, no other country would have been able to maintain a dishonest money system for the simple reason that the peoples of other nations would have seen the great blessings flowing from it; and one nation after another would have cast off the ancient shackles of the private money manipulators.

Government money being non-cancellable, except by the Government itself under proper circumstances, there would be no such thing as mysterious business depressions caused by deliberate and vicious private money cancellation. Business depressions are nothing but the result of private individuals secretly cutting down the supply of money in a nation. When they cut down the supply, prices fall. When that happens they are able to foreclose and scoop in honest men's properties and force laborers into bread lines.

How Silver Was Demonetized in the United States in 1873

Meyer Amschel (Rothschild) had instructed his five sons to induce all countries to adopt *gold* as the single basis for money. In 1818 England demonetized silver. Both gold and silver were originally equally important parts of the money base of England. The very term "pound sterling" referred to silver. As soon as England, through wars, had acquired control of a substantial part of the world's basic sources of gold (mines), silver was demonetized. The reason for demonetizing silver was that other nations controlled a larger amount of the natural silver resources than did England. Once England had established a single gold standard, every possible effort and untold intrigue were used to force other countries to abandon silver as a part of their monetary base.

As a result of the Civil War debt to London, and upon the death of Lincoln, foreign bankers were able to get the United States in their clutches. Their next step, to insure their being able to control the United States, was to demonetize silver. One of the reasons why the United States should never have demonetized silver—as long as it maintained any metal base—is that we have within our own borders some of the greatest silver deposits in the world. Think of it! We abandoned the metal which we possessed and started to acquire a metal, the major part of which England had and held or controlled.

The Constitution of the United States was adopted in 1789. From then until 1873, both gold and silver were equally important as a money base in the United States. Today we are told that a bi-metallic base never "worked."

The act of demonetizing silver was entitled "*An Act Revising and Amending the Law as Relative to the Mints, Assay Offices and Coinage of the United States.*" This Bill was signed by President Grant and eight months later, in a letter dated October 3, 1873, he admitted that he did not understand that the Bill he signed had demonetized silver. That Bill had been *written in London* under the direction of the private money power and a Mr. Ernest Seyd had been sent by them to the United States with $500,000 to aid him in accomplishing his purpose. His methods were effective. Most of the Senators and Representatives in Congress whose votes legalized the demonetizing act, like the President, were innocent of any intention of destroying silver as a part of the monetary base. Any one who cares to carry on the investigation to verify these statements should examine the Congressional Record.

The following quotations are taken from *The Evolution of Banking,* by Robert H. Howe:

"On December 16, 1872, a bill relating to mints, assay offices and coinage was reported to the House from the Senate by Sherman. It had been prepared two years before by the agent of the foreign bankers, the New York Chamber of Commerce, and John J. Knox — who was the Comptroller of the Currency. It provided for a thorough change in our silver coinage; on the plea of equalizing it with that of France. Sherman said the bill had passed the Senate at the last session, and he proposed to modify only a single section. He wished the Senate to pass it without reading. Senator Casserly of California opposed the bill. It was ordered printed and read. When it was put upon its passage in the Senate, January 17, 1873, Sherman added seventeen amendments instead of one. The House disagreed with his amendments; he then moved a conference committee of which he was the head, and, while the bill was being considered by the committee, he introduced the following amendment which was passed: 'That any owner of silver bullion may deposit the same at any mint, to be formed into bars or into dollars of 420 grains Troy, designated as trade dollars, *and no deposit of silver for other coinage shall be received.*'

"These few words abolished the coinage of the old 412½ grain silver dollar by merely omitting that coin from the enumeration of the coins of the United States. It was entitled 'An act revising and amending the laws relative to the mints, assay offices and coinage of the United States,' and bore on its face no suggestion of any change more serious than that of regulating the petty details of mint management.

"While the bill was under consideration in the House, except a mere allusion by Mr. Hooper and Mr. Potter, there is not a single word in the discussion that took place, then or afterward, in the House or in the Senate, indicating that anybody understood that a change was to be made in the standard of value in the United States. The discussion that took place pertained to other matters, such as minor coins, and whether the eagle should be retained on fractional silver pieces or not, etc.

"This law created the *trade dollar,* but limited its legal tender power to any sum not exceeding five dollars in any one payment. Even this slight legal tender power was abolished by an act July 13, 1876, which provided 'that the dollar shall not hereafter be legal tender.'

"As to whether the Congressmen and Senators who voted to pass the bill were ignorant as to the effect its passage would have on the coinage or not, the following quotations ought to set the matter at rest.

"Extract from speech by Hon. W. D. Kelly, Chairman of the Committee on Coinage, made in the House of Congress, March 9, 1878. 'In connection with the charge that I advocated the bill which demonetized the standard silver dollar, I say that, though Chairman of the Committee on Coinage, I was as ignorant of the fact that it would demonetize the silver dollar, or of its dropping the silver from our system of coins, as were those distinguished Senators, Messrs. Blaine and Voorhies, who were then members of the House, and each of whom, a few days since, interrogated the other: "Did you know it was dropped when the bill was passed?" "No," said Mr. Blaine; "did you?" "No," said Mr. Voorhies. "I do not think that there were three members of the House that knew it. I doubt whether Mr. Hooper, who in my absence from the Committee on Coinage, and attendance on the Committee of Ways and Means, managed the bill, knew it. I say this in justice to him."' (Congressional Record, volume 7, part 2, Forty-fifth Congress, second session, page 1605.)

"Extract from speech delivered in the House of Representatives by Mr. Holman, July 13, 1876: 'I have before me the record of the proceedings of the House on the passage of that measure, a record which no man can read without being convinced that the measure and the method of its passage through this House was a "Colossal Swindle." I assert that the measure never had the sanction of this House and did not possess the moral force of law.' (Congressional Record, volume 4, part 6, Forty-fourth Congress, first session, appendix, page 193.)

"Again on August 5, 1876, he said: 'The original bill was simply a bill to organize a bureau of mines and coinage. The bill which finally passed the House and ultimately became a law was certainly not read in this House. It was never considered before this House as it was passed. Up to the time the bill came before this House for final passage, the measure had simply been one to establish a bureau of mines. It came from the Committee on Coinage, Weights and Measures.

" 'The substitute which finally became a law was never read, and is subject to the charge made against it by the gentleman from Missouri (Mr. Bland) that it was passed by the House without a knowledge of its provisions, especially upon that of coinage.

" 'I myself asked the question of Mr. Hooper whether it changed the law in regard to coinage, and the answer of Mr. Hooper left the impression on the whole House that the subject of the coinage was not affected by the bill.' (Congressional Record, volume 4, part 6, Forty-fourth Congress, first session, page 5237.)

"Senator Conkling, in the Senate, March 30, 1876, during the remarks of Senator Bogy on the bill (S. 264) to amend the laws relating to the legal tender of silver coin, in surprise, inquired: 'Will the Senator allow me to ask him or some other Senator a question? Is it true that there is now by law no American dollar?'

"Mr. Bright, of Tennessee, said of the law: 'It passed by fraud in the House, never having been printed in advance, being a substitute for the printed bill, never having been read at the clerk's desk, the reading having been dispensed with by an impression that the bill made no material alteration in the coinage laws, it was passed without discussion, debate having been cut off by operation of the previous question. It was passed, to my certain information, under such circumstances that the fraud escaped the attention of some of the most watchful as well as the ablest statesmen in Congress at the time.' (Congressional Record, volume 7, part 1, second session, Forty-fifth Congress, page 584.)

"General Garfield, in a speech made at Springfield, Ohio, during the fall of 1877, said: 'Perhaps I ought to be ashamed to say so, but it is the truth to say that at the time being Chairman of the Committee on Appropriation, and having my hands over full during all that time with work, I never read the bill. I took it upon the faith of a prominent Democrat and a prominent Republican, and I do not know that I voted at all. There was no demand for the yeas and nays, and no one opposed the bill that I know of. It was put through as dozens of bills are, as my friends and I know, in Congress and on the faith of the report of the Chairman of Committee.'

"Senator Allison said on February 15, 1878: 'But when the secret history of this bill of 1873 comes to be told, it will disclose the fact that the House of Representatives intended to coin both gold and silver, and intended to place both metals on the French relation instead of on our own, which was the true scientific position with reference to this subject in 1873, but that the bill afterward was doctored.' (Congressional Record, volume 7, part 2, Forty-fifth Congress, second session, page 1058.)

"Senator Beck, in a speech made in the Senate, January 10, 1878, said: 'It (the bill demonetizing silver) never was understood by either House of Congress, I say that with full knowledge of the facts. No newspaper reporter — and they are the most vigorous men I ever saw in obtaining information — discovered that it had been done.' (Congressional Record, volume 7, part 1, Forty-fifth Congress, second session, page 260.)

"Mr. Thurman said: 'I cannot say what took

place in the House, but I know when the bill was pending in the Senate, we thought it was simply a bill to reform the mint, regulate coinage, and fix up one thing and another, and there is not a single man in the Senate, I think, unless a member of the Committee from which the bill came, who had the slightest idea that it was even a squint toward demonetization.'

"Here we certainly have a strange state of facts to explain. The whole of official Washington, from President down through the Cabinet, Senate, House of Representatives, officials of the mint, newspaper reporters and correspondents appear to have been totally ignorant of the passage of a bill that abolished the coinage of the silver dollar, which had been coined continuously since 1792."

The following is an affidavit made by a gentleman who knew Mr. Ernest Seyd of London personally. The affidavit speaks for itself:

STATE OF COLORADO }
COUNTY OF ARAPAHOE } ss.

Frederick A. Luckenbach, being first duly sworn on oath, deposes and says: I am 62 years of age. I was born in Bucks County, Pennsylvania. I removed to the City of Philadelphia in the year 1846, and continued to reside there until 1866, when I removed to the City of New York. In Philadelphia I was in the furniture business; in New York I branched into machinery and inventions and am the patentee of Luckenbach's Pneumatic Pulverizer, which machines are now in use generally in the eastern part of the United States and in Europe. I now reside in Denver, having removed there from New York two years ago. I am well known in New York. I have been a member of the Produce Exchange and am well acquainted with many members of that body. I am well known by Erastus Wyman.

In the year 1865 I visited London, England, for the purpose of placing there Pennsylvania Oil properties in which I was interested. I took with me letters of introduction to many gentlemen in London — among them, one to Mr. Ernest Seyd from Robert M. Foust, ex-Treasurer of Philadelphia. I became well acquainted with Mr. Seyd and, with his brother, Richard Seyd, who I understand is yet living. I visited London thereafter every year and at each visit renewed my acquaintance with Mr. Seyd, and upon each occasion became his guest one or more times — joining his family at dinner or other meals.

In February 1874, while on one of these visits and while his guest for dinner, I, among other things, alluded to rumors afloat of Parliamentary Corruption and expressed astonishment that such corruption should exist. In reply to this, he told me he could relate facts about the corruption of the American Congress that would place it far ahead of the English Parliament in that line, so far the conversation was at the dinner table between us. His brother Richard and others were there also, but this was table-talk between Mr. Ernest Seyd and myself. After the dinner ended, he invited me to another room where he resumed the conversation about legislative corruption. He said: "If you will pledge me your honor as a gentleman not to divulge what I am about to tell while I live, I will convince you, that what I said about the corruption of the American Congress is true." I gave him the promise and he then continued, "I went to America in the winter of 1872-1873 authorized to secure, if I could, the passage of a bill demonetizing silver as it was to the interest of those I represented — the Governors of the Bank of

England — to have it done. I took with me £100,000 Sterling, with instructions that if that was not sufficient to accomplish the object, to draw for another £100,000 or as much more as was necessary." He told me German Bankers were also interested in having it accomplished. He said he was the financial advisor of the Bank. He said: "I saw the Committees of the House and Senate and paid the money and stayed in America until I knew the measure was safe." I asked him if he would give me the names of the Members to whom he paid the money — but this he declined to do. He said, "*Your people will not now comprehend the far-reaching extent of that measure — but they will in after years.* Whatever you may think of corruption in the English Parliament, I assure you I would not have dared to make such an attempt here as I did in your country." I expressed my shame to him for my Countrymen in our Legislative Bodies. The conversation drifted into other subjects, and after that — though I met him many times — the matter was never referred to again.

(Signed) FREDERICK A. LUCKENBACH.

Subscribed and sworn to before me at Denver, this 9th day of May, 1892.

(Signed) JAMES A. MILLER,
Clerk, Supreme Court, State of Colorado.

The Congressional Record of April, 1872, page 2032, says:

"Ernest Seyd, of London, a distinguished writer and bullionist, *who is now here,* has given great attention to the subject of mint and coinage. After having *examined* the *first draft of the bill,* he made sensible suggestions which the Committee adopted and embodied in the bill."

The Bankers' Magazine, August 1873, says:

"In 1872, silver being demonetized in France, England and Holland, a capital of $500,000 was raised and Ernest Seyd, of London, was sent to this country with this fund, as the agent of foreign bondholders and capitalists, to effect the same object here, which was accomplished."

The Battle Continued!

The result of the demonetization of silver was such a curtailment in the volume of money in the nation that a terrible depression, lasting several years, was suffered. Senator Ferry of Michigan made the following statement regarding the panic of 1873:

"Millions of people were reduced from good circumstances to penury, or covered with debt, beneath which burden their backs must bend until it is unloaded at the grave, where an innocent posterity must take it up and bear it on."

President Grant admitted before his death that he had been misled in allowing the silver demonetization bill to become law.

The following is a direct quotation from a Resolution introduced to the 63rd Congress by Hon. Charles A. Lindbergh, Sr.:

"In eighteen hundred and seventy-seven, a circular was issued by authority of the Associated Bankers of New York, Philadelphia and Boston. It was signed by one James Buel, Secretary, and was sent out from two hundred and forty-seven Broadway, New York. It was sent to the bankers in all of the States. It read:

> " 'Dear Sir:—It is advisable to do all in your power to sustain such prominent daily and weekly newspapers, especially the Agricultural and Religious Press, as will oppose the greenback is-

sue of paper money, and that you also withhold patronage from all applicants who are not willing to oppose the government issue of money. Let the government issue the coin and the banks issue the paper money of the country, for then we can better protect each other. To repeal the act creating bank notes, or to restore to circulation the government issue of money, *will be to provide the people with money and will therefore seriously affect our individual profit as bankers and lenders.* See your Congressman at once and engage him to support our interests that we may control legislation.' "

Three years after the demonetizing act the general assembly of Ohio demanded that silver be restored as a part of the monetary base. On December 6, 1877, a resolution was introduced in the Senate of the United States and passed by nearly two-thirds majority, after eight weeks of stubborn opposition by the gold party.

The same resolution was passed in the House of Representatives on January 28, 1878. The Bland Allison Act finally passed the Senate on February 28, 1878. It was vetoed by President Hayes, but again passed both Houses and became law. This act provided for the exchange of two to four million dollars per month of United States silver certificates (paper money) for silver bullion. This insured a supply of real money without creating an interest burden. It was an honest method of increasing the money supply. The total silver purchased under the act by the United States Treasury, amounted to about three hundred and seventy-eight million dollars. For twelve years the Bland Silver Law continued in force, during all of which time the gold crowd were doing everything possible to again bring about the demonetization of silver.

The Bland Allison Silver Law was superseded by the Sherman Silver Bill of 1890. The Sherman Act authorized purchase of silver up to 4½ million ounces per month. Through intrigue there was incorporated in the Sherman Bill a provision which made the certificates issued in payment for the silver metal, bought under the provisions of the act, *redeemable in gold*. The cunning internationalists had deliberately incorporated this gold redemption feature in the certificates issued in payment for silver bullion, to be able to disturb the proper relationship as between the gold and silver base in the banking system. It was ridiculous to make those certificates issued in payment for silver bullion redeemable in gold. After this intentional distortion the American people were told that silver had failed in its proper use as a part of the primary money base. The Sherman Silver Bill had been in force only three years when, in 1893, it was repealed. The panic of 1893 followed, because money again became scarce—the accordion was collapsed — and our proper relationships with other natural silver countries were disturbed.

When legislation had to be secured, all manner of dishonorable means were used to *curtail the supply* of money. Just one week after President Cleveland was inaugurated, the "Panic Circular" was issued March 12, 1893. It appealed to the bondholding classes to "advocate an extra session of Congress for the repeal unconditionally of the Sherman Silver Law." It was issued directly from the American Bankers' Association and addressed to all "National" banks throughout the United States.

The following is a direct quotation from a Resolution introduced to the 63rd Congress, First Session, April 29, 1913, by Hon. Charles A. Lindbergh, Sr.:

"In eighteen hundred and ninety-three, a circular was sent out by the American Bankers' Association, an organization in which most bankers hold membership. It is known as the 'Panic circular of eighteen hundred and ninety-three,' bears date March eleventh, eighteen hundred and ninety-three, and was *mailed* to the national banks. It read as follows:

> " 'Dear Sir:—The interests of national banks require immediate financial legislation by Congress. Silver, silver certificates, and Treasury notes must be retired, and National Bank Notes upon a gold basis (the phrase gold basis always means a debt basis) made the only money. This will require the authorization of $500,000,000 to $1,000,000,000 of new bonds (debts) as the basis of circulation. *You will at once retire one-third of your circulation* (your paper money) *and call in one-half of your loans. Be careful to make a monetary stringency among your patrons, especially among influential business men.* Advocate an extra session of Congress to repeal the purchasing clause of the Sherman Law, and act with other banks of your city in securing a large petition to Congress for its unconditional repeal per accompanying form. Use personal influence with your Congressmen and *particularly let your wishes be known to your senators.* The future life of national banks, as fixed and safe investments, depends upon immediate action, as there is an increasing sentiment in favor of government legal-tender notes and silver coinage.' "

It was an undisputed fact that silver, silver certificates, and United States Government legal tender currency had proven very desirable as money since 1878. In the summer of 1893 the American Congress convened in extra session for the very purpose of violating the confidence and the will of the United States. Every one knows that the result was another severe depression.

The following is an excerpt from a confidential bankers' circular issued two years prior to the Panic Circular of 1893:

> "We authorize our loan agents in the western States to loan our funds on real estate to fall due on September 1, 1894, and at no time thereafter. On September 1, 1894, we will not renew our loans under any consideration. On September 1st we will demand our money. We will foreclose and become mortgagees in possession. We can take two-thirds of the farms west of the Mississippi, and thousands of them east of the great Mississippi as well, at our own price . . . We may as well own three-fourths of the farms of the West *and the money* of the country. Then the farmers will become tenants as in England. After September 1st, the interest we receive on coupons will be accumulated. We will not lend any of our funds after that date, as we can make more money by withholding our interest income."

The Gold Clause

After the battle over the dishonest demonetization of silver in the United States had subsided, the international connivers succeeded in passing the so-called Gold Standard Bill. This bill was approved on March 14, 1900. (See United States Statutes at Large, 56th Congress, Session I.)

Under the terms of this bill, unconstitutional in fact, Congress supposedly gave to the United States Treasury itself, and to private individuals, the right to make gold dollar contracts calling for the payment of dollars at future dates, each dollar of which was convertible into 25.8 grains of gold .9 fine.

The falsifiers stated that a dollar consisting of 25.8 grains of gold .9 fine was, henceforth, the standard of value. Thus recently was born "our good old *traditional* gold standard."

Under the banking laws, any private individual could bring gold into the United States, or take gold out of the United States, and hence, at his pleasure, change the volume of gold within this country. Each gold dollar could also be used as a so-called base upon which to build a pyramid of many bank manufactured dollars.

By manipulating the volume of bank manufactured dollars, the actual purchasing power of every dollar in the United States could be altered at the pleasure of a few individuals. Each of these bank manufactured dollars would buy one bushel of wheat, or one-third of a bushel of wheat: one laboring man's shirt or perhaps one-third of a laboring man's shirt, *depending* upon the pleasure of those who could manipulate the volume.

Imagine saying that so many grains of gold constituted a standard of value when as of different dates the currency exchangeable for those grains of gold would vary in its exchangeability for physical goods, according as gold would be added to or withdrawn from the bank reserves.

Human beings do not consume gold. They consume goods. If the dollars returned under a contract will buy relatively as much physical goods as the dollars loaned would have bought, there can be no grounds for a lender contending he has been cheated because he cannot obtain a certain number of grains of gold. Gold is not essential to life.

All contracts involving money payments should call for dollars which are United States legal tender. Conversion into gold was never intended as other than a part of the necessary mechanism for international manipulations. The United States Congress, under the Constitution, has the *sole right* to say what shall be money, and what volume of money shall exist. Neither the United States Government nor any private individual has any right to make any contract binding either the United States Government or a private individual to repay dollars convertible into a specified number of grains of gold. Whatever is legal tender at the time of payment is all that could be humanly and legally used *by the debtor.*

The present agitation (1935) over the gold clause is to create a smoke-screen which, if the people remain deceived, will permit connivers to steal $69.00 for every $100.00 they have in so-called gold contract bonds. Now that they have returned their balances from Europe, through the operations of the "Stabilization" Fund, it is very likely they have placed those balances in United States Government Bonds, and are at present attempting to steal a $69.00 premium for every $100.00 so invested in Government Bonds.

The main reason a so-called fixed conversion of currency dollars into gold was ever set up, was to enable the London gold jugglers to change the currency price of gold arbitrarily in other countries while the price in the United States remained constant.

The "Federal" Reserve System

The panic of 1907 came like a clap of thunder. On the whole, the bankers of the nation, outside of a very small group, seemed to have no hint of the oncoming catastrophe. It is evident that those who created this money stringency deliberately forced this panic upon innocent people. Money was as high as 50% on the floor of the New York Stock Exchange. New York banks refused to honor interior banks' drafts—drafts on their own deposits in those New York banks. Anything and everything was done to tie up the medium of exchange.

With this setting Senator Aldrich, who was at that time sponsoring what later became the Federal Reserve Bank law, started on a tour of the West to tell the American people the benefits of a proposed Reserve Bank. When it became known that the National Bankers' Association favored the Aldrich plan, the farmers and small merchants arose to oppose the Bill. The plan was rewritten and some additions made. The new Bill was known as the Owen-Glass Bill (Federal Reserve Bank Bill). The Bill, approved by the Senate Committee, contained *mandatory provisions* that the Federal Reserve Board see that the price levels were *kept stable. In the House of Representatives this mandatory provision of such far-reaching importance, was stricken out, thereby changing the entire nature and intention of the Act.*

The sponsors of the original Bill in the Senate fought vigorously to have the mandatory provision restored, but they were unable to accomplish their purpose. (See Foreword, by Senator Owen)

The following excerpts from Mr. Paul M. Warburg's own writings indicate that he did a great deal to bring about the passage of the Federal Reserve Act in its final form.

"I do not claim to have originated any new banking principle; but from my arrival in America I have been impelled to urge the adoption of the fundamental principles upon which, under varying forms, were based the practices of every industrially advanced country except the United States. It was owing to the interest I had shown in banking reform that, when the Aldrich Banking & Currency Committee was appointed, I was invited to assist it in formulating a plan providing for the creation of a Central Reserve Association with regional branches." *The Federal Reserve System, Its Origin and Growth* —p. 8.

Mr. Edwin R. A. Seligman, in his introductory remarks of August 1914 to *Essays on Banking Reform in the United States,* by Paul M. Warburg, says:

"For it may be stated without fear of contradiction that in its fundamental features the Federal Reserve Act is the work of Mr. Warburg more than of any other man in the country."

Page 39—"The Currency Committee of the Merchants of New York in a letter dated July 27, 1910, recognizes as Paul M. Warburg's plan the proposed United Reserve Bank (presumably the embryonic name of the Banking Reform), which was *to end all currency famines and money panics, and relieve the national treasury of all responsibility* for the money market, international exchanges and movements of gold."

The relief has been most successful—everybody of everything. Are we to be relieved of our Constitutional Representative Government next?

Mr. Warburg did not tell the American people that the privately owned Central Banks of England, France and Germany were the result of long years of conniving on the part of international money controllers. He did not relate the following facts so honestly told by Huskinson, a famous Briton: "The

'Industrial Revolution,' as it is called, that crowded our industries into factories, is doubtless the spawn of the illicit connection of Government with the 'old harlot of Threadneedle Street' (Bank of England) . . .

". . . In the meantime, several eminent bankers had noticed that every crash was *preceded* by the Bank of England's action on credit in order to strengthen its position. It was seen that the duty of turning the exchanges to bring in bullion rested with the Bank of England alone. The sufferings of the people were not the result of positive fault or mismanagement; but at intervals a natural consequence of the vicious constitution of the Bank of England Charter . . . That the constitution was artificial and that the energies and trade of the whole country could be paralyzed without any reference to the state of the circulation was discovered by a shopkeeper. This man brought about a political crisis. Huskisson (a member of Parliament) had expressed his intention of raising his old demand for clearing off the Government debt to the Bank on the renewal of its charter in 1833 . . . *Huskisson's tragic death prevented his design.* It is curious how the evil fates appear to fight for an evil principle; whenever this question appeared ripe for settlement, when the attention even of the vulgar was directed toward it, some war would intervene, a Ministry would fall, a Parliament expire, or a statesman with the requisite knowledge would die. The attention of the public would then be diverted either by excitement or by the plausible promises of political quackery." *The Bank of England's Charters — the Cause of our Social Distress,* T. W. Huskinson, Page 48.

The foregoing quotations tell some of the facts that the Money Powers neglected to tell the American people regarding the "blessings" of the privately owned central banks of Europe.

In 1844 the Bank Act of England provided that the volume of currency (bill fold money) should vary with the foreign exchanges. In other words, as gold moved out of England, currency would be curtailed. This same type of law was put into effect at the Reichsbank immediately following the Franco-Prussian War in 1870. At that time Germany demonetized silver and tied the rope of a central banking system, based upon the same principles as the Bank of England, around the throats of the real producers of Germany's wealth—the industrialists, the farmers and the laborers.

The International Money Power controlled billions in *liquid* funds, by means of which they could cause gold to flow between nations at will; and, with the aid of these vicious monetary laws, create constant or periodic economic turmoil.

The Federal Reserve Act as passed and later amended and administered was a serious mistake. It turned over to the international bankers complete control over the banking system of this country and, hence, over all business. It was the central control of the credit in the entire nation that resulted in the rapid concentration of ownership in all lines of business. This system is enslaving the unfortunate individuals who are forced to earn their living by being a part of an organization operated from a distant city. These slaves should be liberated for better positions, impossible under our present money system.

Had the money control of this country never been centralized, and had it not been turned over to exploiters, the terrible concentration of control and ownership of wealth could never have been brought about. Some boastfully tell of their "superior business acumen." They say nothing of their control over the money in the nation. There is absolutely no hope of the United States restoring this country to a condition wherein worthy Americans can earn a living in permanent security *unless* the power to create money is restored where it belongs—to the Congress of the United States.

No private individual should ever be allowed the privilege and power of creating and recalling money at will. An individual who counterfeited a few dimes would be sent to the penitentiary and rightfully so, but what about bankers who are given unconstitutional powers to create vast sums of their privately created money and lend it at interest to the United States Government itself? Could anything be more stupid than to permit such a system to continue?

Mr. American! Are any logical suspicions running through your mind, based on the fact that neither in High School, Business School, Correspondence School, College nor University were you ever acquainted with this factual history of American Monetary affairs? Picture the millions it has cost somebody to "persuade" somebody else to omit the truth and substitute a tissue of plausible falsehoods therefor!

Why the International Bankers in 1935 do Not Want Silver Restored as an Important Part of the Monetary Base of the United States

If every important country maintains gold as the single base for its money, and retains a collapsible banking structure, the size of which is dependent upon the size of the gold base, the international bankers can continue to control and manipulate the international flow of gold and, hence, the price levels of the nations—thereby controlling the nations.

As was explained before, with gold the single monetary base, the price of an ounce of gold in London and the size of the gold base in any country, determine both directly and indirectly the price of all raw materials which enter the world markets—because London, under the present money system control, is the world's gold pricing center. When international bankers at London are able to establish the price of an ounce of gold and also determine what gold shall come into or go out of the United States, they are setting the price at which we can sell all raw materials in international markets and at home.

Is it any wonder to the thinking American that the international controllers of London and Paris are ready to resort to any means to prevent silver, which London could *not* control, being restored as an important medium in settling international balances?

As was stated previously, after England had secured control of the world's basic sources of gold (mines), her international financiers were determined to force the United States to stop using silver as a part of the money base. They could not control the United States if silver constituted an important part of the primary money (base) of the United States. Today the battle still rages to prevent the use of silver in an important way.

Many propagandists for international interests have for many years deceitfully told the people of the United States that the United States could not *safely* restore silver as a part of its money base.

Actually, the United States could and should set up a domestic money structure, without either gold or silver as a base, but in the *settlement of international balances* it would be a tremendous advantage, particularly to the United States, to use both gold and silver.

The South American countries are natural silver countries. India and the Far East would also be tremendously benefited if silver could be used as an important medium in settling international balances with the United States. India has always used silver for money domestically. Until 1926 India was also on a silver basis in the settlement of her international balances through London. In 1926, after the "experts" had pronounced its doom, India was put on a gold exchange basis.

This move resulted in the sale of large quantities of silver and of course had the effect of causing a terrible drop in the price of silver. It was predicted by Mr. Montagu Norman, Governor of the Bank of England, what the results in the gold-standard countries would be, if this policy were carried out: "There is (he said) a reaction upon gold prices where an extreme rise or fall takes place in the value of silver, *which is none the less serious because it is indirect and not very apparent on the surface.*

"The consequential changes in prices generally and in trade conditions, which would be produced, the disturbance to the world's economic peace and confidence, . . . the shock to the reliance of a great country like China upon silver as a medium of currency and a common store of value, could not fail to have important effects upon the gold prices of countries in Europe and indeed in America."

The importance of silver in controlling depressions is here made clear. This "interaction between gold and silver" is a power to be controlled. Who will control it? The International Bankers or the Congress of the United States?

The people of the United States have been told

that silver bullion would overwhelm us if we used it, at no fixed price, for settling international trade balances. *Such statements are untrue.* For 57 years silver has been produced at the rate of approximately 13.6 times the amount of gold produced throughout the world. There have been times, particularly during the World War, when silver prices rose substantially, yet, the ratio of silver production to gold did not increase materially.

Until other nations realize that no metal is necessary as "backing" for *lawful* money we could promote world trade by using silver as a commodity at no fixed price to settle foreign trade balances. Such a free silver market would break internationalists' manipulative powers, provided all money were *lawful* and divorced from all metals.

Much propaganda has spread from Washington relative to the Silver Purchase Act of 1934, whereby "the Secretary of the Treasury may purchase silver at a price not in excess of 50 cents per fine ounce until the monetary value of the stocks of silver is greater than 25 percent of the monetary value of stocks of gold and silver". Note the word is *may*, not *must*.

To January 1, 1937, silver purchases paid for with silver certificates have been trifling (about $300 millions) and were made for reasons other than publicized by Washington "experts". Like *all* other New Deal monetary legislation this act made *no attack* on the false money system.

The real reason for the silver purchases was to provide a means for *quietly* increasing the supply of *lawful* money while perpetuating the fraud that sound money requires metal backing.

When all gold coins bearing the Sovereign Stamp were taken from the citizens, and melted into bars, there was *no lawful* money *except* silver coins, silver certificates and United States Notes amounting to *less than* $1.5 billions.

When silver bullion is purchased by the United States Government and *paid for* with paper silver certificates originated and *paid into use* by Congress, those silver certificates are lawful money . . . *lawful* because issued by Congress which has the *sole* right to exercise the sovereign power *to create* money. They *are money* paid into use and not promises-to-pay money, loaned into existence, as are bank credit and Federal Reserve Notes.

Obviously the *cost* of silver purchased with *new* issues of lawful money is the cost of engraving pieces of paper bearing the Sovereign Seal.

It is all important to see through the substitutions (promises-to-pay) now used as a medium for exchange. Bank *credit* is *not* money, it is a promise-to-pay money created by any bank which makes loans. Technically, this credit which the bank *creates to lend* is known as a deposit. This deposit is nothing but a bookkeeping entry. Bankers are *not* dealers in money. The objective of a banker is to create and lend that bank's own private credit and to buy money and debts from its customers by creating and lending its own credit (promises-to-pay) in exchange for customers' money and debts (secured by collateral).

A bank makes its huge profits by creating and issuing its own credit (promise-to-pay money) many times in excess of genuine deposits it receives from those who actually give up earnings by accepting in exchange a right of action against a bank. A bank depositor does *not* have money in the bank. He has merely a right to demand money. If he demands lawful *money,* he must be given, *not* Federal Reserve Notes (promises-to-pay), but *lawful money*.

In 1934, the New Deal Congress made Federal Reserve Notes, which are private promises-to-pay money, Legal Tender-currency that can be legally offered in payment of debt. Federal Reserve Notes are *not lawful* money, as is admitted on each note: — "This note . . . . . is redeemable in lawful money at the United States Treasury or at any Federal Reserve Bank," — a promise-to-pay money substituted for lawful money, and foisted upon the unsuspecting public.

Both the private appropriation of the Sovereign Power and the principle of originating the medium for exchange as loans must be corrected. The *Government* no more than private corporations can establish equitable average prices and maintain them constant so long as the medium for exchange comes into existence when *bank loans* are made (raises prices) and is cancelled out of existence when *bank loans* are repaid (lowers prices).

Transferring the ownership of the Federal Reserve Banks to the Government would in *no* way change the false principle of originating the necessary medium for exchange, as loans, but would only wrongfully enable it to control who might or might not borrow money, thereby destroying all private property rights, the very goal of Karl Marx and Nikolai Lenin.

Congress should originate and pay into use lawful money, not because a borrower is available, but *only* when *more* money is needed to distribute the existing goods and services at the price levels desired. Congress or no branch of the Federal Government should engage in *lending* that lawful U. S. money. Each State should charter *private banks* empowered *only* to accept lawful money as *demand* deposits or time deposits to be loaned.

We American people are going to do some simple, straight thinking before disaster overtakes us.

A Congress backed with strong public opinion, could enact a law which in ninety days from its passage (even considering passage over veto) could restore 75% of all unemployed to work; and in one year there would be no employable adults idle.

The experience of May, June and July 1933, when gold was merely finding a natural price, is but a sample of the real possibilities.

Will Americans Defend the Lives of Their Children?

How much longer will Americans allow themselves and their children to be financially and politically manipulated by a small group of money creators? That group will make our country and our civilization as ghastly as "Russia," unless every courageous loyal American arises and exerts his or her strength to put a stop to their machinations.

We often wonder why Americans, who idolize their children, appear to be unwilling or lack the courage to rescue them from immoral un-economic forces which are bringing destruction. Only deception could cause such lack of action.

Some newspapers have committed an intentional error in making Communism and Bolshevism synonymous terms; the former is an ideal, impossible of attainment until all people would learn to love one another. Bolshevism is camouflaged tyranny; this deliberate and unintelligent confusion of the public mind, if allowed to continue, will cause mobs to arise and destroy one another.

Informed Americans will forget usual partisan politics, for both Democrats and Republicans have, consciously or innocently, been tools; even as Socialist groups which give evidence of being alien-led and internationally financed.

The constitutions of all nations, save ours, are written around powers of private money issue which existed and controlled nations when those constitutions were drawn.

The Constitution of the United States *alone* places the money issue and money value regulation power in the hands of the people's *elected* representatives. America can now constitutionally lead the way out of the monetary slavery which is driving the world into Bolshevism and ultimate subjection by the great money power which seems to aspire to possess the earth.

Other nations must *first* effect constitutional changes, a task hopeless without a shining example to guide their determination. Revolt against private money issues will be fought with every weapon the privileged few can conceive: *but the battle must come.*

Federal Bonds may be sold down to low levels in order to terrify the people, but let them remember that the bonds will be paid off, in real cash, at par. The Stock, Bond and Commodity markets may experience raids, ordered by the money manipulators, but the enlightened American Public, secure in its decision based on common sense in forcing Congress to act, will take for its motto Farragut's immortal exclamation, "*Damn the torpedoes — go ahead!*"

CHAPTER XII

AN HONEST MONEY SYSTEM

THE ONLY HOPE FOR ECONOMIC SECURITY AND PEACE

A scientific money system such as the United States should establish — *must* establish, if we are to perpetuate in the United States of America the Republic founded to grant every citizen the inherent right to life, liberty, and the pursuit of happiness—is explained in this chapter.

A little reflection, and every one understands that wealth is physical, not psychological. Every one understands its properties. Statesmen must recognize that a money system, to function properly, must recognize the laws of physics, not misuse the laws of psychology. The total *quantity* of money in a nation should bear a scientific relation to the volume of consumer goods which the nation has produced and has available for distribution.

Today our money system is based upon debts (*bonds*), *and private bankers' promises-to-pay* (*loans*) and not upon the actual physical goods which we have and want to distribute. The volume of our medium of exchange can be and is expanded or contracted at the will of a few private individuals, without any relation to the actual physical goods which we can and want to produce and distribute. Furthermore, all but a very small part of our money carries an interest burden. Each penny of this *comes into existence* marked with the sign of debt and interest: a far different matter from lending it at interest by one who has acquired it for goods or services. One who so acquires it *does not create it.* Creating it to *lend* is *unsound,* but it is exactly what private groups called banks do today. *Creating* money should be the function of the Government. *Lending* money should be reserved for private individuals who lend real money that has been entrusted to them by private individuals who have earned it.

Creating money to lend into circulation is unsound and is simply public robbery on a grand scale, though "legal." How it was "legalized" is the story we have been telling.

The reader remembers how the strong room keeper, sub-rosa, started to issue receipts for non-existent metal and, through lending them, put them into circulation as money. As time passed, through subterfuge and the teaching of falsehoods, he and his descendants were able to get the dishonest and unscientific system legalized. In 1935 the strong room keeper's sub-rosa system is the principle upon which private individuals fraudulently, though legally, create money and, at their pleasure, destroy it to the ruination of the real producers of wealth.

As time passed, the descendants and apprentices of the original strong room keeper withdrew from local banking as commonly known, leaving that field to the ownership and *apparent* control of local people whom we know today as our domestic bankers. The direct descendants of the medieval strong room keeper concentrated on developing controls over all domestic bankers and engaged in what is commonly called "international banking." They had built fortunes upon many years of collecting interest upon their privately created money and cashing in on foreclosures when the volume of money was curtailed.

They sought profits far larger than possible in the small loan business of the ordinary banker. They engaged in the large loan business of domestic and *inter-*

national underwriting. Their firms acquired gigantic sums, which they kept largely in liquid form (bank balances), by means of which they could dictate the policies to the officers of the largest domestic banks, and by controlling the individuals entrusted with the power to manipulate great Central Banks, create periodic economic stress. By simply converting their large balances into gold, and moving gold from nation to nation, they could influence world price movements. They now had the super-power. The ordinary home city banker, due to their manipulations, lost control over the monetary quantity in his own community. He became a pawn.

Today our monetary system is not set up to be a medium for the exchange of goods. It is a medium of control—control of human beings in a far more inhuman manner than galley slaves were ever controlled at any time in the history of the world. Our money system enables a few unsocial people to control wage levels and to stop or start actual production whenever they please.

The creation of the medium of exchange by which every citizen is enabled to trade in his own services and goods is fundamentally a function of *every citizen*. For universal convenience, all citizens delegated this function, via the Constitution of the United States, to their representatives in the Congress. They did not authorize Congress, and have never authorized Congress, to redelegate this function, either to the Chief Executive or back to a few super-privileged citizens, who by law remained private entities not responsible to Congress or impeachable by Congress.

Establishing a money system recognizing the principles set forth in the Constitution of the United States and following the laws of physics, would be very simple. Every one could understand it.

Necessary Agency to be Established by Congress

Congress should appoint Trustees to carry out the mechanics of providing and maintaining a supply of money adequate to conduct private businesses at equitable price levels. These Trustees should make recommendations to Congress and then be guided solely by the mandates of Congress. The Trustees should in no way interfere with the commercial functions of the individual privately owned banks.

The Qualifications and Functions of the Trustees

1. An American-born citizen, with no past or present connections that would identify the individual or any of his blood relatives as an owner, partner, employee, or adviser of any international bank. An international banking house is any firm, partnership or corporation that has underwritten or sold foreign bonds of any kind, or has maintained foreign balances.

2. Each individual should have an unquestionable record for honesty and integrity. Individuals should have sufficient maturity and practical business experience to realize the grave importance of avoiding wide price gyrations. Service should include Americans who are at least 35 years of age. Their appointment should be for life, with privilege of retirement at 65, or earlier if adjudged incapacitated or for cause. Their compensation should be ample because of the ability and responsibility required for a proper discharge of their Trusteeship. That Trusteeship would intimately affect the life of *every* citizen.

3. These Monetary Trustees should maintain scientific records of prices—price indices which

would reliably indicate at what levels the *aggregate* of raw commodities and aggregate finished goods are changing hands at any particular time. Once raw material price levels had reached a point wherein the nation's productive and business activity had absorbed its unemployed, and the price structure was high enough to afford sufficient national income to carry the legitimate private debt structure of the nation, that price level should be maintained. The fluctuations thereafter should be minor, because the flow of money would always be scientifically related to the actual quantity of physical consumer goods available for distribution. The Government should *not* take any part in controlling prices of individual commodities or goods, but only take cognizance of the *General Averages*.

The result will be *not* a fluctuating dollar as the deceivers shout, but a *stable* dollar, as common sense proves. Stability means *constant purchasing power* of a dollar in terms of things people buy (not gold — did *you* ever buy gold?).

4. As the Nation increased its productive efficiency—was able to turn out more consumer goods per worker—the money stream would have to be increased. The amount of increase necessary would be judged entirely by the movement of prices. If goods were increasing in quantity, but the quantity of the money was lagging behind, prices would decline. Therefore the money quantity would be increased until that situation was corrected. Vice versa; if prices were rising beyond the points considered ample to equitably conduct the nation's business, the volume of currency would have to be decreased.

5. Increases in currency would be made partly to defray expenses of the Government and in lieu of taxation. In case it became necessary to curtail the volume of money, that could be done through taxa-

tion. Retirement via taxation would be easy because of high National income and general activity—little or no unemployment. When the taxes for this purpose were paid to the Government in the form of non-cancellable money, it would be retained in the possession of the United States Treasury for the account of the Monetary Trusteeship, and not reissued until such time as the volume of production and the price levels warranted such action.

The money for paying this so-called tax would always be in the hands of the people; and because it was levied by reason of excessive circulation the tax would not be a burden. *Only a decrease in the volume of consumer goods, due to famine or disaster, would necessitate a decrease in the volume of money.*

Reflection will show that retirement by taxation to control price rises, and reissue in lieu of taxes to control price declines, would be sensible, painless, and beneficial.

6. Individual banks must continue to be *privately owned and managed* but they should *no longer have the power to manufacture and cancel money* (now called expanding and contracting "credit"). They should be depositaries for and lenders of *real money*; should collect a fee for acting as a depositary for private citizens, and for performing all the non-monetary functions which banks now carry on. The basic difference would be that banks would no longer be able to *create* money and to *cancel* money. That prerogative would rest with the United States Government *alone*.

Money—the medium of exchange—would derive its value from its acceptability, as does all money. If the Government accepts it for tax payments at par, that establishes its acceptability, for the United States Government *is* of all the people.

But the power of private individuals to issue and recall money (credit) must be destroyed *forever.* To further centralize this power in one privately owned institution, or to Nationalize the banks—that is, to make money creating and money lending powers *both* a National function—should be *avoided* like the plague. Such type of "Nationalization" is now being advocated by the internationalists, the Socialists, their puppets, and a few sincere people. To Nationalize the banks and retain the *two* functions—money issuance and money lending—as the function of the State, would be *the final step toward turning America over to the Socialists.*

Socialization of banks (including bank-created money which no Socialist, Communist or Bolshevist has ever condemned) would be a fatal mistake. It would be turning over powers now held by many sincere private American bankers to international puppets. Socialism, as well as Bolshevism, is but a weapon of internationalists, to be discarded as soon as their objective is attained.

7. Gold and silver should be used only to settle international balances. They are not necessary as bases for the issuance of domestic money, and are not necessary for domestic exchanges of goods and services. Gold and silver could be used for settling trade balances until other nations have followed our example in revoking the privilege of private issue, and can agree with ourselves and each other on the establishment of an international currency used in settling trade balances. Until that is done silver should be given a more important place in settling international balances. There should be no such thing as international loans. The absurdity of international loans will vanish as other nations also learn to issue

their own currency. Meanwhile, Americans wishing to remove to other lands or climates can transfer their capital in American goods or in money of the country of destination. Arrangements could be made by the United States Government for the transfer of legitimate amounts of money for travel and for reasonable disbursements to dependent relatives in other countries.

The domestic volume of money should not be influenced in any manner whatsoever by international transactions. It is suggested that both gold and silver be used to settle international balances solely because if the United States would restore silver as a part of the medium used in settling international balances, it would destroy the vicious gold control of the internationalists. It would enable the natural silver countries such as South America and India, to trade with the United States. It would be a tremendous benefit to these countries and would help them to get out from under the yoke of the international bankers. China uses silver domestically. China is an importer of silver. The fact that the United States remonetized silver, that is, made it a part of the medium used in settling international balances, would actually benefit China, contrary to all of the false statements by "chinese" (internationalist) unnamed "experts." They have published widespread accounts of China's predicament if the United States were to remonetize silver. Some are *so* concerned about others when it inures to their own benefit. (See Chapter XI)

8. The National Monetary Trustees would be required to file for publication, once a month, an intelligible and easily understood report, which would indicate exactly how much currency was outstanding as of that date. In each Presidential term—there are 48 months—each State, in its turn, could name an

independent firm of public accountants who would audit the books of the Treasury and the records of the Monetary Trusteeship. Each State would have an opportunity, in the course of the 48 months, to verify the Trusteeship Records. At any time currency was issued, the exact amounts and exactly to whom and how issued would be made public information. There is no reason why such reports could not be simple and understandable to every one. The necessity for complicated reports always arises from the desire to conceal the actual truth. "Oh! what a tangled web we weave when first we practice to deceive."

"A system which, for its maintenance, requires that its beneficiaries keep its contributors in ignorance, is fundamentally wrong and, being wrong, is beneath human dignity. We should forego the otherwise inevitable revulsion to its injustice by our voluntary abolition of its practices."

What Steps Should Be Taken to Provide the Initial Supply of U. S. Money; Yet Prevent Destructive Inflation

1. The National Monetary Trustee should first issue U. S. currency to banks to cover total demand deposits and take over the assets securing the loans made to create those demand deposits. As the loans mature and are repaid and the notes cancelled, the money should be immediately paid into use again, in lieu of taxation, and to reduce government debts.

2. The United States could also issue some currency to the aged who have lost, through no fault of their own, their entire resources during the depression. Many are physically unable to again enter industry. Part of the currency issued by the

Monetary Trustees should be issued as a *monthly stipend* to this class of honorable American citizens. It would be very easy to check and learn exactly what men and women would be entitled to such a benefit. The amount thus issued would be negligible and would have no effect upon prices—the sole criterion of monetary quantity. The aged and infirm are entitled to a living. Many have been deprived of their resources through our unjust system.

3. If sufficient currency (demand claims—money) were put into the stream, all of the young adult people of the United States could be employed in the production and distribution of the things American people need to sustain a high standard of living. The only consideration that must always be observed by the Monetary Trustees is that the supply of money be *always* regulated by the actual physical production of consumer goods. All of the employable could be put to work, a condition never heretofore reached outside of war solely because of man-made monetary restrictions; and reached during war by the lifting of such restrictions by those who impose them.

If United States currency were issued in payment of War Bonds just as production could be stepped up, all adults who desire to work could be gainfully employed. This real money would be forced to find profitable use, and if the vicious Securities Act of 1933 were changed and a sufficient amount of money were injected into the stream, the business depression would vanish within a very short time. This Nation has the wherewithal — resources, equipment, and trained human beings, to provide a high standard of living for every person who desires to work. Poverty could be eliminated from the United States if only we American people would do a little

THE CORRECTIVE PROCESS

Object—To set up a non-collapsible honest monetary system

Successive issues of United States legal tender created by Monetary Trustees acting under mandate of the Congress of the United States.

The *Essential* point is illustrated on the right. As U.S. legal tender is paid into use (circulation) the *unconstitutional* privilege of banks to *create* money to lend is progressively restricted. The law of privilege to "money changers" is changed to law of justice for all. Banks' legal reserves, which will be actual U. S. money, will be increased progressively until they have 100% reserves against demand deposits. We will have a de-mystified non-collapsible monetary structure.

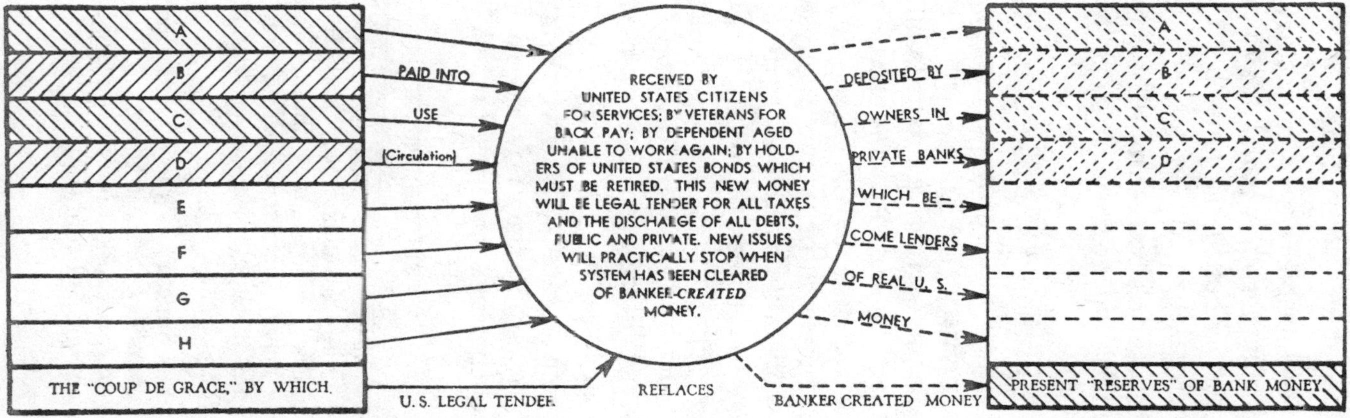

(over)

Business will be undisturbed while correction is being made. *IF* the money changers and their "experts" are not allowed to interfere the price levels can be maintained at whatever level is desirable to afford the Nation, as a whole, sufficient income to support the domestic private debt structure and provide employment for all able-bodied citizens. All that is needed is common honesty and pitiless publicity.

After corrective process is completed bank checks will transfer ownership of legal tender—United States dollars—instead of bankers' private promises-to-pay—mythical amounts of gold.

A non-collapsible honest monetary system can be effected only through *mandatory* laws demanded by the people. These laws must be devoid of trick clauses and weasel words.

The Monetary Trustees must be men of common honesty and intelligence. No present "experts" need apply.

Increases in the volume of money must be widely publicized. Any intelligent person can understand honest statements.

Applying the corrective process will produce the kind of monetary and banking system most people now believe we now have. Once such a system is established, there will be no more "mysteries" which are understood only by the inner few, whose consciences have never been their guides. Such a system could never again be collapsed, for any one who would destroy money would *lose*. Under the present system internationalists *gain*, through foreclosure on real wealth.

Under such a system banks would at last do what the people now think they now do, that is, lend real money which belongs to depositors.

The writer wishes to emphasize that an honest money system would enlarge tremendously both international and domestic trade. Many who are now talking "internationalism" bitterly oppose making changes in the United States money system which are absolutely necessary if we are to trade with other countries.

This writer is opposed to the internationalism which allows foreign countries to stifle trade and dictate our policies, but is strongly in favor of the internationalism which permits us to trade freely with all countries.

simple straight thinking; if we would exercise our good sense and return to the original monetary provisions of the Constitution of the United States.

4. Another way of properly issuing some *real* money with which to replace that cancelled out of the business stream since 1929 by order of the internationalists, would be to pay the Government debt called "Veterans Adjusted Service Certificates" with this new, real United States non-cancellable lawful money. Just why the Veterans Adjusted Service Certificates were made payable in 1946, when many of its should-be beneficiaries shall have passed beyond the need of it, would be worthy of thorough investigation. This "bonus" should be no longer deferred, but paid in the kind of money for which the American soldiers clamored when on their last march to Washington. They had the good sense and the honesty to refuse all other kinds of money than United States Government non-interest bearing notes. Had we joined them in their insistence, instead of cringing in cowardice, moping in ignorance, or parroting the cries of those in *control* of our money system, our soldiers whom we allowed to be duped into the war would now enjoy at least a small part of their just dues. At the same time we would all have been helped toward recovery.

The justification for the payment of United States currency to the veterans is two-fold: this is a legal debt, and acknowledgment of under-pay of the boys in uniform; and secondly, the monetary quantity is today inadequate, so that payment of this debt today would be one step toward rehabilitation of the monetary structure. It would not be disruptive and would cost nothing if paid in new additional full legal tender currency, as a part of the general monetary plan.

Banks Must Remain Private in Ownership and Control

Banks will be private, not government, institutions. They will deal with *real* money. They will loan real money and keep books, but will *not* henceforward ever manufacture a deposit. A Central Bank of issue, whether private or government owned, if it would *lend* money into circulation, and after the system is fully established deal in *credit* money, is to be avoided as the plague.

If these simple rules were observed, poverty could be banished from the United States. Our natural resources are so vast, and our machinery and technical training of such high order, that physical production could be increased to much greater volume than it has attained at the most prosperous period the United States has ever experienced. If this type of simple monetary system were set up, every honest man and woman in the United States could earn a livelihood and accumulate sufficient reserves to educate their children and retire at a reasonable age to enjoy the benefits of a few years of leisure.

As the Providential bounty of nature and progress of science made it possible to produce the raw material to supply more and better food and clothing; better homes and furnishings, etc., the real income of all Americans (their command over units of food, clothing and shelter) could be increased by simply adjusting the quantity of United States money in use. There would be no such thing as "surpluses," and no such thing as business depressions.

Let us not stop with talking about restoring to Congress the function of money issuance. Congress has that power. We must demand that it *resume* the function mandated to it by the Constitution. We have at this time in circulation and held by banks $346,000,000 United States legal tender notes issued by Congress at the time of Abraham Lincoln's administration. Who could hinder a Monetary Trusteeship appointed by Congress from issuing all of the money that is needed?

The International Bankers and their satellites have so far succeeded, but that is *our* fault in not having studied the simple proposition that it is not necessary to pay a rental on what belongs to us, which is what we do when we pay interest to private individuals for using private issues of money.

Our enemies shout that Monetary Trustees answerable to Congress would destroy our banking system. They want to have us stupidly believe that such Trustees could not distinguish between giving a thirsty man a glass of water and drowning him. They will drown us if we remain gullible.

See Chart page 170A

CHAPTER XIII

POWER TO CREATE MONEY IS POWER TO TAX

Why Money Creation Is Rightly The Prerogative of The State

Some will say that it is silly to imagine that money can be created and placed in the blood stream of business by the authorization of the people's representatives. If this be true, is it not equally silly that we accept the fact that money is now created by private individuals? Is that not true? Has it not been done in this country ever since the first violation of the Constitution took place — the first delegation of power by Congress to private individuals to coin money and regulate its value?

Don't be afraid to think! Our fears with respect to so-called financial "mysteries" have been created and nurtured by the Money Creators. Wide-spread public enlightenment on the subject of what money really is, and how it has been used anti-socially by a small group of world-ambitious internationalists *is the one thing they fear and fight with all their power.*

The entire proposition is reducible to this: Should the Congress be compelled to exercise the power given it by the Constitution to issue our money on a scientific basis, i.e., in accordance with the volume *needed* for the Nation's welfare; or should the privilege be left, as now, in private hands to be manipulated for their own selfish purposes and to the Nation's "ill-fare"?

Why should a few private individuals form a corporation, call it a Bank, and thereafter manufacture our money? That right certainly resides primarily in the people, who granted it to Congress. Congress, in violation of the Constitution, passed it on to a *privileged* few.

One cannot give up what one does not possess. If that right existed primarily in the people, it resided secondarily in their Government, and only through unconstitutional delegation by Congress of that power, in the hands of a favored few. Congress *cannot* relinquish that power, given it by the people, through the Constitution, any more than it can give up what it does not possess.

Certainly, the right of the Government to issue money is superior to any right of the few, and the Government must withdraw from the few whatever money-manufacturing powers it has previously granted.

It is a duty we owe ourselves, our dependents and our children, to demand of our Congress that it recall the privilege from private hands and exercise its constitutional mandate.

Here the average sincere person strikes a snag which, however, has been placed in his path by the paid "economists" of the private money powers and their representatives. This is—the question of how the Government may issue money, which is value in the form of purchasing power or medium of exchange, and actually place it in the business stream *without giving it away*.

But what is Government? It is the expression of the common will of the people, and it is vested with the common welfare, subject to human rights. The Government must pay its expenses. That is, any Government set up by a people must levy on its citizens for its subsistence and continued existence. This right is known as the taxing power, without which no Government can exist and perform the functions laid upon it by the people who created it and vested it with power, with the expectation that it would do what they intended.

Remember what money is. It is a demand claim on wealth. Unless you are a banker, you can get money only by producing or rendering some service to society. The money you receive is a piece of paper, inherently worthless to you, until you can exchange it with some one else for goods or services you want.

The abandonment of barter, and the existence of a medium of exchange, necessitates some group getting something for nothing, because whoever issues money creates claims on real wealth. Justice demands that the National Government be the issuer of money, for then the purchasing power created at the original source benefits all.

Money created and paid into use is interest-free at its source. Contrast money that is interest-free and *paid* into use by the Government, with money that is created and *loaned* into use by private individuals. Money loaned into use bears interest at its source, and it may be recalled and cancelled out of use, thereby cutting down the medium of exchange and causing stagnation and foreclosures. Private individuals today exercise the taxing power—they alternately dilute and increase the purchasing power of the money in use.

The Government can regulate new money issues to the annual increase in production *without dilution* of purchasing power.

That can be very readily judged by movements in prices. Prices can be raised to whatever level is necessary to produce a sufficient national income commensurate with the legitimate debt structure in the nation. Equitable price levels require that goods be exchanged at approximately the same levels which prevailed when the major part of the private debt structure of the nation was created. Production can be stepped up to whatever levels are necessary to absorb the labors of all people who want to work. Under an honest money system, for which the Constitution of the United States provides, there would be no such thing as mystifying business depressions.

If, in setting up a system of "civilized money," a government issues lawful money in the first instance to pay its expenses, that is eminently legitimate. Certainly it is more legitimate than to allow private interests called Banks (all of which, unfortunately, are today controlled by foreign manipulators because they are controlled by the Central Banks) to issue loans (create "money"), and collect interest upon their issues, which is allowing them to take *something* for *nothing*. Today banks have the power to create purchasing power. Besides creating purchasing power, they can collect interest thereon, and foreclose on real wealth, if a given number of dollars are not returned to the bank on a given date. Whether or not the dollars returned have a greater purchasing power than the dollars borrowed is not considered, under the present monetary "un-ethics" now in practice. Today private individuals give up valuable goods for privately created money. Thus, the ancient fraud becomes more and more apparent, as repayment becomes more and more impossible.

Another fear fostered by the money creators (in their efforts to strangle money) is the fear very commonly held that once the Government starts to issue money there will be no end to it. But let us reflect upon this libel of the people's own chosen representatives. Let us always remember that the function of Government, and the duty of controlling the money system, must always rest in human beings. Which type of human beings shall we choose — the money creators who now have the power to manipulate the money system, *or* some honestly elected representatives of the people? *Statesmen* would fill our Congressional Halls if the money system were honest.

The stakes are worth billions of dollars per year to the private individuals who now possess money-creation powers. The reason we have many politicians instead of *all* statesmen, and courts of injustice instead of courts of justice, is because the money factor enters. Were the money system honest, bribery could be practically eliminated. Statesmen could then be elected to the highest offices in the Nation, the States, and the Cities. How omnipotent has been the power over this Nation by the private money creators and their wards, who have fattened on the interest collected on the loans of money they created out of *nothing* but a people's ignorance and gullibility.

In 1844 Lord Beaconsfield (Benjamin D'Israeli) cited Lionel Rothschild as saying: "Can anything be more absurd than that a nation should apply to an individual to maintain its credit and, with its credit, its existence as a state, and its comfort as a people?"

Today the United States Government is paying private individuals over *one billion dollars per year* in interest to do exactly what those same private individuals are telling the people the Nation itself *cannot* do. Meekly, the citizens also pay an *invisible* tax levied by the money creators on the medium of exchange, which they create with pen and ink. Yet those privately owned banks have received their power through a delegation of that power by

Congress. Congress received that power from the people. Of course, the delegation of that power is a flagrant violation of the Constitution of the United States.

Would the people rather entrust the power to create and destroy money, without warning and to the serious damage of the nation, to a few private individuals, or to Monetary Trustees placed in power by statesmen, who really represented the people? The Monetary Trusteeship would issue it for *value received. Banks create it for nothing—out of nothing.*

Readers! Do not think that because you own a few bonds or an insurance policy that you would not be benefited by the inauguration of an honest money system. Do not heed the cries of the "Invisible Government" — the financial exploiters who live by your wage slavery and meager incomes — that your accumulated "capital" (money) which is now invested in bonds or insurance companies, would be lessened in value if an honest money system came into being. If the affairs of this nation are allowed to continue as they now are, your bonds and life insurance will become worthless because of the deliberate manipulations of these international financiers. But if an honest money system were brought into existence, the values of all of your properties, including your homes and farms, would be restored, as well as your opportunity to obtain an adequate and decent income. Debts under the present system of control of money by the few, are but chattel slavery; debts you contracted honestly are now calling for dollars of greater purchasing power.

When ancient Greece found itself in a predicament like that of the United States today, it *urged* a Dictatorship on Solon—quite different from thrusting a Dictatorship on the people without any desire on their part for one. Solon's first act was to take over the silver mines and abrogate the privilege of money issue held by the Nobility, which they had abused, just as our money masters have done in our country and, despite humanity's deplorable condition, are still doing.

With the resumption of coinage by the Government of Greece began the era which made Greece great. We confront a similar situation and it devolves upon us whether it shall burst into a cataclysm or whether, by the guiding light of the Spirit and the good sense to return to the original provisions of our Constitution, we shall be able to convert obstacles into opportunities, and *once and for all* establish an honest money system and the regeneration of our national life.

When the single Gold Standard, as now executed, was conceived by the forebears of the world's present privileged interests, Adam Smith was engaged to write *The Wealth of Nations.* His work has come down since the time of the French Revolution as the "Bible" of so-called classical Economics. Sadly, economics did not begin as a science at all. Adam Smith and his followers made human beings mere hirelings to the owners and controllers of gold and government debts. Later John Stuart Mill was engaged to write on the principles of currency. He, too, has been accepted through the years as an unquestioned authority on what has been known as classical, orthodox Economics. John Stuart Mill and his writings have been traced directly to the designs of a small group of people who were then planning, and are still planning, to enslave the rest of humanity. That group is still active behind the scenes directing the social discord necessary to accomplish its goal.

Single Tax advocates, now recognized as a part of the Fabian Movement, should analyze the following pertinent observations of Arthur Kitson:

"Single taxers and land reformers, who see in the monopoly of land the cause of all social misery, should sit down quietly and make a simple comparison of the total amount of annual wealth production paid in rent of land with that extorted in the shape of interest on loans and capital. For, the monopoly of *credit* not only determines the rate of interest on all capital, but it is the chief cause of such interest."

To permit all sincere workers to earn a decent livelihood, only one conquest should have been necessary — the forces of nature. That conquest has been so complete that men and women could all taste the fruits of economic security and leisure to devote themselves to life's higher aims; rather than be enslaved to a constant grind to earn sufficient to sustain life. They cannot reach spiritual heights because they are enchained by a constant grind and bitter struggle to earn sustenance for the body. Having conquered natural forces, our next object of attack is the diabolical forces, which stifle our life in all of its phases and ramifications — now it is forward march or sit down and die.

Those who cling to the writings of Adam Smith, John Stuart Mill, and other so-called classical "economists" have failed to understand and realize that as man conquered the forces of nature, he should have been liberated from slavery. As nature became the slave, man should have become free — free from the everlasting terrors of economic pressure. Science has made production of food, clothing and shelter possible in volume never imagined by the industrialists of a few years ago. Today humanity cannot enjoy the real fruits of scientific progress made possible by industrialists, because of man-made restrictions imposed by deception and continued by keeping the public's eyes filled with the dust of confusing propaganda. The money powers are clinging to the hope of enslaving the world. Such hopes should be destroyed forever. They are inhuman and un-American.

In the multitude of "economic" and "financial" counsellors, there is Babel. The reason for this is that "economics" as taught, and banking as practiced, have all the attributes of magic closely related to the tricks of the well-known Houdini.

Americans! Is it not worth all effort you can put forth to see that every American is informed as to what an honest money system will really do for him, and to see that no American citizen is satisfied until that honest monetary system is established? Its operation would be simple. If we do, America will have permanent prosperity beyond anything ever experienced. Corruption and "legal" rackets would practically disappear. *They exist because we have a dishonest money system.*

An example of how all-important the money system of a nation is, was witnessed from April to July 1933 when, by raising the price of gold, the President, despite the lies shouted ever since by the money powers and their unwitting parrots, caused raw material prices to rise and come into a more equitable relationship with the price of finished goods. If that small step in the right direction was of such tremendous influence, imagine the all-importance of making the entire money system honest.

The invisible forces behind the Government of the United States could be disposed of by the people *demanding* and *obtaining* an honest monetary system, as provided for in the Constitution of the United States. Numerous eminent men in all countries have stated unqualifiedly that "whoever controls the money system of a nation governs the nation." Could there be any doubt as to who controls the money system of the United States? Not only the Federal Reserve Central Banks, but the United States Treasury, and all but a few banks throughout the country, are subject to manipulation and control of policies by those who are subservient to the private money creators.

The selling to the R. F. C. of Preferred Stock (under force) in most of the banks, has practically placed every business man in the United States under control of the internationalists. The control of individual banks by the National Government is very dangerous.

The only hope for the United States is to eliminate bank-created money forever; replace every "credit" dollar with a real legal tender dollar; keep banking separate from government, and restore control of our money creation to Congress. The present un-American control of the United States Money System could be overthrown without war; without disturbing the public peace; without public expense; without interfering with the constitutional rights of any single American; without violating but by observing moral and constitutional law; and without upsetting in any manner or taking any value away from an owner of property in any form, whether it be physical, tangible property or stocks and bonds.

However, the establishing process must be *dual;* real money must be increased, *while private bank created money is intelligently and progressively decreased;* for today each paper currency dollar "reserved" in a bank allows ten to fifteen bank credit dollars to be manufactured and loaned out. The reform should be openly accomplished with monthly statements in plain English, published by the Monetary Trusteeship, so that the price level can be intelligently, openly and properly adjusted. *There is no need for secrecy*: the need is for "pitiless publicity."

Humanity will never be free to enjoy the fruits of our vast natural resources; our scientific discoveries, and the willingness of millions to work peacefully, *while* private banks have two functions: that of creating and destroying money, as well as being custodians and lenders of money. Banks must continue to be privately owned, but they should be custodians of real money which they could lend to worthy borrowers, and *only the nation should have the right and power to create money*. If the power to create money were honestly managed by Monetary Trustees appointed by the representatives of the people, civilization could then actually strive for its Divinely ordained objective — universal peace and brotherhood under the Golden Rule (not of gold) and material plenty, equitably distributed among all who desire to work with brain and hand. An honest money system would free men from slavery and enable them to march toward the better things of life.

The Public must be protected from those who professionally condone and raise a smoke screen around immoral practices of cheating and destroying the medium through which all men's labors must be exchanged. The public does not have to tolerate merchants deciding in advance whether a yard shall be 36 inches or 24 inches or, perhaps, 47 inches, according as they are sellers or buyers. Does not ethics enter into the question as to whether a dollar shall be worth 100 cents or 300 cents in actual exchangeability for physical goods? Would-be inventors and dispensers of fraudulent weighing machines would, like immoral teachers and doctors, be placed under the jurisdiction of prison officials until they thought differently of such activities. The time has certainly arrived for Americans to come to an understanding with those who either innocently or maliciously carry on a "science" of swindling. Many economists are self-deceived, but they can be held responsible for continuing in that state after they have been given proper information.

Americans must direct their attention to the heart of the perversion — private money creation and cancellation powers. There is no need to oppose the *rich* as such. Indeed, real wealth can be accumulated by the *many;* and an adequate livelihood earned by *all.*

America must revert to the money provisions of our Constitution, now in abeyance; restore the prerogative of money creation powers to Congress, and enact laws which treat the issuance or destruction of money by private individuals, as high treason. Our present system has evolved sub-rosa, in violation of the Constitution. Exchangeable wealth itself, and not the question and ownership of debts, must be the factor that determines our volume of money.

Nature being enslaved, men may be free. America has opened the road to the greatest and freest development of the individual. The world money powers, through their weapons—Socialism, Fascism and Communism — are struggling to force it closed. True leaders must lead us away from the terrible economic perversion. Practical Christian leaders cannot justify themselves or their offices unless they are willing to attack the heart of this great moral problem. Beware of those spiritual leaders who "plead" for Social and Economic Justice while they refuse to attack the money problem. A practical millennium is at hand if only leaders will accept their responsibilities and arouse themselves to demand moral and economic justice for a people who have, deeply rooted in their own lives, the proper relation of the individual to his fellows, as man to man, and as between men and women.

The normal channels of education are closed to the dissemination of this truth. *Why?* Because those who possess the power to pervert our economic system also control, directly or by financial pressure —by advertising volume or suggestion—many newspapers, magazines, and publishing companies. The responsibility of dissemination rests on the conscience and the shoulders of every sincere American who himself becomes informed. Individual initiative is powerful. Have we sufficient patriotism and love for our families to exercise all possible influence to win the greatest fight Americans ever waged — *the restoration and preservation of our republic?*

"Life should be a series of festivals, interspersed by honorable labor; instead it is a series of needless battles."—H. V.

By setting the world a good example in the inauguration of a sound money system, the peoples of the world will become so activated in constructive work as to abhor the interruptions of war. Many a war has been precipitated in order to divert people's minds from the money question. By taking the power of issue and the *unearned* interest out of the money masters' hands, the prime incentive to war is eliminated; we can finally have peace on Earth, and the good will that springs from cooperation toward a common purpose: the ennoblement of the races.

The old slogan: "Die for Your Country," will then become reversed to "*Live* for Your Country."

"Though lying for hire is now the primrose path to promotion," there *are* enough courageous Americans to demonstrate to the world that "*honesty is the best policy*"!!

"Let us lift back our monetary system on to the narrow gauge of honesty as the first step to a leap forward on the broad gauge of human progress.

"The monetary system now serves only the convenience of a parasitic and upstart plutocracy practising a worldly wisdom the exact opposite of that which is the foundation of the age. It prefers the dark in times when all men seek the light, and is sowing the seeds of hatred and war in a world weary to death of strife. It is poisoning the wells of Western civilization, and science must turn from the conquest of Nature to deal with a more sinister antagonist, or lose all it has won." — *The Role of Money*, by Frederick Soddy.

Now that we know this sinister antagonist—the private money powers—we must fight it with dauntless courage.

And do not for one moment think that your Congressman or Senator will not listen to you, an individual voter with the initiative to demand an interview, or that he will remain unmoved by what is demanded by you and your friends. After all, you knew him "away back when," and his election to the councils of the Nation has not made him a superman.

Once the international money power is destroyed and the power to coin money and regulate its value is resumed by Congress, as mandated by our Constitution, all of the social experimentation and legislation of the present era; with its high priesthood of theorists, professors, "reformed" speculator stock exchange regulators, Wall Street farmers, professional social "reformers," Judas leaders, Red sympathizers, Constitution ridiculers, college boys, riot agitators, strike agitators, and destructionists in general, can be forgotten as one bad dream.

The abuses that have been sneaked into the Governmental structure of this nation, and of many States and Cities, through the machinations of the international money power to accomplish its own destructive purposes, would be quickly thrown out as relics of a barbarous and almost fatal assault upon the world's only haven of a Government truly "of, by and for the people."

There will never be a Utopia on earth; but conversely it is a moral certainty that the Creator never intended that the earth should be made a premature Hell.

CHAPTER XIV

PRIVATE PROPERTY RIGHTS OR SOCIALISM?

What is Capitalism? What is Socialism? Where Did Its Doctrines Originate? By Whom are Socialistic Principles Fostered?

Today Americans are being intentionally confused by many misleading and malicious discussions of Capitalism and Capitalists. There is an intentional effort on the part of numerous writers to confound the real meaning of Capitalism, and a failure on their part to distinguish between constructive capitalists and international loan mongering "capitalists," who are nothing but money manipulators and, hence, parasites of industrial capitalists.

Kinds of Capitalists

Americans must make careful distinction between the kinds of Capitalists:

(1) National industrial capitalists, who are largely native born Americans and, with rare exception, men of brains, courage and energy, who have built useful businesses. They are engaged in producing and distributing the fundamental necessities of life. The owners of those businesses are constructive patriots who have founded and built businesses which furnish employment and provide the country with finished products. This kind of a capitalist is destroyed by social unrest, and being devoid of intent, is not responsible for the economic pressure which exists today. He and the other Americans of his kind are the type of men who lose when their employees have to be discharged. They are anxious to have an

opportunity to furnish employment and to sell their products. They offer value received and carry the responsibility of conducting the industrial processes necessary to provide the Nation with the physical things society needs.

Indirectly, however, they become responsible for their failure to study the causes of repeated depressions and, upon learning the truth, to demand legislative action for their removal.

The present unbalance between what capital and labor receive as their respective shares in production arises, not out of the greed of the industrialist, but out of the fact that industry cannot operate without borrowed money, for there is (practically speaking) no other kind. The cost of borrowing the medium of exchange into existence is treated as a cost of production, and this sub-rosa drain for the benefit of parasite money-creating banks is far greater than the profits retained in industry for dividends. Let the industrialist keep his profits earned by good management: but let labor be given the unearned interest which now goes to fatten the leeching pocketbooks of money creators ("unearned" is "paid on nothing").

If the agrarian and laboring population is to receive its fair share of the fruits of production, the *birthmark* of interest must not scar our medium of exchange: there must be created a sufficient amount of *freeborn* money to effect the nation's entire business and exchanges.

This will, it is true, deprive banks of much present revenue: but it was never theirs by right. They have kept it solely through having succeeded in keeping the public in ignorance of this secret drain.

(2) The second class of capitalist is the ordinary local American banker, from whom most people and businesses obtain loans of check money. He is

operating under a system handed down through the generations; in blissful unquestioning ignorance of how the system originated, where it is taking him and his "customers," and who are behind the scenes pulling the wires which enable him to grant credit (manufacture money) or force him to curtail it. Most domestic bankers do not realize who are behind the scenes watching that the planned manipulations of the controllers are not interfered with.

(3) The third class of so-called "Capitalist" is the international loan monger who profits by causing vicious price gyrations and economic unrest. To him social unrest, wars and revolutions provide opportunities for exploitation. His kind cause price gyrations and profit thereby. They are the forces, though they are invisible to all but close observers, who guide social unrest and manipulate the money structure of the Nation. This group of misnamed "capitalists" are those who foster socialistic ideas and pay "duped" people to go out and create violence. Besides manipulating the domestic money structure, they destroy the established international price relations existing between the nations by changing the gold value of the various currencies. Their so-called "wealth" or "capital" is not in the instruments of production excepting as a transitory means. They place their funds in various countries and in various businesses only temporarily until they have accomplished some manipulation, when they withdraw their own funds and cause destructive collapses which destroy the honest constructive capitalists who have put their money into plants and equipment and desire to operate their factories for the good of society. These international "capitalists" and their un-American puppets are the actual generators of Socialism. If their object—the overthrow of the United

States Government, is accomplished—they will then own and control all of the physical properties of the Nation, and the honest and constructive capitalists, as well as the professional men and day laborers, will be mere slaves, subject to the complete authority and tyranny of exploiters.

Kinds of Brokers

Americans should carefully distinguish between the legitimate function and place of the underwriter of long-term domestic capital, and the crafty international loan underwriter. The domestic underwriter's function is that of facilitating the investment of funds in the building of factories, railroads, homes, etc. He is *not* a manipulator. He also is the victim of those who manipulate the total amount of money in the Nation and cause vicious price changes.

Americans must also identify those who carry on the necessary functions involved in the distribution and financing of raw commodities in their movements from the fields to the final consumers. These functions are performed by the members of the various commodity exchanges. These individuals execute a necessary part in affording the farmer a daily opportunity to sell his products immediately after production or, if he chooses, many months later. The farmer can obtain cash for his products many months before it is in final form for human consumption. These commodity exchange brokers are frequently victims of international money manipulators. Occasionally, some individual commodity broker may violate the code of ethics and attempt to "corner a market" but that is a rare exception. Individual cases should be dealt with accordingly. Contrasted to the commodity broker, we have the international money manipulator who, by changing the gold value of the various currencies, or by forcing collapses of domestic banking structures, causes destructive gyrations in the prices of raw commodities. Many times farmers have become confused as to the causes of destructive price gyrations. The *commodity* exchanges have been frequently attacked because of the machinations of the international *money* manipulators. Commodity exchanges are a necessary part of the grain marketing machinery. Socialistic regulations of them have done serious damage to American farmers.

Socialistic Isms

Today the American people are being involuntarily hurled from the form of Government guaranteed under the Constitution of the United States toward a Socialistic state.

Socialism and Communism, and their other numerous manifestations found in other countries, such as Fascism in Italy, Bolshevism in Russia and China, Ghandi-ism in India, Nazi-ism in Germany, Fabianism in England and New Dealism (alphabetism) in America, all originated from the same international source. Fundamentally, the object of all of these manifestations or breeds of Socialism is to destroy the rights of private property and deny civil and religious rights to all save a very chosen few.

The masses are led to believe that Socialism is predicated upon all property being vested in the State, or society as a whole, for the benefit of the people, but being vested in the State really means complete control over all properties by a few for the further exploitation of the masses. It creates a gigantic trust and places the internationalists in control in a very secure position. They are able to exercise absolute tyranny over worker and consumer alike. "State" control means *compulsory labor* in return for no monetary remuneration, but merely a ration of food and meager necessities of life. If, then, when the State controllers desire to allow these rations, any of the masses object to the tyranny, they are liquidated—that deceitful word for executed or starved to death.

Besides destroying the individual's rights to own property, Socialism and the other "isms" which have just been named, have other very un-American and vicious objectives. These objectives are:

(1) The abolition of patriotism.
(2) The abolition of religion.
(3) The abolition of the family relationship, which means the abandonment of morality, and State jurisdiction over children.

These phases of Socialism are intended to actually destroy civilization itself for all save the un-social few who are engineering the destruction.

It seems relevant here to relate that in 1934 Edouard de Rothschild of Paris made a speech to the directors of the French Northern Railways, in which he discouraged as useless all opposition to the strong current of State Socialism upon which nations were now rushing toward what he designated as a scourge; which designation suggests that, when State Socialism has been universally established, it will be declared a scourge to justify a change; which, we may assume, will not be a change for the better, but implies an autocratic dictatorship.

There is a historical background for Socialism which has been purposely concealed. All of the theories and practices advanced by the present-day Socialists are copied directly from the organization known as the Illuminati—"enlightened men."

The order of the Illuminati was founded in 1776 by Dr. Adam Weishaupt of Bavaria. Weishaupt spent five years in collaboration with other conspirators and outlined a method for destroying the economic and social order of any country. He aimed at nothing less than World Revolution. His order, and the dupes whom he succeeded in getting to carry out his vicious schemes, advocated abolition of the laws which protected private property; advocated sensual pleasures; abjured Christianity, and called patriotism and loyalty narrow-minded prejudices. They intended to root out all religion and ordinary morality, and break down the bonds of domestic life.

Through a system of intrigue, they inoculated these vicious doctrines in France during the thirteen years prior to the horrible French Revolution. The French people were totally unaware of the motives and objectives of those who led them to destruction. France, as a result of the work of these conspirators, was put through the Reign of Terror five years in which murder and destruction prevailed to a degree previously unheard of in any modern civilization.

The result of the French Revolution was many years of suffering and chaos, and the placing of the control of France in the hands of the internationalists and entirely out of control of the real French people.

Unfortunately, many people in our own country, particularly clergymen, professors, teachers, club members, social workers, etc., appear to have a false impression regarding Socialism. They appear to believe that Socialism has something to do with the philosophy of life; a concept of Christianity; an ethical code; a scientific theory for the production and distribution of goods; a humanitarian movement, etc., etc. Most of this large group of well-meaning individuals do not suspect the identity of the real supporters of Socialism. They do not understand the actual ulterior motives of all those who are the motivating force behind the various queer phenomena which now parade under the terms of Atheism, Radicalism, Liberalism, Pacifism, Internationalism, Socialism, Communism, Bolshevism, Fabianism, Fascism, Nazi-ism and New Dealism (Brain Trustism).

Socialism, once installed, has very definite remedies for unemployment; that is, compulsory conscription of labor, as in Russia. There is no unemployment on a slave plantation. Compulsory labor, with death as its final penalty, is the keystone of Socialism. Until the mirage of Socialism is destroyed, and its underlying intrigue is revealed to the deluded working classes everywhere, there can be no peace or economic security in the world.

The United States has only to return to the monetary principles of its own Constitution and wipe off all of the numerous Socialistic laws which are now fastened like vultures upon humanity itself. A return to the basic Constitution of the United States, particularly the monetary provisions, would enable this country to arrive at the only solution there is to the hideous economic and social conditions which today make life practically unendurable for all save a very few whose sinister objectives are causing them to inflict untold suffering upon constructive and loyal Americans.

"It is lawful for a man to hold private property; and it is necessary for the carrying on of human life."
— St. Thomas of Aquinas.

CHAPTER XV

"RESPECTABLE" DECEPTION

Fraudulent Use of Monetary Terms

Because of the tremendous smoke-screen of fake mysteries, misrepresentations, falsehoods and twisted truths which money creators have long used successfully to befog the mind of a trusting public, it is necessary that we acquaint ourselves with the truths which lie beneath the most familiar deceptive terms. This chapter is intended to aid the reader who has believed, under the stimulus of autosuggestion, that he or she could not understand money. These definitions will enable any intelligent person to recognize when writers are attempting to deceive.

Fiat Money: This term is always used in derision, to suggest that it is wrong for any one to create money. The simple fact is that *all money is fiat money*. The word "fiat" is the Latin, meaning, "so be it." Money is not found in nature. It is an invention, creation and instrumentality of civilized organized society. Either private individuals or a government must create it by fiat. The only question is: By whose fiat shall it be created?

Is it by nature a gift of Providence to the chosen few to use as they please, or is it inherently a prerogative of all of the people and, hence, a prerogative of the government itself? The wise, sagacious, experienced, history-conscious founders of the American Republic recognized that it was *the vital* prerogative of the government. Are we intelligent enough to see what they saw; strong enough to return to the principles they pointed out?

GREENBACKS: This term is used in contempt. It is sufficient for us to recall that honest Abraham Lincoln, noted for common sense and a profound knowledge and appreciation of the Constitution of the United States, was the man behind the issuance of United States notes, which were deceptively termed "greenbacks."

The enemies of the greenbacks were the foreign money creators, the gold crowd, often called international bankers. The depreciation of the non-legal-tender notes was engineered thus: importers had to buy gold to pay import duties; and the government had to buy gold to pay interest on its bonds. The gold bugs named their own price for greenbacks!

COMMODITY DOLLAR: Usually used in contempt. Every effort is made to make the people believe they work to get gold. We know that we work to eat, obtain clothing and maintain shelter. How many readers have ever bought gold? How many have eaten it, slept on it, built a home of it, clothed themselves and their children with it, walked in shoes made of it, ridden in automobiles manufactured from it, etc?

A commodity dollar, when rightfully explained, means a dollar which will, over succeeding generations, purchase about the same average amount of food, clothing, houses, automobiles, etc. The supreme importance of a commodity dollar is shown by the determined resistance of the money creators to all efforts of those who are seeking to force Congress to resume the money creation powers so that stable general average price levels can be maintained.

The enemies of an honest money system are the real enemies of stability. They thrive on instability. Genuine wealth producers thrive on stability. To say that general average price stability is impossible is to assert a falsehood. Manipulators have demonstrated their power to produce wide, wild destruction of prices by means of juggling the secret weapons they possess. Our government, acting through Congress, could honestly utilize those same weapons to prevent such destructive movements.

The general price level *can* be stabilized. It *will* be stabilized when enough people become conscious of this ancient form of robbery, legalized, under which the money creators have for centuries, at frequent intervals, despoiled the producers. They have operated to destroy the confidence of the people in themselves and in their institutions, in the hope that some day a harassed people would welcome a World Dictatorship of money creators.

The question is: Shall we stabilize our money in terms of what every one needs, buys and uses, or in terms of that one thing which is used only by the money creators for juggling purposes — gold — the money creators' weapon?

PROFIT ON REVALUATION: Since it was fallacious to fix the price of gold at $35.00 per ounce, the so-called profit — the difference between $20.67 and $35.00 per ounce, entered on the books of the government — was a mistake. It is small wonder that the people are confused, considering the constant efforts of the money creators to manipulate the financial system.

"CURRENCY WARS": A phrase coined to cover up the operations of international gold jugglers.

No historian can point correctly to a single case in which any *government* has engaged in a currency war with any other *government*.

All such alleged "wars" have in reality been the sham battles indulged in between private gold brokers, by means of which they disrupted world trade and kept all people in economic turmoil and confusion, by shipping gold from one country to another and back again, thereby causing honest and credulous people to believe that something was wrong with their governments.

Something *was* wrong, of course, but not at all what people thought.

When intelligent people who have taken the time to lift the lid of international finance and look beneath see the phrase "currency war" used in the public press, they know that the publication using or countenancing the use of the phrase is merely bowing to palpable untruth ordered into its columns by the world masters, the money creators.

STABILIZATION: What is alleged by the money creators to be stabilization is, in fact, the very ground upon which they continue their depredations. Each sovereign nation should manage its own currency for the benefit of its own people. A free gold market, that is, a price for gold that fluctuates as trade warrants, would take full care of the international value of any nation's currency.

THE QUANTITATIVE THEORY OF MONEY: This is a broadly publicized bit of theorizing intended to show that the quantity of money has no effect upon the general price level. As used, it is a deliberate attempt to conceal a self-evident truth. The perversion strikes at the truth by setting up false premises and then proving that these factors have not borne a relation to prosperity. In general, the false quantitative theory states that business cycles have not been accompanied by changes in the quantity of world gold.

The important element, the bank manufactured money, has been totally ignored. It is this quantity which has been secretly manipulated. The news sources upon which the people rely never call attention to these drastic fluctuations in quantity. The general public is led away from this vital factor to follow herrings drawn across the trail by the money creators, through their pawns, and many "respectable" newspapers and magazines.

SPECULATIVE BOOM:
FICTITIOUS PROSPERITY:
OVER-CONFIDENCE:
"All these cant phrases and the like, so glibly swallowed by supposed impartial students of money in the past, should be now universally recognized as the polite way of informing the initiated that the standard of living of the working class is rising dangerously above *subsistence level,* and the appropriate monkeying with the *quantity* of money is being engineered to bring it down." — *The Role of Money,* by Frederick Soddy.

MONEY MONKEYING:
MONEY TAMPERING:
MONEY TINKERING:
These terms are used to deride all efforts of those who are advocating the honest management of that human institution now called money, for the benefit of the people. Those who decry "money tinkering" are the privileged few who use the human institution called money to exploit the people. The money creators have for centuries reserved to themselves the exclusive right and privilege of doing all the tampering and tinkering for their own selfish gains, with the idea of eventually setting up governments themselves. The tampering and tinkering which is constantly done by the money creators is never mentioned, let alone condemned, by the alleged mouthpieces "of the people." Money tinkering as now conducted by the money creators, is a colossal method of bamboozling and despoiling the public under government protection.

PRINCIPLES NOT PERSONALITIES: Some professional admonishers decry and show the nature and effects of our present money system, only later to sponsor false programs or bills actually intended to hand over all real national controls to the money masters. Test every Bill for yourself. KNOW ! ! (1) Does it mandate Congress to originate all money (*lawful* U. S. Divorced from all metals) and pay into use and keep outstanding a sufficient volume to distribute at just and constant average price levels all that the nation is able to produce or receive in exchange for its products; (2) Separate money creation from lending and restrict lending to State chartered private independent banks, keeping dollar for dollar U. S. money against demand deposits; (3) Mandate Congress to free the foreign exchanges.

Honest reformers have to expose alien banker irresistible anti-social interests and enthusiasts' sheer beginner ignorance as well as vicious confusion and false Bills advocated by traitorous "statesmen" and "religious" admonishers.

SILVER PURCHASES A "DRAIN" ON THE TREASURY: When the Treasury accepts silver and pays for it with newly printed silver certificates, the "drain" is the cost of engraving the paper.

THE LAW OF SUPPLY AND DEMAND: This law is sound and should be permitted to operate on everything man needs and uses, *including money*. The exchange value of money rises when money is made scarce.

There is no excuse for governments' attempting to interfere with, manipulate, change, "adjust," or otherwise juggle the price of any individual commodity, such as wheat, corn, hogs, rubber, sugar, tin, etc., etc. Such and all individual prices should be left to themselves. The *general average* should and can be maintained against destruction by judicious regulation of the quantity of money within the nation.

Changes of "values" do not result from bullish campaigns or bearish raids upon the prices of individual commodities or securities, but by wholesale manipulations of the prices of all physical things through changes in the monetary quantities. This is genuine "high finance." Stock and commodity operations perform necessary functions in the economic system. Attempting to corner a market in any commodity or stock is mere child's play compared with the influence wielded by those who manipulate the money system. Stock market movements, over any length of time, are due entirely to the increase or decrease in the amount of money available for the purchase of securities. This being true, we may well wonder why our trusted public officials in their "investigations" have not directed the searchlight upon the culprits. Is their station too "high" for the people's champions to reach? Who gave them that station? It was built on the nation's strength, surreptitiously appropriated. It can be dissipated only by the force exercised by an enlightened public.

THE "RIGHT" AND "LEFT" IN GOVERNMENT FINANCE: "Left" means radical and "right" means "conservative." Accepting these universal meanings, we quickly see that many writers in the public press are twisting these terms, wittingly or otherwise.

They allege that to turn to a fixed gold content, or a gold price is to turn "conservative." The plain truth is that such a turn is a direct step backward into the clutches of the financial backers of Bolshevism. They are at the center of the abuses of money creation powers, as attested by amazing archives of the United States government.

We can not trust what we read in the daily press about some things being "left" and others "right." This applies not only to finance, but also to other matters, such as those which affect sensible social reforms. This country would need few social reforms if the one important reform were made. The old, the orphans, sick, etc., would need no social charities or other poison pills if the money system were made honest. The use of our brains is the only guide. "If there were more justice, there would be less need for charity." — Henry Ford.

Currency Debauchery: A term used to describe, in money creators' language, the creation and payment into use of legal tender United States currency, or non-interest bearing treasury notes. The term is also used by financial "experts" to describe the ultimate in robbery; namely, the "German" type of inflation, intending to convey the impression that they cannot differentiate between a national issue paid into use in sufficient volume to conduct a nation's business properly, and issues of counterfeit money manufactured by private money creators when they wish to upset a government.

These "experts," whose pay for such experting must indeed be generous to induce them to sink to such depths of misrepresentation, allege that issuance of United States non-cancellable, non-interest bearing money could solve no problems. How can they know? Every time a government has honestly started to issue its own money, in the past 150 years, the private money creators have stepped in and blasted the State apart by counterfeit issues.

The United States Treasury pays for the cost of protecting private money creators against competition, that is, those private individuals who would create money but who are not members of the inner circle called banks. This same department could be used to protect the United States issues against *all* private money creators.

RUBBER DOLLAR: The ability of the money creators to apply ridiculous names to things which the people require, which names, in fact, *apply strictly to their own perverted inventions*, is simply amazing.

The dollar "which does *not* change its purchasing and debt-paying power during succeeding generations" is called by the money creators and their paid "mouthpieces" a "*rubber dollar.*" By contrast, in the light of plain common sense, could any dollar be more rubbery than that unconstitutional dollar with which the American Republic has been inflicted for 150 years? What but rubber in the dollar would permit "mysterious natural forces" to make it worth 50 cents, $2.00, or $3.00 at various times within a few years? It is the rubber in the present money creators' dollar which allows them to wreck values and economic and political stability with which the people have been plagued.

Street hawkers have peddled imitation dollars made of sheet rubber, to impress upon the public mind the ridicule which the money creators have heaped upon the sound dollar which would contain *no* rubber. The origin of these imitations is easily guessed.

Which is better for the people: a dollar which will maintain its power to pay debts and buy what all the people use every day, or a dollar which will always buy the same weight of *gold*, but never a constant quantity of average goods, services, and debt discharge?

If they say that the latter dollar is an impossibility, let them try to explain the stone wall which met the efforts of any man who has tried to get the law written in such a way as to mandate the "Federal Reserve" system to maintain a stable price level!

Applying the Brakes in Time: We Americans have been steeped in the obsession that depressions are as natural as night and day and the seasons of the year; that the way to avoid depressions is to avoid "over-activity."

By over-activity the money creators actually describe a condition in which unemployment is inflicted upon only a few of those willing to work. Such a condition the money creators consider unhealthy — unhealthy for their long range plans, which require that at no time should all of the people be allowed to earn a living. Their system provides periodic intervals at which the unemployed, including enormous numbers of the people, are dispossessed of what they have earned and saved. Only thus can recruiting for bolshevism go forward. Only a discontented people will welcome *any* kind of change, just so it is a change. "Even world dictatorship is better than starvation."

Frequently we are told that bankers have difficulty in restraining themselves and avoiding lending too many of their promises-to-pay, with which the people are able to work, produce and exchange their production into general consumption. Over-expansion of bank manufactured money is the sole basis upon which the money creators have been able to wreck the machinery of civilization at frequent intervals, by destroying such money.

Naturally, when a bank has become over-extended, it is vulnerable to blows — loss of confidence. Any slight disturbance forces it to begin calling in its promises-to-pay which its borrowers are using as money.

Today a small group of private individuals can force it out of existence.

Crashes can be avoided only by eliminating the elements out of which money creators can manufacture crashes.

REDISTRIBUTION OF WEALTH: There is much senseless talk about redistribution of wealth. No honest man wants to take what the other fellow owns. But every citizen wants, and has a right, to the fruits of his own labor.

"Wealth" is too commonly referred to as that which already *is*. We tend to forget that *it is being created every day* by the brains, efforts and labors of men utilizing nature's bounty; aided by science and the inventions of modern times.

No man would look with envy upon the possessions held by his rich contemporaries, provided he knew he was receiving a just compensation for his own honest work. Such reward is what we should begin to regard as the real re-distribution of wealth. Wealth not used in production is useless to its owner or to humanity in general. Production is the sole criterion of real wealth.

A just distribution of the fruits of production, possible only by rationalizing the machinery of distribution — *which is the money system* — is all that any man needs to enable him to receive an adequate and fully satisfactory reward for his own labors, mental or physical.

To get real money into circulation is not to redistribute present wealth, or to change its ownership. Real money in circulation will make it possible to get proper distribution of the fruits of production.

"The function of money is to move goods."—Henry Ford.

Idle Funds Seek Employment: As at present used, this phrase is deceptive.

First, the "funds" are already earning their way because they were *loaned* into existence, at interest.

Second, the so-called idleness is of uncreated bank book money which neither the banker has the confidence to create, nor the business man the courage to borrow by pledging his real assets against the creation of bankers' promises-to-pay. Real money is not idle, for the sore need of the people for money to conduct business has forced them to resort to many kinds of bartering devices.

The so-called "idle" funds do not belong to the depositors. They belong to the banks in a double sense: first, the banks have only loaned them; second, a bank deposit is not a deposit but a *claim* against the bank holding it. The bank has title. Ask your lawyer.

The absolute necessity for more money for exchanges of goods as the basic need of our present mass-production civilization is attested by the many abortive efforts to provide substitutes for money in this and in all previous depressions.

Even Mr. Henry Wallace, the head of the Department of Agriculture, committed to crop destruction, writes in his book *New Frontiers* to this effect: The responsibility for the unemployed rests with the industries of the country. It will be necessary for the government to go ahead with its own devices of rehabilitation if the industries dodge their responsibility. The government, in its method of going ahead, would build out of the unemployed a self-subsistence system of *exchange* co-operatives. This would be outside of the capitalistic system. This is the statement of the "under-plower of agriculture." We cannot quote it directly because of the copyright provisions.

To the informed, "capitalistic," as here used by the Secretary of plow-under agriculture, means *monetary* and nothing else. This is his unwitting confession that it is the monetary system which has failed to function. He would have *primitive bartering* take the place of *money*. Evidently, he has failed to realize or has failed to approach the real cause of the trouble.

In plain English, Mr. Wallace is unwittingly admitting that some system of barter is necessary. If barter is necessary, is not the fundamental trouble a monetary trouble?

SOUND MONEY: Honest sound money is the kind of money advocated by this book — money created not by private individuals but by the national government. Honest sound money was provided for by the founders of this nation. The Constitution is complete in placement of money creation powers. The violations of the money provisions of the Constitution are the cause of our economic distress.

The phrase "sound money" was appropriated by the money creators and misused to designate the kind of money they create and control for private profit. The money creating powers have been used for international destruction. As now used by the gold crowd, it means money that is based 3% on gold and 97% on "confidence," "courage," and other purely psychological and irrelevant factors. It means money, the volume of which can be expanded or collapsed at the will of a few individuals who hold huge liquid funds which they can surreptitiously juggle between the various countries. The public has never understood that an export of one gold dollar potentially destroys thirty "confidence" dollars. As thus misused, sound money means mystery money.

The correct and honest use of the term Sound Money is that meant by the former United States Senator, Robert L. Owen. He means the kind of money which is tangible and contains no "confidence" or "courage." Senator Owen has said:

"I took the ermine robe from the shoulders of the gold bugs and I asked them to come into the public arena, either through the press or on the platform, and in open debate state the facts so that the American people may know that I, and not the gold bugs, use the words Sound Money honestly."

The fact that this country requires somewhere between sixty to seventy-five billion dollars of money in order that the people may effect the exchanges incident to a civilized existence, is proof sufficient that gold is hopelessly inadequate to serve the needs of the people of the world for money. Only a fraction of sixty billions could be converted into gold even if we had all the gold in the entire world. The international liquid capital is capable of demanding all the gold at will, and getting it.

Any money "based" upon an inadequate metal must necessarily contain other ingredients such as "confidence" and "courage"; we have seen repeatedly what happens to the psychological ingredients when the metallic ingredient is slipped out from under the nation's monetary structure.

Foreign Currencies: The reader has been told through the newspapers that when the currency price of gold increases, *devaluation* occurs. But at the same time—the reader is told that when the price of gold in foreign currencies is changed, that is merely an increase in the price of bar gold in the respective nations! Obviously, both are exactly the same thing. The confusion in terms, however, misleads the public and diverts attention from the fact that the currencies of all competing nations are being juggled against the United States.

INTERNATIONAL BANKING: The New York Trust Company issues a monthly publication called "The Index." The September 1934 issue contains an article on "The Balance of International Payments for 1933" which is very illuminating.

There are many people in the United States who have been induced by the autosuggestion of propaganda to believe that any reference to international bankers is the product of disordered minds; that there is no such thing as an international banker. On the contrary, this term is in common use in financial circles and refers definitely to those firms which deal in the moneys of all nations, maintaining gigantic liquid balances wherever their interests dictate.

To show how these international banking accounts have been operated entirely independent of payments representing the normal balances of trade, which the report shows clearly would require transfers of funds *to* the United States, we quote from "The Index":

"The exceptional outflow of funds, which for the *fourth successive year* characterized *short-term* capital movements, was almost entirely due to *transfers in international banking accounts,* which caused the withdrawal of foreign short-term assets totaling $412,000,000. Deposits represented the most important item in this account, those due foreigners, declining heavily."

At the rate of $400,000,000 per year export of capital, this would in four years, equal a total export of over $1,500,000,000 which, under the present system of "gaseous money," would force a collapsing and cancellation of billions of bank created money — the kind that disappears.

Note again, that the New York Trust Company asserts that this outflow of funds was due entirely to transfers in international banking accounts. Therefore, if we have international banking accounts, we must have international bankers.

PAYING OFF "NATIONAL DEBT": The Germans and the shocked world were told that the German inflation was "paying off the internal National debt." Americans will be asked to believe, as in Germany, that it takes thirteen trillion times as many legal tender dollars to pay off the government bonds *as the face value of the bonds call for*.

Will the common sense of Americans stand for this, or will they demand honest sound money for America — honest sound money in sufficient volume to conduct business at equitable price levels? Honest money would cost the people nothing, and would result in the restoration of prosperity.

It will be one thing to "pay off the debt" and *ruin* Americans by overissues of Federal Reserve private bankers' promises-to-pay: and quite another to *pay off the debt* and *redeem* America with United States *government* legal tender.

SCRIPT MONEY AND CLEARING HOUSE CERTIFICATES: These have been used at times solely because the banking system, on ancient precedent, never required that bank "reserves" amount to 100% of deposit liabilities. This was true because "there never was enough currency in the banking system to pay off those who had deposit claims." Why this has been the case has always been omitted from the published discussions. In a sensible banking system, clearing house certificates or script money would never be necessary. In a system where banks dealt in actual money, the depositors could actually be "paid off."

Why not? Legal tender is a manufactured product. Are we in this day of "over-capacity" and "over-production" unable to produce enough legal tender to satisfy this requirement?

PRICE LEVELS: Falsifiers say that the volume of money can have no effect on prices. Since prices are the index or pointer which indicate the actual relation between the quantity of goods and the quantity of money, we raise this question when faced with price changes: "In order to raise prices shall we destroy a portion of what nature alone can produce, or shall we add to the quantity of money which man alone can produce?" As was told the President: "We can eat pigs; but we cannot eat prices." As yet, the world has never had a surplus of anything but misinformation and resultant evils.

A RECENT CLASSIC EXAMPLE OF DECEPTION IN TERMS: *The Chicago Tribune* on December 12, 1934, quoted Senator Carter Glass:

"Do you think the banks are doing their part now," he was asked.

He answered, "Well, what are the banks supposed to do? Their job is to loan money and it is not their own money. It's money that belongs to depositors, and they should exact adequate security for their loans."

Hon. Carter Glass claims to be one of the sponsors of the Federal Reserve Act. He has also set himself up as a money authority in the United States Senate.

Is Senator Glass deliberately trying to befog simple truths and mislead the people, or is he so grossly ignorant of the nature and workings of the banking system as to believe the statements he made?

As has been shown in this book, banks *create* the credits they loan by merely making deposit credit entries on one side of the ledger and debiting loans and discounts on the opposite side. Is this lending other people's money? It most certainly is not. The banks create the money. All but a negligible amount of the money in the United States has been created by the banks. Bank credit is not *real* money, but it is what we have been taught to use as money.

We agree with Hon. Carter Glass that banks should exact adequate security for loans, but why should banks create out of nothing money to lend?

Something for Nothing: The propaganda artists frequently shout that those who favor government money are trying to create something out of nothing. This is *what has been done* and *what has to be done* in order to have money, a man-made instrumentality. The only question is: Shall its creation be by the people, acting through their duly chosen representatives for the benefit of all of the people, or by the private money creators for their own personal benefit?

Over-production:
Under-consumption:
Glut:
Surpluses:
No Markets:

All these terms are used to hide a condition of unnecessary suffering and misery, the real obstacle of human progress.

Consumer's Strike: "In our day it is not the agitator fomenting class-hatred who can start, nor the airmen raining down bombs that can stop, a revolution. But empty milk into the Potomac; import pests to destroy the cotton crop; burn wheat as fuel; restrict production; set up tariff barriers; permit trusts, federations, cartels, and lock-outs; allow trade unions to develop ca'canny methods to reduce output; maintain in misery, insecurity, and idleness masses of unemployed who are not allowed to better their lot by making the very things of which they stand in need; and revolution in some form is not probable, but certain.

"Their institutions, so far from protecting them in their peaceful avocations on which they rely for their livelihood, appear leagued together to keep them in traditional and unnecessary servitude and dependence. The people soon begin to realize that they are officered by the enemy.

"Nor will any means avail to terminate or defeat such a revolution . . . unless and until the barriers that oppose the free and full distribution of wealth from the producer to the ultimate user and consumer are broken down and the flow of wealth again fulfills the purpose for which men have striven to create it.

"It is money alone that can effect the exchange of wealth and the continuous flow of goods and services throughout the nation, for money is the life-blood of the community, and for each individual a veritable license to live at all."—*The Role of Money,* by Frederick Soddy.

Until the American people learn the exact nature of the money power, there is little hope that bolshevism can be stemmed, for it is only continued gross economic injustices that can drive men into the arms of the proletariat, who, in simple ignorance, believe they can lose "nothing" by revolution.

"So long as we have simple folk displaying a pathetic acquiescence in the piety that renders thanks for all the good things of life and ascribes them to the bounty of Providence, along with anything but simple folk who totally disbelieve anything of the kind, but nevertheless do still believe implicitly in practicing much more forcible methods of obtaining them; so long will civilization be a happy hunting ground for the predatory and acquisitive, and a *wilderness* for the original and the creative." — *The Role of Money,* by Frederick Soddy.

An honest money system would make it easier to "render unto Caesar the things that are Caesar's and unto God the things that are God's."

"Phoney" Money Plans

For the sake of the reader who has not had the time to examine the various monetary plans which are being advocated in various quarters and are coming out of suspicious sources, the following description of a few of them is given:

The Labor Dollar: This would be issued at the rate of say $1.00 per hour of labor expended by every laborer. This is predicated on the theory that labor is the source of all wealth. There would be no limit set to the quantity as long as labor goes on. Evidently, the quantity of money would soon outrun what it is supposed to buy. In reality, it would result in the break-down via the vicious inflation route.

This theory further ignores the plain fact that men do not labor for labor's sake, but to produce what they need to live. Production of goods is the sole objective of industry, for it is goods that are used to sustain life. A monetary system that ignores the plain fact that stability depends upon the steadiness of the general price averages of the things people use in living, is thoroughly unsound and "phoney."

THE MONEY OF TECHNOCRACY: Some years ago Mr. Thorstein Veblen, an engineer who had long been disgusted with the failure of the financiers to keep step with the progress of science and engineering, wrote a book called *The Engineers and the Price System*. Actually, this was a satire upon the inconsistency with which life has been filled. As science advanced, the retrogression of finance and the increase of the debt burden made it impossible for people to live better, as scientific progress warranted.

After Veblen's death, and during the current "depression," his theories were taken up by a group of men, one of whom coined the word "technocracy."

Technocracy would, according to its own propaganda, put out by a political organization using the name technocracy as a shield for the sponsors who finance it, pay laborers in money which would be "purchasing power in the form of some kind of energy certificate."

This has exactly the same errors as the labor dollar. There would be no limit to the quantity issued. Furthermore, this money would be based on the energy expended instead of the things actually produced and needed for living — consumer goods.

DIRECT CREDITS: There have been spread throughout the country pamphlets purporting to explain a method through which the government would issue credits directly to individuals. Apparently, under this scheme, the national government would *lend* money to individuals. This scheme carries the basic fallacy that the money would be loaned into circulation and not paid into circulation. It would be subject to exactly the same manipulation, except on a far larger scale, as the present system. It could easily be used as the guise for a vicious inflation of the money structure of the nation.

Actual money itself should be issued; paid into circulation by the Monetary Trusteeship in actual scientific relationship to the physical consumer goods available for distribution. The reader will note that all of the "phoney" money schemes have some base other than the consumer goods which men need to live. A genuine system based upon scientific and honest principles must be based upon just those things, for money is merely the medium of exchange for those things. When made the medium for control, or the accumulation of property by the vested interests, perversion is inevitable.

The Socialists' Money

Many students hold the opinion that the motives of the leaders of socialism and communism, as political movements, are open to serious question; and this writer holds the considered opinion that the rank and file members of these organizations are the victims of the money creators, both economically and theoretically. They have been driven to the extreme of economic pressure and, in desperation, have been forced to accept *some* doctrine of escape. They have accepted these false doctrines, which seem plausible, but which are being held out to them by the actual agents of the money creators. To such sincere advocates of economic justice, the following thought is directed: If they are now the victims of a money system, is their economic situation likely to be improved by perpetuating the system which made present conditions possible?

It is demonstrated that the monetary mechanism is the weapon with which men are driven into the arms of bolshevism. None of the various shades of bolshevist thought have even intimated that the present vicious mechanism will be destroyed upon their ascendency to power. No, it will simply be turned over completely to their manipulations. The weapon will not be destroyed, but the fingers at the trigger will be fully entrenched with tyrannical powers. In the past, it has not been the fingers that brought the destruction but the weapon itself. Nothing can stop the destruction except the destruction of the weapon.

The thousands of sincere socialists, communists and reformers in general are therefore invited to examine the monetary question in the light of true liberty which they say they advocate. They are entitled to fair warning that their false leaders (secretly the money creators), have already set out bait of all kinds on this question. Some kinds would result in complete destruction of exchanges. *They carefully avoid touching upon the system of imaginary money,* which is what we must uproot. Many varieties of the bait are based upon treacherous foundations, such as labor hours, or anything at all which helps to obscure the real issue — which is the stabilization of general average prices. All must beware of false leadership.

A PREDICTED OBJECTION: Apologists for the present mysterious system, and its deceptive mechanism, always treat the "reserves" of a bank — its actual money — as something which is only necessary because some of the clientele of the bank want to use actual currency instead of checks. To this school of thought the idea of having every bank's deposits matched dollar for dollar by legal tender some place in the banking system is abhorrent. They assert that this would be waste — a waste in that something is being allowed or required to lie "idle" or "sterilized."

But even a casual examination of the question discloses the fallacy of this idea. Does legal tender in the money system mean that energy (the accepted basis of wealth creation) is being wasted—allowed to expend itself without fulfilling its function? Is it like a pile of coal burning unchecked in the open air? Is it like the waste of a forest fire? Most obviously, it is not.

Unless there would be a *deterioration* in the system described, there would obviously be no waste and, hence, no valid objection. The objections come from those, or the mouthpieces of those, who are petrified in their conviction that no money should exist that they have not themselves created for the purpose of lending it at interest; to be cancelled out of existence the moment interest fails to accrue to them.

The idea that money must make money in order to be of any use is the child of usury. Henry Ford has effectually set that idea to rest by saying: "The function of money is not to make money but to move goods." If moving goods earns a profit, that is desirable; but it is another matter.

Ridicule

Ridicule is the standard weapon of the money creators used on all fronts. They have come to the full realization that ordinary Americans can stand any kind of attack except ridicule. Ridicule is, therefore, used to nullify the efforts of honest people who attempt to tell the truth regarding honest money policies and honest legislation.

Ridicule is used to silence those who have arisen to spread the alarm regarding the distinct threat against American institutions raised by the bolshevist movement.

Ridicule is used to divert the public mind from the fact that Karl Marx, the so-called founder of bolshevism, never attacked the gold standard. Ridicule is used to screen the fact that the red organs of publicity, while aiming their shafts at "bankers" and "bosses" *never* utter a single word against the international private money creators.

The American public must now steel its mind against ridicule; must stand for what it knows is plain common sense. It must be prepared to stand for its principles in the face of all the ridicule that devilish ingenuity can invent. Only unselfish courage can make it possible for this nation to live for what is worthy, noble and good.

Personal Attacks: Another malicious weapon resorted to is personal attacks through controlled newspapers upon any who, having found the truth, raise their voices to spread it.

It is a very ordinary thing to find that a person who has actually told plain truths in a public address is subsequently misquoted in the public prints. If actual misquotations are not resorted to, for fear of legal consequences, excerpts from the address are given which create an impression of superficiality by avoiding the essence of what the speaker was discussing.

Persons subjected to attacks of this kind have no opportunity to answer because the newspapers which publish the attacks refuse to publish the answers and the facts advanced by those maligned, unless the latter are equipped with huge funds with which to proceed through successful legal action.

One of the most clever forms in which this weapon of personal attack appears is that in which the points of issue raised by the speaker are utterly ignored because they are unanswerable, and the reply instead is twisted into an attack upon the individual himself. Whenever the public sees this done, it is the part of wisdom to carefully examine what the speaker has actually said, because it is probably the truth, stated in such a form that any attempt to refute it would merely emphasize its truthfulness.

A great modern scientist writes, relative to the monetary question, "Lying for hire is the primrose path to promotion." Many people have long wondered how it has happened that so many utterly mediocre, if not actually small caliber people, have become so prominent and "successful."

America is surfeited with fake "big shots," "experts" and false leaders in civil, religious and commercial posts, whose utterances are paraded before us in the public press to the exclusion of plain truth and common sense.

WHAT LIES AHEAD? The press resounds with frequent frantic assertions by "experts" and "confidence" money men that the present course is leading us straight to the precipice of uncontrolled inflation of the currency, which will destroy the value of every dollar, life insurance policy, bond, mortgage, etc. — the value of every debt. This is true — alas, too true. If uncontrolled inflation of the currency takes place, not only will the value of every dollar, every life insurance policy, every bond and mortgage be destroyed, but the United States Government itself will be destroyed, and the people will find themselves chained body and soul to the tyranny of a dictator.

The public mind is being prepared for uncontrolled inflation. The banks are being loaded with government bonds, which they are buying with their private "credit," not with money. They hold over ten billion in government bonds. Insurance companies and trust funds hold a large portion of the balance.

The banks have been forced to manufacture their credit with which to absorb still more of these improper governmental obligations. When the time is ripe, the money creators will start their privately controlled printing presses and turn out private money by the bale, as was done in Germany in the early 1920's.

The alleged excuse for such steps will be that they are "paying off the public debt." Every bank will be ruined, together with their depositors.

The falsehood in this "debt payment" becomes apparent when we consider that after the "German" inflation, which was alleged to have been required in order to pay off the government debt, *the holders of certain bonds were given other bonds in exchange.* If, in contrast to this destructive program, an honest monetary policy is pursued, the public debt would actually be paid off in new United States currency, which common sense tells us is exactly as good as the bonds it would replace. These bonds would not be paid off with new currency at a rate such as would cause vicious price gyrations. *While the bonds were being scientifically replaced with actual currency, the power of the banks to create money by lending their book money would be systematically curtailed. They would eventually have reserves equal to their demand deposit liabilities.* In other words, the total demand deposits in the bank would be backed by the same number of dollars of currency existing some place in the banking system. The result would be pleasing to all except the present holders of the money fiat privileges.

Under this policy not a bond owner would be injured; not a trust fund dollar would be lost; not one life insurance policy sacrificed; not one mortgagee robbed, and not one dollar of currency would become valueless. All of the things which are now so freely predicted by the paid scribes of the money creators in their efforts to throw the public off the scent of the real perpetrators of such destruction, *will* happen, if the present powers are permitted to be retained.

After the present condition is rectified, that is, after the transition period, the amount of *freeborn* money must thereafter be geared to the supplies of goods, so that no matter how high they mount, the general average price level will never fall. Why should it, when all that is required is to avoid destroying money and to increase its quantity as goods increase?

By abolishing credit money, imaginary money, and substituting legal tender, he who destroys any will lose what he destroys: the direct opposite of the present system.

However, it may be fully expected that the money creators will not surrender their ancient privileges without a struggle. The depth to which they will dip to drag forth new schemes with which to plague the people can be easily appreciated by those who will take a little time and have the fortitude for such exposures.

CHAPTER XVI

PRECEDENTS

Readers who have not had the opportunity to study sources of information upon the money of earlier times, are of course open to accepting the deceptive statements coming from suspicious sources relative to the failure of all money of all times to meet the needs of commerce *except* that issued, controlled, and recalled from time to time by the saintly money creators.

In order to disabuse the mind of any reader of the notion that the kind of money advocated by this book is a new invention of an obscure crank of the present day, there are listed below some of the instances in history where the principle was used and operated with total success until the early money creators succeeded in destroying it for the purpose of substituting their own private issues.

It cannot be too often repeated that the right to issue national money is as much a power — and *obligation* — of a sovereign government as the taxing power itself; it being in fact the *most important* form of the taxing power, though "legally" delegated to private individuals. This basic principle of political science has been recognized through the ages, dating back to Solon, the Caesars of Rome, etc. It was also recognized by the framers of the Constitution of the United States, that unmatched Charter of Liberties which has never been equaled in all history in a recognition of all that a constitution ought to be. It is the "key to the science of government." Why are we such "easy marks"?

THE BANK OF VENICE: This institution was founded in the year 1171. It grew out of the necessity of the government to raise funds for wars. The government called upon all citizens to bring their precious metals, etc., and lend them to the government. In return the government credited each lender with an entry on the books of the bank, which entry could be transferred at will on order of the creditor.

Note well that the government *paid* interest on these credits for 176 years. The credits were *owned* by, not loaned to, the persons listed. A much different matter from the custom today.

The real assets of the bank were given over to the government, and, we are told, were used to purchase materials of war in foreign countries. Very soon the bank had *no assets* except the credit of the government, which of course was purely and simply its taxing power.

For the last 450 years of the bank's existence, there was no interest paid to the creditors, the *owners* of the book credits, yet these credits stood so high in the estimation of the public, *both domestic and foreign,* that they were worth for many years, 30% more than coins of actual precious metal.

Note that this bank never made any loans. It did not *loan* money or credit into existence. First it monetized the assets of those who brought in their assets for this purpose; but later, after these assets had left the possession of the bank, the credits resulting from the monetization process remained, backed by the taxing power. Obviously the government *could* have created this final money *for domestic purposes* without monetizing so-called precious metal.

This bank served the people of Venice with its national money, issued without *charging* interest but under *payment* of interest — the exact reverse of today's circumstances — for 626 years; and ceased to function only when the Venetian Republic was destroyed by Napoleon Bonaparte, in 1797.

Napoleon attacked Venice in order to obtain the huge treasure which his backers believed to be in its vaults. He obtained nothing but a lesson in Politico-financial science — assuming that he was not aware of the real nature of the Venetian money, which may be doubted.

Thus, we see the money of the Bank of Venice was destroyed by Napoleon who never fought the money creators, but was aided by them. The Bank of Venice, which was actually a government bank of issue, had served the needs of the Venetians for many years. It was destroyed not because it had proven unsuccessful, but because the private money creators, having gained power, wanted to usurp the most important national prerogative for themselves.

ENGLISH TALLIES: This form of national money was adopted in England as the means of financing the government, by Henry the First, fourth son of William the Conqueror. Henry I ascended the throne in the year 1100 A.D.

The "tallies" were made of wood, being four-sided rods of hazel or linden wood about an inch thick. The amount due from the state to the payee was designated by notches cut into one of the flat sides, and also written in ink on the two adjacent sides. The piece was then split lengthwise through the notches, so that each piece carried ink markings of the value.

One piece was paid out to the payee; the matching piece being retained in the treasury as a method of preventing counterfeiting.

All who served the king or state were paid in these tallies, enough being issued so that they could be paid out until tax collection time again brought in this money for state use. Supplies for the royal household were also purchased by issue of these tallies, which circulated among merchants and people, being used in the exchange of commodities and services.

At tax collection time the sheriff of each county called all who had exchequer tallies to present them and obtain allowance for them. They were matched with the counter-tallies. When the edges matched they were said to "tally," hence the name.

Their sole value was derived from their acceptability by the people in payment for any kind of goods and services, which in turn was derived solely from their acceptability as taxes by the government which had paid them into circulation in the first place.

These tallies were used as money by the people of England for 594 years, exclusively; for the next 89 years partially, and for another 43 years unofficially, a total of 726 years. This is a tribute to their usefulness and acceptability, and political soundness, which may well be marked by the advocates of the gold standard, an infant in comparison. It will be noted that the incidence of violent depressions is traced back, in all modern treatises, only a little over one hundred years; which period corresponds accurately with the use of the gold standard.

The Bank "of England" was chartered in 1694. There were then about $70,000,000 in wooden tallies in circulation. The new bank was given the original privilege of issuing paper money, *loaning* it into circulation, and collecting interest on its creations. The plain fact was that there were not enough tallies in circulation! At any rate, the new private money did not seem dangerous, because no one could get it without paying interest. It turned out, however, to be a case of the camel being allowed first to put his toe inside the tent, which was followed by further extension of privilege until the camel alone was *in* the tent, the master having been crowded out.

A weak king could not defend himself; parliamentary hirelings of the money creators did the rest.

Naturally, the use of the more convenient paper bank money after a time displaced the cumbersome wooden tallies, some of which were two to four feet in length.

In 1783 the use of tallies was abolished by Act of Parliament. America was free but England sank deeper into false money principles and hence slavery!

In spite of this, however, tallies were continued until 1826. In 1830 the heaps of broken tallies were ordered burned in the furnaces of the Houses of Parliament. A defective or overheated flue started a fire which completely destroyed the buildings.

One of the tallies is still preserved in the British Museum. Edmund Burke mentions tallies in his Speech of Conciliation.

And note well, that the value of the tallies was acknowledged by the incorporators of the Bank "of England," for, in 1697, when the capital was increased, $800,000 of the new capital was paid for with the wooden tallies. They were accepted at par.

The English tallies were another form of sound money maneuvered out of existence by the privately owned Bank of England. The Bank of England usurped the prerogative of money issuance, and its owners caused the tallies to be taken out of use.

EARLY SWEDISH MONEY: Paper bank notes were first introduced into Europe by Sweden. The Swedes are noted for financial sagacity.

The money of Sweden consisted of large plates of copper, 3/8″ thick. A two-daler piece, for instance, was 7½″ square and weighed 3½ pounds. This was so inconvenient that a bank of deposit was established at Stockholm. This bank gave out paper notes to those who brought in their copper dalers for deposit.

These paper notes were then used in all transactions for making payments.

They were *not* loaned into circulation.

They could not be recalled at the will of the bank.

Their existence depended upon something else than the creation of a promise-to-pay by some money creator.

They were forerunners of our silver certificates, and all other similar instruments.

THE CURRENCY OF KUBLA KHAN: Marco Polo wrote: "Kubla Khan, the great Mogul emperor, makes his money of the bark of the mulberry tree, and this they cut up into something resembling paper, but black . . . Everyone takes it readily, for wherever a person shall go he will find these pieces of paper current, and be able to transact all business."

The first issue was in 1260 A.D. A "secret of alchemy" prevented counterfeiting, according to the narrator.

GUERNSEY MONEY: At the close of the Napoleonic wars, the Island of Guernsey, one of the Channel Isles, was in pitiful condition, both physically and financially. Public works such as sea walls, roads, etc., although badly needed, were not undertaken because of the scarcity of money. The money used by the people consisted of the notes of the Bank "of

England," which were very scarce because of the customary post-war panic. The money creators had, as usual, seized the opportunity to contract their promises-to-pay after they had accomplished the destruction necessary to a satisfactory war.

Though the Island was blessed with abundant natural resources such as building stone and other materials, as well as good farm lands, the people could imagine no way in which to lift themselves out of their stagnation until, at last, in discussing the great desirability of a new market house, they visited the governor to learn if he could suggest a way out.

The Island has an autonomous government, and its parliament is known as "The States of Guernsey." Being self-governing, it had certain inherent rights, the chief of which had never been exercised both because the people had never before been at such an extremity, and because former governors had not been awake to certain basic principles of political science.

"We need a new Market, but we have no money," said the committee to the governor.

"Have you the stone, the materials for making bricks and mortar, the lumber, etc., as well as workmen who are idle though willing to work?" asked the governor.

Receiving a reply in the affirmative, he asked why they did not go to work, and was again reminded of the lack of that great essential, money.

He countered by suggesting that the "States" (parliament) issue the money. This had never occurred to the committeemen, who had never had an opportunity to make a study of the basic functions of government.

An estimate of the cost, in terms of honest money, was prepared, and the States printed the money required, which was paid to those who either worked on the project or furnished materials for it.

The new Market House was completed and opened on October 12, 1822. Meanwhile, as the new currency was paid out into circulation among the people, general activity sprang up. As it became possible for the people to make exchanges by means of the new currency, people began to do things that had long been neglected because there had been a scarcity of the means with which to effect the exchanges.

The new "States" currency was accepted on all hands because with its issue, a tax was levied, based upon the rental values expected from lessees of stalls; thus, the always acknowledged taxing power of the sovereign state was the real security behind this money. The money was to be cancelled when the entire issue had been collected in the form of taxes.

This issue of money was retired on schedule, but it proved so successful in producing general activity, by expediting the exchanges of goods and services of citizens who had nothing at all to do with the public project directly, that other issues were brought out for other public works and legitimate, if unusual, public outlays.

At the time of original issue, there was no bank upon the Island, hence no opposition to the issue of state money. Ten years after the first issue, however, the general activity on the Island aroused the ambitions of certain men, who saw that opportunities were being overlooked. They wanted to drive out of circulation the state money, which had been *paid* into circulation as dictated by the first principles of political science, and to substitute for it their private issues, which they would create and *lend* into circulation. This would not only give them an interest-income from their special-privilege creations, but would enable them, from time to time, to take over the fruits of the labors of the people, now become used to productive activity and therefore very useful from a money creator's standpoint.

The subsequent history does not at this point in this work concern us. Needless to say, they got what they wanted. However, they have not to this day been able to kill off all of the state notes, or public money, but they have succeeded in preventing all new issues for public purposes. The deficiency has to be supplied by private issues, *loaned* into existence. The amount of Guernsey money outstanding at this date is about $200,000.

The Guernsey money was prevented from coming into full use and expanding with the growth of modern commerce by means of arrangements which were made off the record by the representatives "of the people," and those who wanted to get the privilege of creating private money. This occurred in the period from September 21 to October 9, 1836. The advocates "of the people" abdicated their firm stand against private money creation and the result was the curtailment of the issue of public money, and an increase in privately created money.

THE ASSIGNATS: During the "French" Revolution (there is good reason for using quotation marks to designate these various flashes of redism), the revolutionary government found itself running short of money. In December, 1789, it confiscated the lands and properties of the Church. Shortly afterwards, it issued money backed by these properties as security; that is, backed by the productive power of these properties, the revenues, earnings; these being comparable to taxes in this case.

These assignats, as they were called, were the money which financed the wars fought with other nations by the revolutionaries.

The fact that they were destroyed as money by the gigantic counterfeiting operations of the money creators later, does not detract from their validity.

Napoleon Bonaparte put down the revolution, but did not attempt to issue national money. The lack of money creator opposition, if not its actual co-operation, doubtless accounts for much of Napoleon's success. The Bank "of France" was born in 1800.

"Miracles" can be worked with money.

The assignats were destroyed by counterfeiting. This counterfeit money was issued by the same people who were guiding the revolutionary forces which destroyed the French government. Napoleon, who at last put down the revolution, did not attempt to issue government money. Whose servant was he?

THE CONTINENTAL CURRENCY: We learn the truth about this much-maligned money through the famous letters of Benjamin Franklin.

The colonists lacking a medium of exchange, each colony created and paid into use, via public expenses, its own currency. This generated so much activity that it aroused the fears as well as the avarice of the London money creators, who had by now practically succeeded in driving the tallies out of use, forcing the people to make use of promises-to-pay created and loaned at interest by the money creators.

The money manipulators, upon learning from Benjamin Franklin the reason for the great prosperity and general employment in the colonies, demanded and obtained from Parliament laws abolishing colonial money. The last of these laws was passed in 1773.

In two years the colonists went to war, driven to it chiefly by these selfishly inspired monetary laws, according to Franklin.

Our histories tell us that the war was the result of a long list of British acts which irked the colonists, but they failed to list any of these acts except Taxation without Representation. This statement was a silly evasion of something real. Every man, woman, and child had been made to feel monetary strangulation caused by the system under which every shilling used by the colonists had to be created by London bankers and loaned into use in the colonies. This was indeed "Taxation without Representation" — with a vengeance!!

It is exactly what we have today; the money creators having out-maneuvered the honest respresentatives of the people who demanded rational, honest, national money. They have deceived the people by false ideas transmitted by means entirely at their own disposal. They have fastened upon this nation a system of money creation and cancellation which has brought us to the verge of revolution by a people who have been forced to grow discouraged with representative government. Representative government, in our country, has not been in practice for many years, being shunted aside by the skill of the money creators. The money creators are those who control the political machines in all of the states and cities, and it is they who have prevented our having a representative government.

TAXATION WITHOUT REPRESENTATION!! How much representation have you, dear reader, on the Federal Reserve Board; the American Bankers' Association; Investment Bankers' Association; the Federal Advisory Council, or any other monetary body?

UNITED STATES NOTES— ABRAHAM LINCOLN MONEY: As explained elsewhere herein, these notes were issued at the insistence of Abraham Lincoln. The first issue of $150,000,000 was full legal tender. The subsequent issues ordered by Lincoln were hamstrung with the infamous "exception clause" by means of which the money creators (called bullion brokers in those days) throttled the issuance of honest money.

In another chapter of this book we have discussed how the fate of these United States notes was engineered. When the money creators were ready, these notes returned to full parity with all money, and have continued in use by the people. They drew no interest *on their creation* and they could not be recalled. Hence, they avoided the two basic fallacies in practically all of the rest of our money. Money created through some one making a loan involves the eventual payment of the principal as well as the payment of interest. To pay the principal itself destroys the money itself, hence, destroys the people's medium of exchange.

It is a startling fact that from the time of the first issuance of the Lincoln money down to June 20, 1933, the total interest saved to the United States government on just this small issue of money was $11,378,000,000. Is it any mystery to people how wealth has become concentrated? The answer would be simple to any school child given the facts.

Did you know that until recently you seldom saw a United States note? Why? Because these United States notes — in deceptive ridicule called "greenbacks" — were used, whenever possible, by the banks as their legal reserves at the Central Banks. They bore no interest. Hence, banks put into use in the hands of the public, whenever possible, Federal Reserve notes whose very existence forced interest payments.

British Treasury Notes: In the Hearings before the Subcommittee of the Committee on Banking and Currency, House of Representatives, 73rd Congress, Second Session, on the Bill to establish the Federal Monetary Authority, hearing held January 30 to March 8, 1934, Page 43, we find Honorable O. H. Cross of Texas testifying substantially as follows:

The Bank "of England" had the legal right to create fifty-five million paper pounds sterling and the right to put into circulation thirty million paper pounds. When the war broke out, the bank found its gold reserve had dropped. Then, in the distress in which England found herself, the *treasury* was permitted to issue paper money and did issue it to the extent of three hundred twenty million paper pounds, in units of pounds and of ten shillings each.

Then, when England went back on the gold standard in 1925, these three hundred twenty million paper pounds which had been issued by the treasury were not put on the gold standard: this was done when these three hundred twenty million pounds were "taken over" by the Bank of England in 1928.

Needless to say, these three hundred twenty million paper pounds not only up to 1925, but from 1925 to 1928, were accepted as real money and were real money.

We see here exemplified the principle that the private money creators will permit a sovereign government to create all the legal tender required in order to carry on as destructive a war as possible (by which the money creators profit through their munitions agencies), but after the destruction is over, they then prate piously that this money should be cancelled out or taken over: thus we have during every war the expansion of money required to produce the destruction, and after the war is over there is invariably a deflation sufficiently drastic to put the entire monetary power back into the hands of private parties once more.

There are other instances of financially and politically sound issues of money in history, but those already listed are sufficient to absolve this writer from trying to save the world by a personal invention. The sole effort now is to bring the subject out for discussion in every possible circle; in every possible light; so that the plain, reliable common sense of the American people, coupled with their determination that their children will not be enslaved in violation of the faith of those who founded this country, may operate to the final rational solution of the one outstanding problem of this day and age.

Findings of a Great Scientist: Except for a firm belief that the American people are always ready to accept plain truths, and for a high confidence in their famous Common Sense, this writer would not attempt such a work as this. Other writers have tried it before, and have reached only a small section of the people.

That the readers of this are not leaning exclusively upon the findings of one investigator has already been shown.

That any reader who so wishes may find a genuinely scientific essay upon and examination of monetary science, will be reassuring to those who are, mayhap, a bit timid about relying even upon their own agreement with what this writer has asserted and recommends.

Such a purely scientific examination and report

is to be found under the title *Wealth, Virtual Wealth, and Debt,* by Frederick Soddy.

It is interesting, amusing, or disturbing, according to the viewpoint, to find that certain men who are now prominent New Dealers, not more than eight years ago enthusiastically endorsed this work by Frederick Soddy. These men are professors also, and to one who has been through college, it is amusing, nothing less, to find that these men who read and endorsed this treatise eight years ago, have proved themselves either incapable of absorbing its principles and becoming apostles on its side, or have found it expedient to forget the truths they once endorsed, and come out on the side of the money creators who are manipulating what the people fondly believe is a new deal.

Professor Soddy is a world-famous chemist, winner of the Nobel Prize in Chemistry in 1921. He observed, however, that while science and industry removed the natural obstacles to a greater enjoyment of material civilization, something else seemed to raise an *unnatural* and still greater obstacle, which prevented the attainment of what seemed well within reach.

What was this mysterious something which, apparently, laid a curse upon man's apparent conquest of nature?

Was science accursed?

He laid aside his chemistry, and, bringing into play that capacity for pure research which had been sharpened under the great Lord Rutherford, and which had enabled him to delve deep into the nature of radio-activity and the structure of the atom, he delved into economics and immediately found, to his surprise and puzzlement, that not one examination of the subject could be found which treated economics as a pure science.

Every text book differed from the next. There were no scientific fundamentals.

Not one treatise dealt with the essence of the matter, which is Money, in such a way as to tell whence it comes, and where it goes; every other science treats its subject matter in this manner.

When Professor Soddy finished with the subject, it had been reduced to a science. Anyone familiar with his book, and fully understanding it, is thenceforth his own economist, and need no more examine every new book on the subject, hoping for daylight, as has been the case up to now.

So National Money, Honest Sound Money, Rational Money, Abraham Lincoln Money, or whatever you may choose to call it, now has the endorsement, not only of history, but of science as well; and the few who do not quite trust their own instinctive common sense may now go forward with those who do, secure in the knowledge that they are *right*.

It is difficult for most Americans to realize that for many years there has been on foot a movement which is diametrically opposed to the great concept of American life—*do as you would be done by*.

Most Americans believe that unless they deliberately enter the markets of trade, speculation or investment, there is no danger from an aggressor. They hesitate to believe that any American who takes his pay in the medium of exchange; any American who buys or sells anything from personal services and the necessities of life to mere paper evidences of indebtedness, is *not free* from the baleful influence and grasping power of the money creators, yet, there is the record to consider. To convince any intelligent person that there is an aggressive power deliberately exercising an influence against the private business affairs of every person who handles the medium of exchange, or uses it in any way, it is only necessary to consider the instances named in this chapter to realize how this influence is operated with the intention of creating havoc. This havoc has been inflicted upon the real producers of wealth, and has resulted in suffering caused by artificial manipulations—not by any natural forces, such as the manipulators would like to have us believe.

MONEY VERSUS BANKING: The current discussions about national control of all banks is a natural accompaniment to the failure of the money system to function properly.

This writer believes that national control of all banks should be avoided like the plague. If money were created and issued solely under a trusteeship, acting with authority from Congress, as provided by our national Constitution, and *paid* into use by legitimate governmental expenditures, it can readily be seen that there would be no necessity for any national control of the banks. The United States Constitution says nothing about controlling individual banks.

Every bank should be privately owned. It should be a lender of real money—money which has actually been brought to it by those who have earned it in producing the things civilization needs. Many people raise the question: "Do you mean to do away with credit?" The answer is, "No." Real money would be loaned. This writer is simply advocating doing away with the private creation of money now called "bank credit," but the privilege of a business man to borrow real money from his banker to carry on business *should not be interfered with in any way.*

If banks were not permitted to deal in their own creations of what the people have to use as money, they would then be free to serve their local communities without Federal interference. Why should a group in Washington or New York have the power to operate controls which can force every banker to call loans and curtail the supply of money?

This writer favors complete localization of banking, and the complete abolition of all Federal interference in banking. Such results could be obtained if money creation were divorced from money lending, and all of the money existing in the nation had been *paid* into circulation, was non-cancellable, and without mystery. Such money is dictated by the necessity of our scientific age and by our Constitution—so long violated in this most important respect.

National money, issued by a Monetary Trusteeship, would enable the nation to do away with all Federal Bank laws, all of which arose out of the vicious system of misnamed "national" banks, and the Federal Reserve System.

Each state would then regain the right to regulate its own internal affairs, including the banks, which are inherently state creations, being corporations which the states have the natural, as well as the constitutional right and obligation to charter.

Let money creation and banking be properly separated, and we shall embark upon an era of economic freedom and general prosperity for all such as we have never before even been permitted to imagine. Bankers themselves, in the long run, would earn more profits. They are entitled to a reasonable fee for handling accounts, and for acting as agent in the lending of real money. They would then no longer suffer such terrific losses as always occur when the banking system is collapsed, due to the operation of national controls. The small banker would, for the first time, have assurance that "mysterious" forces would not cause him to bankrupt his customers and, in many cases, to lose his own bank.

If this action is not taken within a very short time, there will not be a single independent bank left in the United States. Bankers with vision already see this but, unfortunately, have not, in many cases, had the time to ferret out the real forces which are bringing an end to the very desirable and legitimate business of small banking, without which there can be no local prosperity anywhere.

Meyer Amschel Rothschild, who founded the great international banking house of Rothschild which, through its affiliation with the European Central Banks, still dominates the financial policies of practically every country in the world, said:

"Permit me to issue and control the money of a nation, and I care not who makes its laws."

CHAPTER XVII

SUMMARY OF PRINCIPLES

Honest Money and an Honest Money System

The people constituting a nation produce and must exchange goods and services with each other. If primitive barter is to be avoided, a convenient mechanism or ticket system must be used. In the last analysis, money is the people's bookkeeping reduced to its simplest possible form. It has been ably defined as follows: Money is the *nothing* you get for *something* before you can get *anything*.

Let us consider the meaning of this definition, Money is the nothing. It is a piece of paper inherently worth nothing but which entitles you, upon surrendering it, to claim some valuable goods. You received it (unless you are one of the privileged who has a right to create it) by giving up your time and services in some productive enterprise. If you are working for a weekly wage, you gave up so many hours a day of your time, and so much of your mental and physical energy in the production of something useful to society. The money you received in return for your work is of no value to you until you give it up for some physical goods or service.

All producers give up their time and energy to help provide goods and services useful to society. The things which they produce, but do not themselves consume, are made available for society as a whole. They give up goods of value for *nothing* but a claim to receive other goods upon demand.

Money is a demand claim on physical goods or services. The amount of demand claims (money) must bear a scientific relation to the amount of consumer goods produced and ready for consumption. If the amount of demand claims is either decreased or increased, the holders of demand claims are either secretly benefited or secretly robbed. If a given volume of consumer goods are in the hopper ready for consumption, and some "mysterious" force increases the number of demand claims in the possession of the people, each dollar's worth of demand claims will be exchangeable for a relatively smaller part of the physical units of goods; in other words, prices will rise and each demand claim becomes exchangeable for physical goods or services of less value. If the opposite takes place — the number of demand claims is suddenly and "mysteriously" decreased — the reverse situation prevails. Then, each demand claim in existence is exchangeable for more units of physical goods than it was previously. Under those conditions, the holders of demand claims gain an advantage.

When private individuals called banks manufacture money (demand claims) they, in reality, rob all of the people then possessing demand claims. Vice versa, when they destroy money they give an advantage to all holders of demand claims, but they work an unfair hardship on all who have borrowed demand claims (money) on long-term contracts, and who are called upon to pay back money which will claim a greater amount of physical goods.

Since every citizen must use money, which is nothing other than general bookkeeping, its establishment is primarily a function of every citizen: that is, every citizen has an inherent natural right with every other citizen to create money. Why should the producers of the nation be victimized by a few private individuals delegated with the unjust power to create money, while other individuals can only obtain it by engaging in actual productive work?

In order to bring into existence a medium of exchange, which is acceptable everywhere in the land, honesty demands that money be the creation of a representative body which has been authorized by the people to act for them in this respect. The Constitution of the United States is so written, but by perversion, the body authorized by the people to perform that most important function, has abdicated its powers, surrendering them against the expressed will of the people to private individuals; thus giving to privileged persons a right which properly belongs to all. This right has been gained through trickery and stealth, as is perfectly obvious to any one who will study the methods through which monetary legislation has been put through Congress.

Now the creation of money is the creation of purchasing power, for money is a demand claim and will command physical goods upon demand. Therefore, those who are endowed with the privilege of money fiat are *endowed with the privilege of creating purchasing power*. This power *must* exist for all money is created — created by man. Money is not a mysterious institution designed and operated by the Almighty. Those endowed with the special privilege of creating money would like to have us believe that money is like the sunshine and rainfall — a part of the designs of the Creator, over which mankind has no control and of which mankind knows little.

The question is, therefore, since all money or purchasing power must come into existence by the act of man, who shall be entitled to so act and thus be given the original power to purchase what the new money will buy? Obviously, such original purchasing power should rest with the people at large.

The people at large, in civilization, act through government.

It is their government which should first create the money, and all of the people should have the benefit of its original purchasing power. Only the people, as a whole, should share the benefits and the advantages involved in a change in the volume of money in existence in a nation. By placing this first buying power in the government, the benefits fall to all of the people, for by whatever amount the new money is issued, tax collections may be correspondingly reduced.

This statement can be twisted into the thought that taxes can be abolished by merely issuing money *ad infinitum*. This is fallacious, for new money should be paid into use (circulation) only as the total stock of consumer goods — the things the people have produced and need in civilization — has been increased by expanded production.

The point to be kept in mind is, therefore, that since money must be used by all of the people in daily life to effect their exchanges, and since money is merely popular accepted bookkeeping and since it must be created, the original privilege of spending it should in all justice rest with the people as a whole. It should be injected into general use (circulation) via the government buying with it whatever is authorized by the people's will, expressed in law.

It requires nothing more than a knowledge of simple arithmetic and the possession of plain common sense to see that as a nation grows, and its people, through science and invention, are able to produce more goods and services in civilization, more money is needed to effect the exchanges.

Why should a small group of private individuals have the right to create money originally and, worse than that, the right to manipulate the volume of money in existence; hence, enriching themselves periodically at the expense and to the sorrow of all the real producers of wealth and services?

The national government — the people as a whole — must exercise the prerogative of money creation and, hence, control over the total volume of money in the nation.

The national government should have nothing whatever to do with the merchandising of real money. Bankers should be merchandisers of real money. Every bank should be privately owned and privately controlled. They should receive real money on deposit and lend real money. *They should have no power to create money.*

The most dangerous thing that could be done would be to place the merchandising of money in the hands of the national government. Such a step would give the internationalists their final weapon to destroy property and personal rights of loyal Americans. The internationalists are secretly seeking to make just such a move at this time. Watch their movements carefully and be on the alert that they do not put over legislation which would nationalize the banks, as they call it — in other words, make every bank in the United States a branch office of the Federal Government.

The Essentials of An Honest Money System

1. Every bank should be an independent, privately owned corporation, having legal authority to accept United States legal tender on deposit.

2. The power to create money should be vested in a Monetary Trusteeship appointed by and answerable to the United States Congress. This Trusteeship should pay actual legal tender into use. Original

issues of money by a sovereignty should always be paid into the money system in exchange for goods or services. Privately owned banks should have the power to loan real money into use, upon its having been deposited with them by people who have themselves earned it. The creation by private individuals of money to lend, is usurping the taxing power of a government.

3. The amount of money paid into use should always be determined by the productivity and price levels existing in the nation. The volume necessary to move the consumer goods in existence in the nation at equitable price levels should be the sole determinant of the amounts of money in use at any time.

4. The Monetary Trusteeship should be completely divorced from the Treasury Department of the United States. The Treasury Department should, properly, be a collector of the nation's revenues, and the dispenser of the revenues so collected. It should have nothing whatever to do with the issuance of the money in use in the nation.

5. The Monetary Trustees should maintain accurate records of production and price levels of raw materials and finished goods. As soon as general prices, then safeguarded from manipulation, have reached equitable levels, they should be watched, and any increases in the volume of money should be governed entirely by the volume of consumer goods available for distribution. There should be no price fixing whatsoever. Attempting to fix the price of any one product, whether it be raw material or finished goods, is a violation of one of the most basic economic principles.

6. Neither gold nor silver should play any part in the domestic money structure. Only United States legal tender should be used in the settlement of all

domestic obligations. Gold and silver (until other nations adopt an honest money system) should be used only for settlement of international balances. It is essential that silver be used with gold for that purpose, in order to destroy the gold controllers' power to manipulate the financial systems of other countries. It is also essential that the price of an ounce of gold in terms of United States currency, be put on a parity with the price of an ounce of gold in the currencies of other raw material producing and exporting countries. It would be simple to establish a ratio between gold and silver to be used in the settlement of international balances.

7. The use of bank checks should be continued by individuals and corporations for making payments of money. The checking system for the transfer of bank balances is a convenient mechanism which should most certainly be retained. Banks should settle their clearing house balances with real money, which is what the people, through misinformation, believe is the case today. The individual check user would notice no difference in his monetary settlements. Banks should also be lenders of real money for business purposes. Banks would then actually be doing what most people believe they now do!

8. All unjust artificial restrictions on the flow of investment money must be eliminated. The Securities Act of 1933 must have important alterations. As it is now written, it prevents the flow of legitimate private money into investment channels. The one essential which must be observed in long-term investment loans is that the loans be repaid out of the earnings from the properties during the actual period of usefulness of the property.

9. Federal control of commodity exchanges must be abolished. If the volume of money is not manipu-

lated, the commodity exchanges will be operated in an honest and equitable manner. Federal control causes injury to the producers of raw materials, and places unfair power in the hands of secret forces.

10. The Monetary Trustees will be mandated by Congress to replace bankers' credit money with United States Government money; to establish mandated price level; and in every way operate *as ordered* by Congress.

Under a Monetary Trusteeship, with the power to create money vested in that authority, and divorced from all banking functions, the money system would be placed beyond the manipulation of a small group of internationalists, who have operated the raw material markets to suit their own pleasure. Such a money system would be independent and free from foreign intrigue and manipulation. It could be understood, and its operations followed, by every individual capable of reading simple figures.

How much money should be paid into use? What price levels are equitable? To know, consider the functions performed by money.

As a country develops, direct barter decreases. The amount of fixed capital in use, division of labor, and the volume of goods in process, increases.

Remember, fixed capital—factories, machinery, etc.—are not consumed directly by human beings. They are instruments to lighten human labor and facilitate production and distribution. They are worthless unless utilized.

The owners of fixed capital share the products resulting from its use. In other words, a flow of new wealth is being created when the fixed capital is in use. Fixed capital represents a debt of the community because its owners are rightfully entitled to claim a part of the goods produced. Fixed capital is actually non-repayable debt as long as it is in use. The fact that fixed capital may change ownership does not alter its status, for the new owner is entitled to the same share in the products. This share is paid in the form of profits or interest. It is profits when the fixed capital is owned. It is interest when the investment in the fixed capital is a loan.

As the fixed capital, the volume of goods in process and the finished goods ready for consumption increases, more money (demand claims) is required to carry out the exchanges involved in the production of new fixed capital, and the production and distribution of consumer goods.

The amounts to be paid into the money stream should be determined by the movement of price levels. Fixed capital owners obtain an equitable share of the products of industry when price levels approximate those prevailing when the major part of the investments were made. If price levels are too low, too large a share of the products goes to satisfy those who own claims on the fixed assets; and those engaged in actual production receive less than would enable them to consume the products of industry.

After the desired price level is reached, money should be paid into the stream by the Monetary Trusteeship only as goods appear ready for distribution, which goods cannot be moved into consumption at the existing price levels without additional money.

Given an adequate supply of money, the volume of goods distributable at a given price level would be limited only by the capacity of the nation to produce the goods. The volume of goods produced would be limited only by the amount of natural resources, fixed capital, and the number of workers available.

The money created and *paid* into use by the nation must be non-interest bearing at source and non-cancellable, except by recalling it through taxation.

How would foreign trade be affected by a scientific money system?

The money of any country is a demand claim on the goods of that community alone. It cannot be used in another country, but can merely be exchanged for the money of another country.

For the exchange ratio to remain constant, without precious metal flowing between the respective countries, the value of sales of goods from one country must be equal to the value of the sales of goods by the other. The value of imports must equal the value of exports. In any country, in so far as the value of imports is offset by exports, the trade is really barter and does not involve any exchange of the moneys of the countries at all, for the importers pay the exporters in each country. If they do not offset each other, it is the unbalanced residuum that matters. That residuum may be taken care of by moving precious metals.

Under a scientific money system the exchanges should be left to adjust themselves. There will then be no advantage gained by buying in a foreign country products produced more efficiently in one's own country.

If the foreign exchanges were free to adjust themselves, and a country were importing more than it is exporting, the cost of exchanging for the money of other countries would rise. The ensuing rise would make it more profitable for the buyer to avoid the exchange of moneys and buy the goods in his own country.

In inaugurating the system and reducing foreign exchange to the settlement of actual *trade* balances,

America's war debt claims could be used to offset money balances in this country belonging to foreigners. If foreign international bankers have large cash balances in this country, let the foreign governments of which they are citizens pay them in the money of their own country and take an offsetting credit on the war debt payments owed to America.

We have only to allow the exchange ratio of our money for other moneys to rise or fall as demand for dollars rises or falls in the settlement of *trade* balances. The price of gold should rise as the general price level rises, and should be used only as a commodity for ironing out exchange fluctuations. This country could also buy silver in both the domestic and world market, and use it similarly in the settlement of *trade* balances. A scientific money system would expand our foreign as well as our domestic trade.

We can enjoy the benefits of a scientific age, and restore peace and prosperity in America if we will but make our money system perform its proper function; recognize physical realities and demand that the nation provide an adequate volume of non-repayable money interest-free *at source*—liberated from secret manipulations—and *paid into use in relief of taxation* when production makes a larger volume of money necessary. The fundamental principles are very simple.

America stands on the threshold! The choice is ours —either a permanent state of poverty and degradation, or the full enjoyment of what science has made possible.

Will natural leaders in every community rise to the occasion, spread the truth, and lead their local forces in demanding that our money system be made honest? Those in control of our government have no alternative but to recognize what the people demand. Do we Americans possess enlightened self-interest, or shall we continue to be willing slaves to intrigue?

BIBLIOGRAPHY

The Open Review, Vols. 1-2, by Arthur Kitson, published May 1909—March 1910, by Frank Palmer, London, England.

History of the Bank of England, by A. Andreades, published in 1909.

Real Money Versus Banks of Issue Promises-to-Pay, by T. Cushing Daniel, published in 1911.

High Cost of Living, by T. Cushing Daniel, published in 1912.

Banking and Currency and the Money Trust, by Charles A. Lindbergh, Sr., published in 1913.

The Bank of England's Charters—The Cause of Social Distress, by Thomas W. Huskinson, published in 1912 by P. S. King & Son, London, England.

A Fraudulent Standard, by Arthur Kitson, published in 1917 by P. S. King & Son, London, England.

Wealth, Virtual Wealth and Debt, by Frederick Soddy, M.A., F.R.S., 1st Edition, published May 5, 1926, E. P. Dutton & Co., New York. (Read the revised edition with the Foreword to the American Nation, printed in the United States in 1933.)

The Role of Money—What It Should Be Contrasted With What It Has Become, by Frederick Soddy, published in 1934 by George Routledge & Sons, Ltd., London, England.

The writer suggests that interested Americans club together and subscribe for the Congressional Record. (Write to Superintendent of Documents, Washington, D.C.) The cost is $1.50 per month while Congress is in session — about $7.50 per session. The revelations will be decidedly worth while. One can learn which congressmen and senators are sincere and honest.

INDEX

INDEX

INDEX